# Expedition

# Expedition

## FASHION FROM THE EXTREME

◇

Thames & Hudson

To our brilliant editor and colleague, Julian Clark

First published in the United States of America in 2017 by Thames & Hudson Inc.,
500 Fifth Avenue, New York, NY 10110

thamesandhudsonusa.com

First published in the United Kingdom in 2017 by Thames & Hudson Ltd,
181A High Holborn, London, WC1V 7QX

www.thamesandhudson.com

Library of Congress Control Number 2017934766

British Library Cataloguing-in-Publication Data:
A catalogue record of this book is available from the British Library.

ISBN 978-0-500-51997-4

Design by Paul Sloman | +SUBTRACT
Printed and bound in China

(frontispiece) CHANEL, fall/winter 2010 ready-to-wear collection,
photograph by Stephane Cardinale

# Contents

———◇———

———◇———

# Expedition

## FASHION FROM THE EXTREME

### Patricia Mears

———◇———

We live in an era when people wear parkas, puffer coats, and backpacks as a matter of course, as well as clothing made of technologically advanced materials such as neoprene and Mylar. Although ubiquitous, the ways in which these items and innovative textiles became a part of our daily wardrobes are little known. Few ponder the reality that they were inspired by the so-called "heroic era" of polar navigation, extreme mountain climbing, deep-sea exploration, and journeys to outer space. *Expedition: Fashion from the Extreme* investigates how clothing made for survival in the most inhospitable environments on earth and beyond found its way onto high-fashion runways and into magazine editorials. This book is a companion to an exhibition of the same title organized at the Museum at FIT in New York. It is the first major study to address the relationship between these two incongruent types of garments—survival wear and high fashion.

The idea for this book and exhibition came to me when I saw the fall/winter 2011 collection of the young designer, Joseph Altuzarra. Then a relative newcomer to the international fashion scene, the French Basque/Chinese-American creator had just relocated to New York City from Paris and was presenting a collection in the United States for the first time. Altuzarra's riff on the midcentury American military parka—known as the fishtail—was a hit as he artfully blended diametrically opposed entities: survival gear and chicness (fig. 2). The following year, he repeated this seemingly incongruous blend in his 2012 fall/winter collection (fig. 3), although these parkas were inspired by those of Arctic peoples. Not only did his parkas garner a healthy amount of press from the moment they appeared on the runways—street-style stars kept the coats in the news months later, in February 2013, during New York Fashion Week.

Exploration to the most remote places on earth—the North and South Poles (the Arctic and Antarctica respectively)—increasingly relied on new technologies throughout the twentieth century. Yet the first Europeans to successfully make inroads to the poles were equally indebted to the ancient sartorial traditions of indigenous Arctic peoples and to their reliance on natural materials. Both these extremes—the very new and the very old—formed the

**1**

Yeti coat by Issey Miyake,
fall/winter 1990–1991, photograph by Irving Penn,
*Yeti (Front View)*, New York, 1990

2

Joseph Altuzarra, fall/winter 2011

foundation of clothing design for explorers and, decades later, the world of high fashion.

The "athleisure" phenomenon in fashion (a blend of athletic wear with street style) has become popular in recent years, parallel to the fusion of expedition-inspired clothing and high style, creating a frisson of activity in global clothing design. Altuzarra is among a growing cadre of influential designers appropriating expedition wear for their seasonal collections. For two decades, Issey Miyake (fig. 1), Yohji Yamamoto, Karl Lagerfeld for Chanel, Chitoso Abe for Sacai, and Giambattista Valli for Moncler have

produced clothing and elaborate fashion shows that bring to life the drama and beauty of Inuit innovations.

A portion of this book documents the arduous treks in the nineteenth and twentieth centuries to remote areas of the North and South Poles, and early attempts to scale peaks such as Mount Everest. Clothing worn by European pioneers included items that ranged from bespoke menswear by Savile Row tailors to innovative fur garments created by indigenous peoples of the Arctic. Later, synthetics and other technologically experimental fabrics were engineered for these journeys, as well as for deep-sea and space exploration. These collective influences began to make their marks on high fashion as early as World War I. The phenomenon culminated during the 1960s, an era that produced some of the most fantastic and outrageous fashions ever made and documented. For the remainder of the twentieth century and into the twenty-first, expedition clothing continued to permeate all levels of attire, from cutting-edge street style to glittery, high fashion. Extreme expeditions and modern high fashion—an urban, industrially driven entity—both began to emerge and take shape during the mid-nineteenth century.

How did extreme expeditions come to be? These new endeavors, especially the explorations to the poles, were unlike earlier human treks to unknown lands. Those had often been commercially or politically motivated, undertaken, for example, in order to discover more expedient access routes to coveted goods in distant lands. It can be argued that exploration of the North and South Poles was spurred in large part to developments in science, and especially the work of Charles Darwin (1809–1882). His seminal publication, *On the Origin of Species* (1859), helped establish the field of evolutionary biology and was part of a larger scientific movement that swept across much of Europe during the Victorian era.

Darwin, a Cambridge-educated geologist and naturalist, was not the first scientist to challenge prevailing notions about the origins of life. Numerous pioneers in both France and Britain—including geologist Charles Lyell and Alfred

Russel Wallace (a naturalist who independently conceived the theory of evolution through natural selection and jointly published his findings with some of Charles Darwin's writings in 1858)—spearheaded what would become extended scientific expeditions to far-flung locations. It was during one of those expeditions—specifically the 1831–1836 trek on the HMS *Beagle*—that Darwin was inspired to create his revolutionary theories. While other prominent scientists were publishing pioneering works that challenged the prevailing notions of creation throughout the nineteenth century, *On the Origin of Species* is credited as the most important single work that set into motion the mania for scientific discovery.

The rise of science and its increasingly important role in society, however, created anxiety among many throughout the Victorian era. Thomas Hardy's poem "God's Funeral" poignantly describes the struggle by many people and institutions grappling with the simultaneous decline of religious devotion and the rise of science. Two of its seventeen stanzas sum up the anxiety about the loss of faith and the question of what would take its place:

XI

How sweet it was in years far hied
To start the wheels of day with trustful prayer,
To lie down liegely at the eventide
And feel a blest assurance he was there!

XII

And who or what shall fill his place?
Whither will wanderers turn distracted eyes
For some fixed star to stimulate their pace
Towards the goal of their enterprise?

Written between 1908 and 1910, "God's Funeral" summarized the nineteenth-century debates between the so-called modernists—who included philosophers and writers such as Thomas Carlyle (1795–1881), Matthew Arnold (1822–1888), and Alfred, Lord Tennyson (1809–1892)—and strident defenders of Christian orthodoxy such as Cardinal John Henry Newman (1801–1890)—who was a leader of the Oxford movement—and those known as fundamentalists who became entrenched in dogma. By the time Hardy published "God's Funeral," the impact of science and the role of expeditions was widely known and was increasingly being accepted in Western society.

Darwin and his fellow scientists also inspired a new literary genre: science fiction. French author Jules Verne (1828–1905) was an avid lover of the natural sciences and did much to glamorize and popularize the idea of extreme travel—so much so that he is widely regarded as the founder of science fiction. His adventure books, such as *Vingt mille*

**3**
Joseph Altuzarra, fall/winter 2012

*lieues sous les mers: Tour du monde sous-marin* (or *Twenty Thousand Leagues under the Sea: An Underwater Tour of the World*), published in 1870, and *Le tour du monde en quatre-vingts jours* (or *Around the World in Eighty Days*), published in 1873, may have been fiction, but they were based on Verne's rigorous and devoted research of the latest scientific discoveries.

Expeditions to the poles, the deep sea, and outer space were all topics expounded upon by Verne. Trained as an attorney, he abandoned his legal practice when his earliest publications proved popular. Most of his work detailed travel to extreme locations, including his 1870 masterpiece, *Twenty Thousand Leagues under the Sea*, and *De la terre à la lune* (*From the Earth to the Moon*), published in 1865. An avid researcher who spent many hours in the Bibliothèque Nationale de France, Verne scrupulously and passionately devoured information about the latest scientific discoveries, especially in geography, and befriended the illustrious geographer and explorer Jacques Arago. Verne's novels and short stories were highly successful, and he is among the most widely translated writers in history, situated between Agatha Christie and William Shakespeare. It should be noted that while Verne is lauded internationally as the father of science fiction, he is also a major literary figure in his native France. He had profound influence on his generation's avant-garde writers and, later, on the surrealists. Unfortunately, the poor quality of the English versions of his books limited his scholarly reputation outside of France for decades.

Nevertheless, Verne's works inspired an array of scientists and explorers. *Twenty Thousand Leagues under the Sea*, for example, had a huge impact on Jacques Cousteau, the father of deep-sea research, who referred to the novel as his "shipboard bible,"[1] and on the pioneering submarine designer, Simon Lake. Lake wrote in his autobiography: "Jules Verne was in a sense the director-general of my life."[2] This book even inspired Antarctic explorer Sir Ernest Shackleton.

Perhaps one of the reasons Verne's works resonated with later generations is that they were remarkably prescient. *From the Earth to the Moon*, for example, stated that Americans (with their engineering predilections) would be the first to land on the earth's satellite, and that they would launch their spacecraft from Florida or Texas, as their locations were ideal in terms of proximity to the moon and atmospheric conditions. The primary NASA locations reside in those two states. Rocketry inventors Konstantin Tsiolkovsky, Robert Goddard, and Hermann Oberth were also inspired by this work. So too was Apollo 8 astronaut, Frank Borman, who noted that in "a very real sense, Jules Verne is one of the pioneers of the space age."[3] Salyut 6 cosmonaut Georgi Grechko likewise stated that his colleagues had all read Verne, "a visionary who saw flights in space. I'd say this flight too was predicted by Jules Verne."[4]

Polar explorer Richard E. Byrd, who flew over the South Pole on November 29, 1929, stated that it was "Jules Verne who launched me on this trip."[5] *A Winter Amid the Ice* (1855), *The Adventures of Captain Hattaras* (1864), and *An Antarctic Mystery* (1897) were likely additional sources of inspiration for Byrd. Interestingly, *An Antarctic Mystery*, which takes place in 1839, was a response to Edgar Allan Poe's 1838 novel, *The Narrative of Arthur Gordon Pym of Nantucket*, perhaps the first work to place its protagonists at the earth's southern extreme.

There seems to have been no viable influence of expeditions on high fashion during Darwin's or Verne's lifetime. However, imagery illustrating expeditions' movement into other areas of popular culture does exist. A unique photograph, dating to circa 1880 and in the collection of the Library of Congress, shows the celebrated French actress Sarah Bernhardt dressed fashionably in a "full-length portrait, seated, facing slightly right, with a person in deep sea diving gear standing alongside" (fig. 4). A second photograph amusingly captures Bernhardt wearing the deep-sea suit herself and is labeled the "Ocean Empress" (fig. 5). What the images represent—costumes from a play or a promotional event—is unknown. This deep-sea suit appears to be the version designed by Augustus Siebe and is described in Ariele Elia's essay.

It was not until World War I that expedition-influenced fashions and related imagery began to emerge. Both fashion

4
Sarah Bernhardt, seated, alongside person
in deep-sea diving gear, circa 1880

—

moon-inspired ensembles, and fur suits and pants that were decidedly new and sometimes bizarre. Meanwhile, fashion publications not only increased the number of fashion spreads photographed "on location," but began to seek environments that were decidedly extreme.

Before beginning an analysis of extreme expedition clothing and its influence, specifically garments from the Arctic, it is prudent to address the terminology used to describe the various indigenous groups that have inhabited that region for millennia. One of the most potent of the commonly used words to describe the indigenous, nomadic peoples living north of the Arctic Circle is "Eskimo." Although the name is commonly used in Alaska to refer to Inuit and Yupik people, it is considered derogatory in other parts of the region. Used by non-Inuit people, including early European explorers, it was reportedly thought to mean "eater of raw meat." Linguists now believe that "Eskimo" is derived from an Ojibwa word meaning "to net snowshoes."

The people of Canada and Greenland prefer other names. "Inuit," meaning "people," is used in most of Canada, and the language is called "Inuktitut" in eastern Canada. The Inuit people of Greenland refer to themselves as "Greenlanders" or "Kalaallit" in their language, which they call "Greenlandic" or "Kalaallisut." Most Alaskans continue to accept the name "Eskimo," particularly because "Inuit" refers only to the Iñupiat of northern Alaska, the Inuit of Canada, and the Kalaallit of Greenland, and is not a word in the Yupik languages of Alaska and Siberia.

I am indebted to Sarah Pickman, a doctoral candidate at Yale University researching the vitally important role clothing has played in the history of expeditions, for tackling the issue of terminology. Her essay, based on her unpublished master's thesis, not only addresses the complexity of racial terminology, it also dissects the reasons some heroic-age explorers rejected the appropriation of indigenous Arctic clothing, while others more readily adopted it. Pickman also addresses the relationship between the indigenous peoples of this newly discovered region and the European explorers. Issues from the practical nature of furs and animal skins (and their ability to allow humans to withstand the harsh

magazines and designers took the first steps toward appropriating material from the Arctic around 1916–1917. Over the coming decades, fashion slowly began to incorporate more extreme clothing elements as expeditions gained greater political relevance, and technological developments increased and spread.

The space race between the Soviet Union and the United States dominated national agendas, while successful climbs to the highest and most challenging mountains in the world—Mount Everest and K2—occurred in the 1950s. By the 1960s, the correlation between expedition clothing and high fashion reached a creative peak. Popular interest in expeditions surged; therefore, it is no wonder that designers—both established names and newcomers—created

5
Sarah Bernhardt in deep-sea diving costume
as the "Ocean Empress," circa 1880

cold), to racial and cultural discrimination and exploitation, are addressed in her groundbreaking essay.

Furthermore, because this book focuses on fashion, the fashion specialists who have contributed do not give lengthy and detailed descriptions of expeditions. Such documentation is covered not only by Sarah Pickman, but also by Lacey Flint, curator of The Explorers Club in New York. Flint's essay documents the rich history of this pioneering organization and its role as a science-driven entity. The phenomena that led to its creation and its mission are described, as well as the significant "first" feats of its most celebrated members and their collective contributions to exploration.

The fashion historians, Ariele Elia and Elizabeth "Liz" Way, members of the curatorial team at the Museum at FIT, write about the impact of deep-sea and outer-space exploration on fashion, respectively. Elia investigates topics such as the influence of ocean navigation and extreme diving on both fashion design and photography; the recent popularity of new materials such as neoprene; and even how new species, such as bioluminescent animals found only in the deepest parts of the ocean, have influenced avant-garde fashion collections. Way explores the fascination with travel beyond our planet, a phenomenon that reached its zenith during the mid-twentieth century. The height of the Cold War space race between the Soviet Union and the United States (from the late 1950s to the early 1970s) captured the imaginations of young fashion designers and photographers. Way documents how cutting-edge technology of actual space clothing inspired an array of lunar-like fashions and photographs at the middle of the twentieth century.

My own essay focuses primarily on the influence of polar expeditions and extreme mountain climbing on high-style clothing and fashion imagery from the 1910s to the present. It also addresses the growth of firms that were created to provide expedition-worthy clothing and gear, beginning in the early twentieth century, and the inroads they made to high style. The essay is arranged both chronologically and thematically, as developments in expeditions and technology often inform and overlap with the fashion trends they inspire.

It is understood that many of the objects discussed in this book—mainly the furs and animal products used by the fashion industry—are controversial. In no way are we historians attempting to popularize or glamorize the often grizzly culling of furs. While it can be argued that the indigenous peoples of the Arctic maintained a balanced relationship with nature—as they only hunted and harvested enough wildlife to sustain their small, nomadic populations—the same cannot be said for contemporary Western purveyors of luxury goods inspired by groups such as the Inuit.

Dr. Jonathan Faiers, a fashion scholar and theorist, has begun an extensive study of fur and its relationship to fashion and human consumption. His essay is a condensed version of his forthcoming publication addressing many issues surrounding the allure of fur, as well as its pivotal developments in the long and controversial relationship between humans and the animals they coveted and harvested for profit.

We recognize that most scientists agree that the earth's climate has been undergoing dramatic changes. The Arctic and its indigenous wildlife are already being directly impacted by climate change. While this phenomenon is not a primary focus of this project, mankind's exploitation of natural resources is indeed an underlying aspect that is eerily, if quietly, ever present in our collective research and findings.

The urge to explore—both the greater world and one's internal landscape—is also the primary and underlying force of this project. Like the burgeoning scientific endeavors that inspired expeditions in the nineteenth century, this book is an early, preliminary investigation of the rich and varied world of extreme exploration, and the many ways it has made its mark on high fashion. It is by no means a comprehensive study of either field as the topics are incalculably vast. All the contributors readily recognize that we are at only the outset of a long journey of exploration and discovery—a journey we hope will continue in the centuries to come.

# 1

# The Explorers Club

## A BRIEF HISTORY

### Lacey Flint

———————◇———————

At 46 East Seventieth Street in Manhattan stands a Jacobean-manor-style town house that is the headquarters of a unique and storied institution, The Explorers Club. Founded in 1904, it is an international, multidisciplinary, professional organization that is dedicated to advancements in scientific exploration and field research. The Club's core philosophy is to preserve humankind's instinct to explore land, sea, air, and space.

Prior to the nineteenth century, exploration was motivated by conquest (political, geographic, and religious) and by trade. With the rise of science during the Victorian era—especially the natural sciences—exploration began to assume its modern purpose. This new motivation had a not insignificant competitive edge, which was notably manifested at the turn of the twentieth century with the race to the North Pole. Countries around the world were mounting expeditions to locate "farthest North," going beyond what previous parties had managed.

Realizing that such endeavors would require teamwork and collaboration, Henry Collins Walsh, newspaper editor and war correspondent for the *New York Herald* and

*Harper's Weekly*, imagined a club whose members would push the boundaries of human exploration. In his invitation to join his newly formed Explorers Club, he wrote that its purpose would be:

> to further general exploration, to spread knowledge of the same, and to encourage explorers in their work by evincing interest and sympathy, and especially by bringing them in personal contact and binding them in the bonds of good fellowship.

The Explorers Club was by no means the only organization dedicated to scientific discovery. The United Kingdom's Royal Geographical Society, created in 1830, was (and still is) dedicated to the development and promotion of geographical knowledge. Its American counterpart, the National Geographic Society, based in Washington, DC, and founded in 1888, likewise seeks "to increase and diffuse geographic knowledge." And in New York, the American Museum of Natural History, one of the world's preeminent scientific and cultural institutions, was established in 1869 with a global mission to "discover, interpret,

6
The interior of The Explorers Club Library,
which features a ceiling from a fifteenth-century
Italian monastery

and disseminate information about human cultures, the natural world, and the universe through a wide-ranging program of scientific research, education, and exhibition."

But the vision and earnest approach of The Explorers Club is unique. Since its inception, members of The Club have dedicated themselves to the mission of supporting some of the most daring expeditionary efforts of the twentieth century. These expeditions have come to be recognized as The Club's "Famous Firsts." Robert Peary, The Club's third president, and Matthew Henson "discovered" the North Pole in 1909. The discovery of the South Pole by member Roald Amundsen followed soon after, in 1911. Club members Sir Edmund Hillary and Tenzing Norgay were the first to summit Mount Everest in 1953, and Mariana Trench, the lowest point on earth, was attained by our Honorary President Don Walsh and Club Fellow Jacques Piccard in 1960. Neil Armstrong, Edwin "Buzz" Aldrin, and Michael Collins reached the moon in 1969, while carrying The Explorers Club Flag. This essay examines these landmark expeditions and will briefly touch upon some of the foundational efforts and discoveries that led ultimately to the success of the "Famous Firsts" expeditions.

### The Long and Icy Trail Northward

The race to the North Pole gave rise to some of the most famous expeditions in history. The Explorers Club members

Robert Peary and Matthew Henson are credited with being the first to reach the Pole in 1909. Some, however, argued that their attempt to stand on the earth's most northern extreme was not successful. For example, Arctic explorer Frederick A. Cook infamously asserted that he had beaten Peary and Henson to the Pole by nearly a full year. Cook's claim was later discredited, but the controversy of his declaration raised significant questions about the validity of Peary and Henson's conquest.

Over the past century, numerous accounts and studies have attempted to either discredit or prove the outcome of the 1909 expedition. While some have concluded that neither expedition was successful in reaching the North Pole, others back Peary and Henson's claim. For example, a 1988 report published in *National Geographic* proclaimed that the Peary/Henson expedition fell thirty to sixty miles short of the Pole. Conversely and somewhat ironically, in 1989, a 230-page report from the National Geographic Society reasserted the claim that Peary and Henson did in fact make it. As recently as 2005, Bruce Henderson, a reporter and field producer, marshaled evidence in *True North: Peary, Cook, and the Race to the Pole* that Cook was successful in his attempt. Ultimately, although The Explorers Club recognizes that there will never be enough evidence to determine beyond a reasonable doubt that the 1909 expedition actually reached the North Pole, it celebrates the Peary/Henson expedition all the same.

Humanity's fascination with finding the farthest point north was documented as early as circa 320 BC: the Greek Pytheas is said to have discovered a northern land, Thule, which might have been Norway, Iceland, or Greenland. The Norse explored and settled in Greenland in AD 900. However, nothing has ever fed humanity's fascination with the Far North like the competition to reach the North Pole at the outset of the twentieth century.

The race for the North Pole was a fervent one. On the Lady Franklin Bay Expedition (1881–1884), American Lieutenant Adolphus W. Greely, who would later become The Explorers Club's first president, reached a new farthest-north point at

7
Explorers Club Flag 161 is the only object to ever have traveled to both the highest and lowest points on earth, summiting Mount Everest in 1981 and descending into the Mariana Trench in 2012.

**8**
Hand-colored lantern slide
taken at the North Pole

**9**

Artist in Exploration Albert Operti's rendering of
Matthew Henson, Robert Peary, and their team
at the North Pole, April 9, 1909

83°. In 1893, Peary attempted the Pole in the first of what would be eight expeditions, including that of Norwegian Fridtjof Nansen. All of these expeditions served as learning opportunities, filled with trial and error. They ultimately formed the foundation for Peary and Henson's 1909 expedition.

In July 1908, the SS *Roosevelt* departed from New York City's Twenty-Forth Street pier headed for Cape Sheridan on Ellesmere Island, the winter base from which Robert Peary and Matthew Henson's North Pole attempt would be launched. After arriving at Cape Sheridan on September 5, the team spent the Arctic winter readying themselves for their final destination. Under Henson's supervision, sledges were built using a modified design: long runners that curved upward to better negotiate inequalities of ice were lashed together with sealskin thongs. Measuring twelve feet long by two feet wide, the large size would allow for a more even distribution of weight. Upon completion, teams would sledge supplies ninety-three miles northwest to Cape Columbia in preparation for their journey to the Pole.

On March 1, 1909, the expedition departed Cape Columbia, stepped off land, and set out across the frozen polar waters. The Pole lay more than 400 miles to the north across the glacial landscape, the Big Lead fault line, and pack ice. The expedition traveled in a series of relays, each party blazing a trail some distance farther than the last and turning back sporadically. On April 1, 1908, Captain Robert A. Bartlett and the final supporting party would turn back toward Cape Sheridan after reaching 87° north. It was up to Peary, Henson, and their team of four Inuit, named Ootah, Ooqueah, Seegloo, and Egingwah, to continue northward. On April 6, 1909, Camp Jesup was established at the North Pole.

## South Polar Pioneers

Documented South Polar expeditions began long ago, in 1773, when British explorer Captain James Cook reached 71°10' south in the Antarctic, crossing the Antarctic Circle. In his expedition papers, Captain Cook claimed, "I can be bold enough to say that no man will ever venture farther than I have done and that the lands which may lie to the south will never be explored." Cook may have been a world-class adventurer, but he was certainly not prescient: two parties reached the South Pole in 1912.

The outset of exploration to the South Pole formally began in 1895, when the Sixth International Geographical Congress meeting in London adopted a resolution. It stated:

> That the Congress record its opinion that the exploration of the Antarctic Regions is the greatest piece of geographical exploration still to be undertaken. That in the view of the additions to knowledge in almost every branch of science which would result from such a scientific exploration, the Congress recommends that the scientific societies throughout the world should urge in whatever way seems to them most effective, that this work should be undertaken before the close of the century.

The resolution and attention to Antarctic exploration was perhaps inspired by Norwegian Leonard Kristensen. On January 24, 1895, Kristensen and six men were the first to step on the continent of Antarctica after sailing through the Ross Sea in search of whales. Continuing to push the boundaries of southward exploration, in 1897, Adrien de Gerlache of Belgium wintered below the Antarctic Circle. Roald Amundsen, the legendary Norwegian explorer whose team would later become the first to reach the South Pole, was a member of de Gerlache's party.

Antarctic exploration continued. During the 1901–1904 *Discovery* expedition, led by Captain Robert Falcon Scott of Great Britain, the existence of the only snow-free Antarctic valleys was discovered, one of which contained Antarctica's longest river. Scott's additional achievements included the discoveries of the Cape Crozier emperor penguin colony, King Edward VII Land, and the Polar Plateau on which the South Pole is located.

From 1907 to 1909 Ernest Shackleton, a member of Scott's *Discovery* expedition, led the *Nimrod* expedition within ninety-seven miles of the South Pole and determined a new farthest south at latitude 88° south. In 1908, a member of the

**10**

Hand-colored lantern slide from the *Terra Nova* Antarctic
expedition (1910–1913), photograph by Herbert Ponting

—

*Nimrod* expedition, Australian Douglas Mawson, reached the South Magnetic Pole—the wandering point on the Southern Hemisphere that shifts with Earth's magnetic field—and was the first to attain the summit of Mount Erebus.

The heroic age of exploration reached its pinnacle when Roald Amundsen and his team became the first to arrive at the South Pole on December 14, 1911. Amundsen was a veteran explorer who had, among his many credits, pioneered the Northwest Passage (1903–1905). As of 1909, it was the North Pole that was his primary goal. In preparation for the journey northward, Amundsen gathered a crew and secured a ship, only to hear news at the last moment that Robert Peary had already reached 90° north. In his 1927 autobiography, *My Life as an Explorer*, Amundsen wrote, "This was a blow indeed! If I was going to maintain my prestige as an explorer I must quickly achieve a sensational success of some sort."

Amundsen would not be stopped—but he was redirected. Within a year of the news of Peary and Henson's success, Amundsen sailed for the uncharted terrain of the South Pole with the same crew and ship he had planned to take north. The privately revised expedition schedule required the schooner *Fram* to leave Norway in August 1910 and sail to Madeira in the Atlantic, its only port of call. From there the ship would proceed directly to the Ross Sea in Antarctica, heading for the Bay of Whales, an inlet on the Ross Ice Shelf where Amundsen intended to make his base camp.

Despite the fact that the South Pole had not been Amundsen's original target, his team quickly shifted tack and adjusted its preparations. Amundsen and his team meticulously calculated the direction and distance to be covered each day, predicting changes in the weight of supplies and in the strength and number of sled dogs, in order to get to the Pole and back. On October 20, 1911, Amundsen, Helmer Hanssen, Sverre Hassel, Oscar Wisting, Olav Bjaaland, and fifty-two sled dogs set out, southward bound.

On December 14, 1911, at approximately three o'clock in the afternoon, the team halted and raised the Norwegian flag. As Amundsen wrote in *The South Pole*, "Of course, every one of us knew that we were not standing on the absolute spot . . . but we were so near it that the few miles which possibly separated us from it could not be of the slightest importance." For good measure, and perhaps to assuage the doubts that the North Pole discovery had faced, two men trekked forward another twelve and a half miles along the trajectory of the march, one at a 90° angle to the left, and one to the right. Additional readings taken in ensuing days assured them that those extra miles had indeed covered the Pole.

Captain Scott, the leader of the *Terra Nova* expedition and Amundsen's chief rival for conquest of the South Pole, set sail for the Antarctic Circle ahead of Amundsen in June 1910, with a team of sixty-five men and an array of ponies. Amundsen was a sporting, gentleman explorer in the best tradition of The Explorers Club, and he wired Scott to inform him that he, too, was en route and in pursuit. Amundsen had learned much about surviving on the ice from natives of the Arctic Circle; in the end, he overtook Scott and beat him to the South Pole by thirty-four days. Everyone under Amundsen's command survived the journey. But Scott was less fortunate: when he and four of his men reached the Pole on January 16, 1912, they found a Norwegian flag flying next to Amundsen's tent, and then all five of them, including Scott, perished in the attempt to make their way back.

## The Journey to the Top

In 1885, Clinton Thomas Dent, president of the Alpine Club, declared that because of successful ascents in the Alps,

climbing Mount Everest was also plausible. Expeditions to Everest were soon thereafter launched, but it was not until the 1921 British Reconnaissance Expedition that the northern approach to the mountain was discovered by George Mallory and Guy Bullock.

On June 8, 1924, Mallory and another member of the British Mount Everest Expedition, Andrew Irvine, made an attempt on the summit via the North Col route. The two climbers never returned and the search for their remains commenced. Irvine's ice ax was found in 1933 near depleted oxygen cylinders, and in 1936, sightings of what could have been a human corpse were recorded. On May 1, 1999, the Mallory and Irvine Research Expedition found Mallory's body, well preserved and intact because of the climate, on the North Face in a snow basin below and to the west of the traditional site of Camp VI, the last camp before the summit, at approximately 26,000 feet. Controversy has raged in the mountaineering community whether one or both of them reached the summit twenty-nine years before the confirmed ascent of Everest by Edmund Hillary and

Tenzing Norgay in 1953. Ultimately, although it would have been possible, it is unlikely that either Mallory or Irvine ever reached the summit.

The Swiss Expedition of 1952, led by Edouard Wyss-Dunant, was granted permission to attempt a climb from Nepal. The expedition established a route through the Khumbu Icefall and ascended to the South Col at an elevation of 26,201 feet. Raymond Lambert, a Swiss mountaineer, and Nepalese Sherpa Tenzing Norgay were able to reach a then record height of 28,199 feet on the southeast ridge. The duo was forced to turn back about 820 feet from the summit because of harsh conditions and malfunctioning oxygen tanks. On this expedition, no attempt at a final ascent of Everest was deemed practicable. The team was there for reconnaissance and to open up a new path for future expeditions. Norgay's experience would prove invaluable when he was hired to be part of the British Expedition with Hillary in 1953.

At 11:30 a.m. on May 29, 1953, Norgay and New Zealander Edmund Hillary reached the summit of Mount Everest,

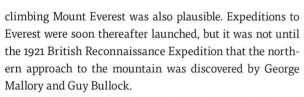

**12**
Edmund Hillary and Sherpa Tenzing Norgay
on expedition to Mount Everest in 1953.

the world's highest peak. The two men smiled and shook hands more than 29,000 feet above sea level. Their expedition had begun three months previously, in early March, in Kathmandu, Nepal, under the command of John Hunt. The team of twelve climbers were accompanied by an army of low-altitude porters and high-altitude Sherpas who, according to plan, dwindled from 450 men to zero as supplies were consumed, the terrain rose, and the air thinned to one-third of the amount of oxygen found at sea level.

Overcoming the treacherous, shifting glacial ice of the Khumbu Icefall at 18,000 feet, the expedition established Advanced Base Camp at 21,200 feet, in the Western Cwm canyon beneath the icy face of Mount Lhotse, one of the tallest mountains in the Himalayan chain. The climbing team and nineteen Sherpas reached the South Col, the 28,500-foot-high midpoint in the ridge connecting Lhotse and Everest. When bad weather brought the team to a halt on the Lhotse Face, Hillary convinced Hunt to allow him, Norgay, and Wilfrid Noyce to forge ahead alone.

The time had come for the final assault on the summit. Hillary and Norgay were prepared to make the attempt, and Hunt agreed. Trudging up the avalanche-prone soft snows of the South Summit, Hillary and Norgay encountered a forty-foot, vertical, rock wall. Clinging to a fissure in the rock, Hillary made his way up and over the wall, now known as the Hillary Step, and then belayed the rope for Norgay, who followed.

The last great physical obstacle had been overcome, but now an unexpected snag loomed. "We couldn't find the summit," Hillary later phrased it in an interview for *Life* magazine's *The 100 Greatest Adventures of All Time (The Explorers Club 100th Anniversary Edition)*:

> It wasn't until we came to a place where we could see that the ridge ahead dropped away, and we could see Tibet in front of us, that I realized we must be pretty close to the summit. Up above us the snow rounded off into a dome, and we realized that that must be the top.

In the years after reaching the top of the world, Tenzing Norgay traveled widely and served for twenty-two years as field director of the Himalayan Mountaineering Institute. Sir Edmund Hillary, knighted for his achievement, dedicated much of his life to building hospitals and schools to better the lives of the people of the Himalayas through his Himalayan Trust. The year of the summit victory, Hillary, Norgay, and Hunt were elected as Honorary Members of The Explorers Club, the most esteemed classification for membership.

## Diving Deeper

Oceanography may be one of the newer fields of science, but its roots extend back several tens of thousands of years, to when people began to venture from their coastlines via waterways. It was not until about 850 BC that early naturalists and philosophers began attempting to understand the enormous bodies of water they saw from land. Early exploration of the oceans was primarily for cartography and was limited mainly to the waters' surfaces and whatever was collected by fishermen.

The foundation of modern oceanography can be attributed to various expeditions, but most notably the research conducted during the *Challenger* expedition (1872–1876), whose circumnavigation of the globe was paramount. Fundamental analyses regarding salinity, density, and temperature of seawater, as well as ocean currents, sediment, and metrology were undertaken. Additionally, hundreds of new species of underwater life were discovered, and underwater mountain chains were documented.

As technology developed, so too did the study of oceans. In 1934, American William Beebe was lowered in a tethered bathyscaphe to a depth of 3,028 feet, marking the advent of manned exploration of the ocean depths. During World War II, electronic navigation systems were developed that transformed ocean travel. It was during this period that deep-ocean camera systems, early magnetometers, side-scan sonar instruments, and early technology for guiding remotely operated underwater vehicles (ROVs) also emerged.

In a significant step toward making the descent into the Mariana Trench possible, on February 15, 1954, the French research submersible FNRS III dove to 13,257 feet off the coast of Dakar, Africa. This submersible vessel, known as a bathyscaphe, was piloted by Georges Houot and Pierre Willm, and was invented by noted physicist Auguste Piccard. Their success thus ushered in the era of manned, untethered research submersibles.

On January 23, 1960, US Navy Lieutenant Don Walsh and Swiss engineer Jacques Piccard (Auguste Piccard's son) set a record for the deepest descent below the ocean's surface. After being towed for four days by a US Navy tugboat, the navigable submersible *Trieste*, a 150-ton steel bathyscaphe, sat atop a rough sea, prepared to plunge. Walsh and Piccard descended at a fast pace, four feet per second. So great was the depth, however, that their voyage took five hours to complete. The seabed of the Mariana Trench, located in the Pacific Ocean off the island of Guam, lies more than 36,000 feet below the surface. The *Trieste* ultimately reached a depth of 35,800 feet. In his account of the expedition, *Seven Miles Down: The Story of the Bathyscaph Trieste*, Jacques Piccard recalls, "And as we were settling into this final fathom, I saw a wonderful thing. Here, in an instant, was the

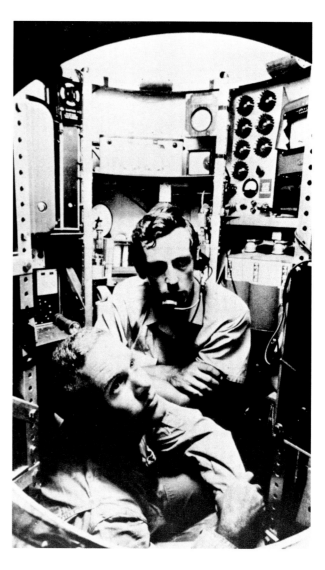

answer. Could life exist in the greatest depths of the ocean? It could!" The expedition found that sea life can exist at these amazing depths, where the pressure is eight tons per square inch. Out the window of the bathyscaphe, Piccard observed what was later determined to be a sea cucumber.

Unlike The Club's other "Famous Firsts," there has only been one other manned attempt at descending the Mariana

13
William Beebe (left) and Otis Barton with Explorers Club Flag 23 on expedition, testing their bathyscaphe in the Sargasso Sea in 1934

14
Don Walsh and Jacques Piccard inside the bathyscaphe *Trieste* on descent into the Mariana Trench, January 23, 1960

Trench. On March 26, 2012, the film director James Cameron became the third person to make the dive in the deep-submergence vehicle (DSV) *Deepsea Challenger*, carrying Explorers Club Flag 161.

**Racing into the Future: The Journey to Space**

The steps to the moon began with man's ability to fly. The first hot air balloon, *Aerostat Reveillon*, was flown in 1783 by scientist Jean-François Pilâtre de Rozier. Less than two months later, Joseph-Michel and Jacques-Étienne Montgolfier attempted the first manned balloon ride, ultimately realizing the dream of putting humans in flight. Motorized flight would come in the century to follow.

Wilbur Wright predicted in 1901 that men would not fly for another thousand years. This proclamation came shortly after a test of the glider that he and his brother Orville had built yielded a less than stellar performance. Their 1902 glider, however, disproved that hypothesis when it made a record 622½-foot flight. By 1903, the Wright Brothers had added a motor to the *Flyer*, their 600-pound plane made of wood, muslin, and wire. On December 17, 1903, with Orville piloting, their craft flew 120 feet for a total of twelve seconds. Human flight was now more feasible than ever.

Building upon feats of aviation and the early rocket science inspired by World War II, explorers fixed their sights on space. On October 4, 1957, a 184-pound satellite, *Sputnik I*, became the first man-made object ever to orbit Earth. The Soviet Union's aluminum sphere spent three months circling the Earth, transmitting radio signals that were analyzed to gather data about the upper atmosphere. *Sputnik I*'s importance was less scientific than symbolic. With the Cold War prevalent, the launch of the satellite was nothing less than the space shot heard around the world. The space race between the United States and the Soviet Union was on.

The first US satellite, *Explorer 1*, went into orbit on January 31, 1958. In 1961, Russian Lieutenant Yuri Gagarin became the first human to orbit Earth in *Vostok 1*. On February 20, 1962, John Glenn's historic flight on *Friendship 7* made him the first American to orbit Earth. Throughout the twentieth century, space exploration has continued to push boundaries. Scientists maintain that research of the universe is vitally important and only in its infancy. As Steven J. Dick, NASA's chief historian, thoughtfully addressed the issue in *The Importance of Exploration*: "Is space exploration really desirable at a time when so much needs doing on Earth? The argument is exploration, and that we should undertake it for the most basic of reasons, our self-preservation as a creative, as opposed to stagnating, society."

The world stood breathless as Neil Armstrong announced, "One small step for a man, one giant leap for mankind." On July 20, 1969, astronauts Armstrong and Edwin "Buzz" Aldrin walked on the moon. Onboard Apollo 11, a miniature version of The Explorers Club Flag accompanied the mission. Apollo 11 was the pinnacle of the Apollo program, set in motion eight years earlier by President John F. Kennedy with one simple goal: to reach the surface of the moon.

The lunar module *Eagle*, with Armstrong and Aldrin aboard, separated from the command and service module *Columbia*, piloted by Michael Collins. The *Eagle* descended to the lunar surface as the *Columbia* circled above. The module's autopilot nearly carried its crew into a rocky crater, but Armstrong switched to manual control and guided the craft to its intended destination, the level bed of the dusty Sea of Tranquility. After exiting the *Eagle*, the two men explored the lunar landscape on foot for two hours and thirty-one minutes. During that time, they collected soil samples. They deployed a seismometer to measure tremors and deployed a reflector allowing a laser beam shot from Earth to bounce back. The beam's round-trip travel time yielded a precise measurement of the moon's distance from our planet: 238,856 miles. They also planted an American flag.

The return trip was three days' silent cruise through space, then a 25,000-mile-per-hour ride through Earth's atmosphere at a blazing 4000°F hull temperature, followed by parachute deployment and splashdown. From the Sea of Tranquility to the Pacific Ocean, from one world to another, the crew of Apollo 11 had returned home. Upon reflection,

**15**
An image of the Apollo 11 moon landing, together with the
miniature Explorers Club Flag that Neil Armstrong carried
in the pocket of his space suit during the mission

Buzz Aldrin remarked in *Famous First Flights that Changed History*, "The future of space exploration is limited only by our ability to imagine."

## Women at The Explorers Club

According to The Explorers Club Bylaws, adopted October 25, 1905:

> Persons eligible for active membership shall be men who have engaged in exploration, or who have added to the geographical knowledge of the world; travelers who have done some distinctive work, and who have added to the world's store of knowledge concerning the countries they have visited, as, for instance, by the publication of a notable book or articles . . .

"Persons eligible for active membership shall be men" was staunchly enforced. It was not until 1981, following an impassioned letter from noted astrophysicist Carl Sagan, that this component of the Bylaws was amended and women were finally permitted access to applications. In that year, the first class of twenty women was elected to membership. Included in those ranks were aquanaut Sylvia Earle; former NASA astronaut and the first American woman to walk in space, Kathy Sullivan; and archaeologist Anna Roosevelt.

Little has been done, however, to assess what involvement women may have had in The Club despite their lack of membership. It would be all too easy to assume that they had none, that The Club believed women's accomplishments to be of no value, and that their words were unworthy of note. That would be a grave mistake. Women may not have been among our earlier members, but as explorers, and supporters of exploration, they were celebrated.

Polar wives, as they were sometimes called, were often important fixtures on Arctic expeditions. Eva Nansen, Emily Shackleton, and Kathleen Scott joined their husbands on expedition on multiple occasions. Josephine Peary gave birth to her first daughter, Marie, 13° south of the North Pole, while on the Second US North Greenland Expedition

AMELIA EARHART
OUR GUEST OF HONOR

EXPLORERS CLUB
LADIES NIGHT
NOVEMBER 7th, 1932

(1893–1895) with her husband, Robert Peary. She accompanied him on six of his Arctic expeditions and was an accomplished author who detailed her time in the North.

In the early years of The Club, events were frequently arranged to acknowledge the accomplishments of particular explorers. On December 22, 1912, The Club hosted its first female guest of honor, the English travel author Ethel Brilliana Tweedie, who wrote as Mrs. Alec Tweedie. Tweedie traveled extensively in the Arctic, beginning in 1886.

Perhaps one of the most famous women explorers honored by The Club was Amelia Earhart. After accomplishing various feats of aviation, plans were developed for Earhart to become the first woman and the second person to fly solo across the Atlantic. On May 20, 1932, five years to the day after Charles Lindbergh's historic transatlantic flight, she

**16**
Program cover featuring Amelia Earhart's presentation
at The Explorers Club on November 7, 1932

took off from Harbor Grace, Newfoundland, with plans to land in Paris. Although strong north winds, icy conditions, and mechanical problems plagued the flight and forced her to land in a pasture near Londonderry in Ireland, Earhart felt the flight proved that men and women were equal in "jobs requiring intelligence, coordination, speed, coolness, and willpower."

Filled with genuine admiration for her exploits, The Club determined to recognize Earhart's accomplishment and hold an event in her honor. As excerpted from the Board Minutes of June 2, 1932:

> Whereas Amelia Earhart, in being the first woman to fly alone across the Atlantic Ocean, has added to an already distinguished career a truly great pioneering feat of air exploration; and

> Whereas she flew across the Atlantic Ocean in 1928 as the first woman passenger, and is thus the only person to have twice flown this ocean; and

> Whereas no woman has done more than she has to demonstrate the safety and practicality of air travel for all people; and

> Whereas Amelia Earhart, as an air pilot of the first rank, has brought honor to her country and to her fellow countrymen: therefore be it

> Resolved: That we, the members of the Board of Directors of the Explorers Club, give expression of admiration and respect felt by the members of the Club for her splendid accomplishments and for her acts of calm courage; and be it further

> Resolved: That this Resolution be spread upon the records of The Explorers Club and an engrossed copy be presented to Ms. Earhart.

Earhart would host the first Ladies' Night in the new Club headquarters located at 10 West Seventy-Second Street on November 7, 1932. In her memoir, *The Fun of It*, Amelia Earhart wrote: "'I think I'd like to fly,' I told the family casually that evening, knowing full well I'd die if I didn't." That innate compulsion to explore embodies the explorer. Exploration and the need to discover is inherent. It is not exclusive to any one category of person.

## Continuing the Legacy

There is a notion today that, since the highest mountains have all been climbed and the poles have both been reached, there are no more adventures to be had. I could not disagree more. Adventure is in the individual. It is as close as putting on your boots in the morning and heading out the door. And it is not about the prize, the trophy, the goal, the gold. Robert Service in his poem "The Spell of the Yukon" put it perfectly: "Yet it isn't the gold that I'm wanting / so much as just finding the gold." That is adventure—the finding of it.

Although The Club does differentiate between adventure and exploration, Arctic explorer Will Steger encapsulates that feeling of curiosity as quoted in *Life* magazine's *The 100 Greatest Adventures of All Time (The Explorers Club 100th Anniversary Edition)*: "The Club is composed of individuals who are curious about our planet and our universe, and membership is open to qualified individuals and corporate leaders who promote The Club's mission by undertaking significant roles in the fields of science and exploration."

Our 3,500 current members represent more than sixty countries and range in age from sixteen to ninety-seven. Although this essay only examined the "Famous Firsts," our members go on upward of six hundred expeditions each year and encompass all fields of science. Club members are constantly finding new and creative research to undertake. From discovering fungi used to treat cancer, using citizen science to fill fundamental ocean information gaps, or rapelling into an active volcano to gather data, Club members remain vigilant and determined to explore.

The Explorers Club cherishes its past but is also firmly focused on the future. The well-being of our planet will soon

be in the hands of the young explorers and scientists trained today. A primary objective of the Club is to identify the next generation of explorers and foster the vision, courage, and tenacity necessary for successful exploration. The beckoning horizon of exploration has long been open, and new discoveries abound. The importance of The Explorers Club's mission remains as powerful as ever: to inspire exploration and the protection of wild places from our backwoods to our oceans, mountain peaks, and distant galaxies, while sustaining a spirit of fellowship among all explorers.

**17**
The Explorers Club seal

# 2

# Dress, Image, and Cultural Encounter

## IN THE HEROIC AGE OF POLAR EXPLORATION

Sarah Pickman

———◇———

## Introduction

Mountaineers have a saying: "The best gear is invisible." Proper equipment allows climbers to reach their goals without encumbering them or distracting them from the task at hand. Yet sometimes, even in the most extreme environments on earth, the best gear is both invisible and highly conspicuous at the same time. For explorers during what is often called the "heroic age" of polar exploration—roughly 1890 to 1922—clothing met these dual requirements.

Clothes were an essential part of an explorer's kit. Obviously they protected the wearer from the fury of a polar climate, yet the explorer's garments were more than merely functional. In the Arctic and Antarctica, where one might expect the clothes to reflect practical considerations above all else, exploration garb was as much about self-presentation as protection from the elements. Clothes that might be thought of only as tools for staying warm and dry and nothing more were a means for explorers to project themselves as they wished to be seen, to reflect the cultures they came from, and establish themselves as professional explorers. While they may not have described their garb in terms of "fashion," they were concerned about image as well as function, even at the edges of the world.

Of course, Western explorers were not the first people to confront the challenges of dressing for polar landscapes. For centuries, the indigenous peoples of the Arctic have relied on clothes made from the furs and skins of local animals to survive in an unforgiving environment. As polar historian Barbara Schweger has discussed, over the course of the nineteenth century an increasing number of Western explorers, whalers, and fur traders who ventured into the Arctic acknowledged the superiority of native Inuit-style fur clothing over Western textile clothing for survival in that region, in both materials and construction.[1] However, even at the turn of the twentieth century, some polar explorers rejected indigenous dress and continued to primarily

18
Robert Peary on return from the North Pole, 1909,
photograph by Donald Baxter MacMillan, courtesy of
the Peary-MacMillan Arctic Museum, Bowdoin College

use Western—or in Inuit terms, "Southern"—garb on their expeditions. Why would some outsiders choose not to wear these protective garments?

Many modern accounts of polar explorers from the heroic age have ascribed a one-to-one correspondence between the adoption or rejection of Inuit dress by these men to their attitudes toward the Inuit themselves. Supposedly, those explorers who wore native-style fur clothing did so because they respected Inuit knowledge and experience of the Arctic environment, while those who did not held racist biases against indigenous peoples, dismissing them and their goods as primitive or uncivilized. Yet the actions and writings of some explorers, including those who lived intimately with Inuit communities, challenge these assumptions. Explorers' preference for native Arctic clothing did not always reflect respect for native Arctic peoples. Nor was a rejection of fur clothing a complete rejection of indigenous technology.

Rather, explorers' clothing at this time echoed a complex web of Western ideas about race, exoticism, nationalism, and anxieties surrounding "over-civilization." Additionally, exploration during this era was not limited to daring quests or an insatiable thirst for knowledge and discovery, even if explorers discussed it in these ways. Exploration was a profession, and the successful explorer needed to raise funds for expeditions through lecture tours, book sales, expedition subscriptions, and product endorsements.[2] Photography was an increasingly important part of expeditions, and explorers could use photos of themselves from the field to market their work to publishers and patrons. And the business of exploration required expedition leaders to dress the part. Under the right conditions, clothing could be a tool for the explorer both to achieve his goals in the field and to sculpt a compelling—indeed, a "heroic"—image back home. The right outfits would help a polar explorer survive on the ice floes and tundra *and* in the capitalist jungles of New York and London. Even those who admired Inuit clothing used this appreciation to build their public images and to lend authority to their efforts as explorers. By doing so, these men masked native contributions to polar exploration, even as they literally wore the evidence of these contributions on their bodies.

The relationship between these men and their clothes was further complicated by the politically ambiguous nature of the polar regions. Western exploration across the globe was often a precursor to government-backed colonizing efforts, from North America to Africa to Asia. Items from colonies, including food, artistic styles, and textiles, could become quintessential parts of the culture of the colonizer nations (think of chintz fabrics in Great Britain, or Native American buckskin as part of Euro-American "frontier wear"). Anthropologist Nicholas Thomas has argued that appropriating indigenous objects by appreciating them aesthetically in this way is "one of the obvious routes to national distinctiveness" for colonizing or settler nations.[3]

But the polar regions presented unique challenges to the colonial powers of Europe and the United States. Because their climates were deemed unfit for large-scale colonial settlement, the status of the Arctic and Antarctica as potential colonies was unclear. So what role did native clothing play in situations where colonial relationships were less clear-cut, and where attitudes toward native people were notably ambivalent? What could Westerners hope to gain by dressing like native polar peoples?

Regardless of whether certain explorers chose to adopt native dress or not, there is no doubt that even today clothing still forms a large part of the popular memory of the heroic age. Robert Peary's weather-worn face peeking out from a luxuriant fur hood, Robert Falcon Scott and his men posing in gabardine smocks, Roald Amundsen's stern visage emerging from a fur parka: these images have become iconic of this era, polar history, and exploration in general. Why have these garments become such an integral part of the *idea,* as well as the practice, of the polar explorer? What do they reveal about larger cultural beliefs at the turn of the twentieth century, and how do they challenge simplistic ideas about Westerners appropriating non-Western dress? And how do they represent concerns about style as much as function?

**19**
Roald Amundsen, circa 1920s

In the words of art historian Ruth Phillips, they are the kind of objects that form a "record of historical processes by which ideas of cultural difference have been constructed. They illuminate many individual acts of negotiation and cross-cultural appropriation that are not recorded in any other place."[4] This melding of appreciation and appropriation through dress is a topic that has been extensively discussed in many other geographic areas. However, the same subject has received comparatively little attention in the case of the Inuit and other indigenous Arctic peoples. Case studies of the three aforementioned explorers—Peary, Amundsen, and Scott—show how these "individual acts of negotiation" played out in a climate where native garb held great practical—indeed, potentially life-saving—advantages. They also challenge the simplistic adoption/respect versus rejection/prejudice dichotomy that links attitudes regarding dress with those toward indigenous people themselves.

This essay is divided into several sections. First, it outlines the technological and design factors that made native circumpolar clothing well suited to polar climates, primarily focusing on the garments of the North American Inuit, which most often served as the model for exploration gear.[5] Rather than offering an exhaustive survey of traditional native Arctic clothing, this section highlights some of the advantages native outfits had over the available Western clothing of the early twentieth century, which made such indigenous ensembles advantageous in polar regions.[6] I will only briefly touch on clothing's role

**20**
Kiota in sealskin shirt, 1913–1917, photograph by
Donald Baxter MacMillan, courtesy of the Peary-MacMillan
Arctic Museum, Bowdoin College

**21**
Inuit caribou parka with hood trimmed in polar-bear fur
(part of MacMillan's outfit, with polar-bear-fur pants, fig. 23),
courtesy of the Peary-MacMillan Arctic Museum,
Bowdoin College

in earlier nineteenth-century encounters between native polar peoples and Westerners, a topic that is the subject of an exhaustive survey by Schweger.[7]

The main section of this essay provides case studies of three of the most well-known polar explorers of the late nineteenth and early twentieth centuries: American Robert Peary, Briton Robert Falcon Scott, and Norwegian Roald Amundsen. Each employed a different strategy for selecting clothing for his expeditions and cultivating his own public image. These three men will be analyzed in the larger context of the "polar mania" at the turn of the twentieth century; contemporaneous ideas about masculinity, race, and civilization; and the financial realities that underpinned Victorian and Edwardian-era exploration. As historian Marionne Cronin has written, studying explorers' fur clothing can be a way to more fully reinsert native Arctic peoples into the story of exploration—a story in which their participation has typically been minimized or erased.[8] However, this essay will show how Peary, Amundsen, and Scott established their credibility as explorers by framing their ability to appreciate or reject Inuit technology and labor as part of *their own* skill as explorers. On the bodies of American and European adventurers, Inuit fur clothes embody Thomas's assertion that, "objects are not what they were made to be but what they have become."[9]

This essay will deal almost exclusively with the indigenous peoples of North America, especially of eastern and central Canada and Greenland. Terms such as "Arctic peoples" and "polar peoples" should therefore be understood to refer to North American Inuit—"Inuit" being the generally preferred term for native circumpolar peoples as a broad group—except where clearly noted.[10]

## Inuit Clothing and Cold-Weather Technology

Inuit clothing has never been uniform across all of North America, and ornamentation and materials especially have always differed from region to region, with decorative features often serving to delineate different groups of people.[11]

However, the basic forms of fur clothes have typically been similar across the high north, a testament to their effectiveness at preserving human life in these places. Traditionally, a typical winter outfit for both men and women included a parka, a long-sleeved fur outer garment with a built-in hood that fits loosely around the torso and is tighter in the sleeves. Parka hoods were finished with "ruffs" of fur around the opening, which buffered the wearer's face from cold and wind. The parka, which sat on top of fur or skin undershirts, was worn over fur trousers with fur boots and mittens. For extremely wet conditions, the parka might be topped with a waterproof outer garment made from animal intestines or fish skin.[12]

In a climate that cannot support the cultivation of fibrous plants or domesticated wool-bearing animals, fur and skin from animals such as caribou, seals, and polar bears are the only truly local material for clothes. Yet these furs and skins, if treated properly, are exceptionally suited for human wear in cold conditions. Animal furs and skins are not heat-generating materials in and of themselves, but good insulators with the ability to trap heat naturally lost from the wearer's body in pockets of air against the skin. Wearing multiple layers—for example, an inner layer with fur turned toward the body and an outer layer with fur turned away—traps multiple levels of warmed air. However, the clothes cannot be so tight that the air cannot circulate, and a slightly loose fit is necessary in order not to cut off air flow or blood circulation. Looser parkas also allow the wearer to pull his or her arms and hands out from the sleeves easily, and wrap them around the torso to warm them if needed.[13]

Traditional garment forms have a minimum of seams and openings, to decrease the areas where cold air might seep in, in contrast to Euro-American outerwear of the nineteenth and early twentieth centuries, which typically closed with buttons or toggles. Seams were sewn with animal sinew, which swelled when wet and provided an even tighter seal against moisture that might otherwise seep in along seams. Fur's major drawback is that it can be quite bulky and become heavy when damp. However, snow and ice crystals

can easily be brushed off fur, and damp fur garments can either be dried over a heat source or left outside so that the moisture freezes on the fur; it can then be scraped off. In contrast, when woven or knitted textiles absorb moisture and are not thoroughly dried, the moisture freezes into the cloth itself, making it extremely stiff, heavy, and cold, and reducing the cloth's insulating properties.[14]

Besides cold temperatures and wind chill, a great enemy of human activity in polar regions is perspiration. Without a method of escape, sweat trapped against the skin by heavy fur clothing will linger, causing the clothing to become damp (thereby reducing its insulating abilities) while conducting heat away from the body. To combat perspiration caused by physical activity, parkas allow the wearer to quickly throw back the hood or pull the bottom hem away from the body. This allows cold air to briefly "vent" under the parka to cool down the wearer.[15] Yet Inuit modes of physical activity also worked against the threat of perspiration. Fur clothing is ideal for protecting the body during prolonged periods of physical stillness outside, such as traditional methods of ice fishing or seal hunting, which required hours spent sitting patiently without moving.[16] Indigenous practices of wearing layers of highly insulating clothing while mitigating the effects of perspiration would later be adopted—with varying degrees of understanding and success—by explorers.

## Southerners Come to the Poles: Natives, Outsiders, and Ambivalence

The heroic age of polar exploration was the climax of a century of intense European and American probing in the Arctic and Antarctic regions. Initially, European interest in finding the Northwest Passage, an imagined route via water to the goods and economic markets of Asia, led most explorers to the Arctic, and by the mid-nineteenth century they were also joined by fur traders, whalers, and missionaries. Perhaps ironically, it was clothing that helped drive outsiders to the Arctic, as whale baleen—used for making corsets—sealskins, and Arctic fox furs became extremely

**22, 23**
(top) Inuit sealskin parka with decorative points, associated with Captain Robert A. Bartlett, circa 1908; (bottom) Inuit polar-bear-fur pants with sealskin (part of MacMillan's outfit with caribou jacket, fig. 21), courtesy of the Peary-MacMillan Arctic Museum, Bowdoin College

valuable raw materials for the Western fashion market. By the early nineteenth century, explorers, whalers, and sealers also began to systematically investigate the southernmost continent, observing and mapping small sections of coastline before being pushed back by sea ice.[17]

Many Western expeditions to the Arctic initially set out equipped with wool and cotton garments. This might be explained by the fact that many of these expeditions were officially military ventures. Polar exploration emerged at the same time as Euro-American colonial expansion into many other parts of the globe, and in the nineteenth century, national governments—especially that of Great Britain—were initially the primary backers of polar expeditions. These expeditions were usually outfitted by standard military contractors, who were used to sending soldiers and sailors to the field in cotton and wool clothing and leather boots.[18]

Some have argued that these government expeditions, particularly those sponsored by the British Royal Navy, were outfitted with textile clothing instead of fur only because of cultural prejudice. Historians Charles Officer and Jake Page have written:

> The [British Royal] navy largely [held beliefs that] … made the Inuit too low and barbaric to emulate. So, for example, the Royal Navy went forth in the wrong kind of clothes for the climate, evidently in the belief that they could bring their own climate with them.[19]

Indeed, cultural prejudice *was* a factor in dressing in the larger European and American colonial world. In the nineteenth century, at the same time that polar explorers were selecting their clothing, explorers in sub-Saharan Africa, Asia, and South America were likewise donning specific outfits, typically safari-style, khaki ensembles from suppliers such as Abercrombie & Fitch in New York and Benjamin Edgington in London. These ensembles often came complete with accessories like spine pads and pith helmets, thought to prevent a host of illnesses that would befall Caucasians overexposed to tropical sun and heat.[20] Not surprisingly, these outfits resembled the actual uniforms of British soldiers, who enforced colonial rule in many of these areas.[21] Similarly, European settlers in African and Asian colonies often tried to maintain the style of dress they were familiar with from home. There are numerous examples from colonial India, for example, of British administrators and expatriates suffering through heat and humidity in heavy European-style clothes.[22]

Yet as Schweger has noted, once in the Arctic, explorers often found that Western-style woolen or leather garments offered poor protection against the harsh climate. Some American and British explorers, including Elisha Kent Kane (active 1850–1855), John Rae (active 1846–1854) and Charles Francis Hall (active 1860–1871) began to trade with local Inuit for clothing or to commission Inuit women to sew garments for them, while noting in their diaries and published accounts the superiority of indigenous garments for coping with the climate.[23] Although some may have been prejudiced toward the Inuit on an individual level, this did not always prevent them from wanting to swap the clothes they had brought for the warmer furs. Within military and exploration circles, expedition leaders began to share information about fur clothing, even if their voyages still set out with stores of textile clothing for their crews.[24]

Given that explorers in other regions upheld Western ways of dressing, why did some polar explorers feel comfortable donning fur items or entire fur outfits? Besides protection from the extreme environment, perhaps the ambiguous status of the polar regions as potential colonies also helped enable such willingness to adopt native-style dress. The Arctic had wealth in furs and whales that could be exploited by small groups of traders and sailors, yet its harsh climate and lack of arable land discouraged large-scale colonial settlement. The status of Antarctica as a colony was even less clear-cut, since it lacked even fur-bearing land animals that might be valuable. Since the polar regions were not suitable as settler colonies, and there were few—if any—other Westerners there, explorers might have felt free from needing to "keep up appearances" in Euro-American style clothing.

This ambivalence toward the environment extended to indigenous polar people. As anthropologist Ann Fienup-Riordan has written, Victorian ideas of Manifest Destiny and industrial progress tinged the perception of other indigenous groups—for example, Native Americans—as savages who needed to be tamed and removed from land that Westerners wanted to settle. Yet, "Well after the press of civilization had crushed the 'wild Indian,' [the idea of ] 'noble Eskimos' prospered because they were perceived as no real threat."[25] In contrast to indigenous peoples further south, the Inuit represented "pure primitives," who were not as sophisticated as Euro-Americans but whose closeness to nature and fitness for their environment, as interpreted through prevailing Rousseauian and Darwinian ideas of civilization, were seen as somewhat commendable. Contemporary Western commentators focused on the Inuit's "hardiness and the rigors of their homeland. Whereas ... Indians were perceived to have a choice between savagism and civilization, Eskimos were described in more elemental terms. Their choice was between starvation and survival."[26]

Thus for explorers, "going native" through dress may have been seen as permissible in this ambiguous context. Visited by few outsiders, Americans and Europeans viewed the polar regions as so far at the edges of the global map that they were almost not of this world. In discussing the Arctic, though his analysis can also be applied to Antarctica as well,

24
Three Inuit women in fur and skin parkas,
Selawik, Alaska, circa 1929, photograph by Edward Curtis

Russell Potter writes, "The Far North has remained, despite its ostensible 'discovery,' a largely *unseen* country.... For this reason, the stakes in the visual depiction of the Arctic have always been different from those for nearly any other place on earth."[27] In terms of how they presented themselves visually, explorers approached these ambiguous regions with the ability to choose their garb according to their own goals, perhaps freed from some of the cultural constraints that followed explorers to other parts of the world. Yet this freedom only extended so far, as explorers in the field still had obligations to audiences and patrons at home.

## Cold Fever: Exploration and Polar Mania

Historian Stuart Weaver has noted that after the 1870s, instances of national governments acting as the sole backers of polar expeditions decreased. Aspiring explorers therefore needed to raise funds from other sources for transportation, supplies, and the salaries of their crews. This was increasingly accomplished through media engagement and private or commercial patronage. Prior to setting off, explorers could sell exclusive publication rights to the stories of any discoveries to newspapers. They could also solicit donations from the public, including large gifts from wealthy donors that came with the implied promise of naming a natural feature after the patron. After returning, explorers tried to recoup financial losses and generate profit through lecturing and publishing book accounts of their journeys. The lecture and publication circuit especially was a crucial part of exploration in the late nineteenth and early twentieth centuries.[28] The glory did not always belong to the man who had accomplished the greatest feat, but to the man who could get back to civilization, alive, with a unique (and salable) story to capture the public imagination.

And the public imagination *was* captured, so much so that by the end of the nineteenth century, being an explorer and making money by tapping into this fascination had become a viable, if unorthodox, profession. Polar explorers especially captivated the public. As the frontiers of the globe known

to Westerners expanded further and further, the Arctic and Antarctica became final frontiers, the proverbial ends of the earth, to be reached by Western civilization. At the same time, the exhibition of Arctic peoples at world's fairs and expositions in Chicago (1893), St. Louis (1904), Seattle (1909), and other cities helped ignite a frenzy of interest in the Arctic around the turn of the twentieth century. "Northerns," a genre of silent films focused on stories of Inuit people, fur trappers, and Klondike gold prospectors, were extremely popular, culminating in Robert Flaherty's classic documentary *Nanook of the North* in 1922 (fig. 45).[29] Audiences packed lecture halls around the world to hear talks by explorers, and their exploits filled the pages of popular periodicals. As historian Beau Riffenburgh has detailed in *The Myth of the Explorer,* newspaper publishers especially were intimately involved in exploration. For example, Riffenburgh has argued convincingly that as much as the 1909 controversy over the first explorer to claim the North Pole was a feud between Peary and his rival Dr. Frederick Cook, it was also a battle between their associated media partners, the *New York Times* and the *New York Herald.*[30]

Part of their popularity stemmed from the belief that these men, like explorers in Africa, South America, and elsewhere, embodied prevailing ideas about the need to preserve manliness in the face of "over-civilization" brought on by increased urbanization and industrialization.[31] What could prove a better antidote to the sheltered, civilized world of industrial America or Europe than braving harsh conditions at the end of the earth, with no one but perhaps "primitive Eskimos" for company? As Lisa Bloom has written, "The difficulty of life in desolate and freezing regions provided the ideal mythic site where men could show themselves as heroes capable of superhuman feats."[32] In the United States especially, wealthy patrons flocked to associate themselves with these heroes and fuel their own fascination with wilderness. Myriad summer camps, scouting organizations, and tourism companies urged young, urban, white American men to spend time playing at "being natives," lest their city lives make them too soft and unmanly.[33] By 1900, in New

York alone, there were at least half a dozen elite social clubs devoted to exploration, mountaineering, and other outdoor activities, including two devoted exclusively to polar exploration. One of these, the Peary Arctic Club, was formed solely to back Peary's attempts to reach the geographic North Pole.[34]

To men like American president Teddy Roosevelt—perhaps the most famous advocate of white men "roughing it" in the wilderness—to combat the ills of over-civilization, polar exploration and the attainment of goals such as reaching the "furthest north" latitude were tests of rugged manliness and national might. In a display of quintessential Victorian racial sentiment, Roosevelt himself once praised Peary as "a man who by his achievements makes it evident that in some of the [white] race, at least, there has been no loss of hardier virtues."[35]

## Clothes Make the Man: Lieutenant Robert E. Peary

What did Peary do to deserve Roosevelt's praise as the embodiment of the rugged, hardy yet civilized, white man? And how was his clothing an essential part of this image? Boastful, controversial, but undoubtedly prolific in his exploits, Robert Edwin Peary (1856–1920) is today one of the most widely known explorers of the early twentieth century. By 1909, the year he claimed to reach the North Pole with his assistant Matthew Henson and four Greenlandic Inuit men, Ooqueah, Ootah, Egingwah, and Seegloo, Peary's adventures and dashing persona had turned him into a national hero in the United States.

Peary, an American naval officer, conducted a short expedition onto the Greenland Ice Sheet in 1886, with six months of leave from his military post and a $500 loan from his mother.[36] By this time, Peary was ravenous for the fame that would result from daring polar exploits; as a young man he wrote in an oft-quoted letter to his mother, "I *must* have fame . . . while yet I have youth and strength and capacity to enjoy it to the utmost."[37] Once home, he began cultivating financial support for his bid for the North Pole, from organizations such as the American Geographical Society and wealthy individuals, many of whom coalesced into the Peary Arctic Club in 1898.[38]

In order to attract media attention and patrons, Peary promoted the attainment of the North Pole as a matter of American national pride. For example, he announced his achievement by cabling the Associated Press, "Stars and Stripes nailed to the North Pole."[39] Riffenburgh, who examined Peary's 1909 diary, notes that the explorer's own notes also show another, more private motivation. Even while marching northward across ice floes, Peary scribbled his plans for book deals, product endorsements, and promotional photos once he returned home.[40]

Peary spoke of the benefits of wearing fur clothing in the Arctic throughout his entire career. As early as the mid-1880s, when he made his first expeditions to Greenland, Peary touted the superiority of Inuit clothing for Arctic life, writing that, "The traveler who goes upon the ice-cap without fur clothing does so either from ignorance or because he is reckless."[41] From then on, his expedition plans always included procuring locally made fur clothing; commissioning Inuit women to make clothes for him and his team, while their husbands worked as hunters and guides. In his 1917 part memoir, part manual for aspiring explorers, *Secrets of Polar Travel*, Peary devoted an entire chapter to clothing. It opened with the statement:

> Many, finding the fur clothing of their own particular expeditions unsatisfactory for the purposes to which they put it, have drawn general instead of specific conclusions in regard to the value of fur. . . . British explorers seem to have been specially averse to the use of fur in Arctic work, their aversion to this style of clothing being as pronounced as their antipathy to the Eskimo dog for traction power.[42]

Peary went on to describe his typical ensemble and claimed that thus properly clothed, he had survived outdoors in temperatures of –50°F (–45°C).

Yet beyond protection in the field, Peary found that his Inuit gear could be a big draw for audiences at home. On his

Commander Peary
in Arctic dress.

final expedition in 1909, Peary made a note in his diary for his ideal promotional photo: "Have [photographer George] Borup take a . . . focus portrait of me in deer [caribou] coat (face unshaven) with bear roll [of fur, on hood], & keep on till satisfactory one obtained."[43] At his public lectures he prominently displayed Inuit objects, including furs and skins, and sometimes came on stage wearing furs.[44] On other occasions he had Henson burst onto the stage in the middle of the talk, clad in furs and leading a team of sled dogs, to thunderous applause.[45] Widely circulated photos

of Peary in furs were reproduced on posters to advertise his lectures.

In this self-fashioning, Peary was one in a long line of Americans who embraced indigenous clothing for their own goals. During the nineteenth and early twentieth century, Americans from Meriwether Lewis and William Clark to George Custer and William "Buffalo Bill" Cody appeared in public or posed for paintings and photographs wearing articles of Native American clothing, sometimes full ensembles, as a way to prove their credibility as frontiersmen,

**25**
"Commander Peary in Arctic dress," 1909,
paper postcard, courtesy of the Peary-MacMillan
Arctic Museum, Bowdoin College

**26**
Robert Peary on the deck of the steamship
*Roosevelt*, possibly near Ellesmere Island,
Nunavut, Canada, 1909

attract attention from Euro-American audiences through exoticism, and visually "assimilate" native peoples into mainstream American culture.[46] Peary recognized that fur clothing was key for survival in the Arctic, but in choosing to wear it he also embodied a preexisting model of what James Hanson has called American "frontier cross-dressing."[47] Peary took this model from the American West and moved it further north.

But while Peary admired and used Inuit clothing—for his own varied aims—his admiration for the indigenous people of the Arctic themselves was more selective. He would famously praise the Greenlandic Inuit who became his guides, to whom he owed his survival, by writing that, "with their racial inheritance of ice technic and their ability to handle sledges and dogs, [they] were more necessary to me . . . than any white man could have been. Of course they could not lead, but they could follow and drive dogs better than any white man."[48] He later remarked, "I have often been asked, of what use are the Eskimos to the world? . . . But let us not forget that these people . . . will yet prove their value to the world. With their help, the world shall discover the Pole."[49] A litany of Peary's exploitative actions toward the Inughuit Inuit community in northwestern Greenland, the people he considered "his Eskimos," has already been catalogued in Kenn Harper's *Give Me My Father's Body*. Here, it is important to note that like fur ensembles, Peary understood the value of Inuit people themselves as tools, to both accomplish his goals in the field and create a sensation at home to boost his own fame.[50] Tellingly, despite spending about twelve years in total in the Arctic, Peary learned only a very small amount of Inuktitut, limiting his ability to communicate directly with the local people he lived among. Matthew Henson, who learned to speak Inuktitut fluently, carried out much of the daily conversation with the Inuit guides.[51]

Ultimately, though Peary owed his success as an explorer—and moreover, his very life—to his Inuit guides and companions, he continued to characterize them and their technology, including fur clothing, as tools to be used in the

service of achieving the fame he craved. Peary even tried to claim that one of his greatest strengths as an explorer was his groundbreaking ability to recognize and exploit Inuit technology. According to Riffenburgh, Peary "frequently claimed credit for the initial adoption [by whites] of Eskimo clothing, methods of travel, and living techniques. These were [not] his development . . . having been used by [nineteenth-century British and American explorers] Rae, Hall, Schwatka, Gilder and others before Peary ever considered going north."[52] Although Peary enthusiastically embraced and promoted Inuit clothing, he viewed it, and its makers, as valuable only as a tool for achieving his own goals.

## A Race and a Clothes Call: Amundsen and Scott

In contrast to Peary, the explorers who sought the South Pole did not encounter any indigenous people there. Instead of relying on local native populations, they had to bring all of their own gear, chosen from among Western or Inuit models. As with Peary, the clothing these men chose for their expeditions has become an integral part of their legend as explorers.

Historians and biographers have often cast the "race to the South Pole"—the concurrent 1910–1912 expeditions of Norwegian Roald Amundsen (1872–1928) and Briton Robert Falcon Scott (1868–1912)—as a contest of gear that was in turn a microcosm of leadership styles. Amundsen's champions have cited his embrace of Inuit clothing as a reflection of his openness to other cultures as well as practical planning for the environment.[53] Criticisms of Scott have characterized his planning methods, including his choice of clothes, as part of a strain of romantic but outdated British attitudes toward exploration. At worst, they have been described as symbols of his own personal incompetence as a leader, or emblematic of stubborn, racist, and antiquated thinking that supposedly permeated a crumbling British empire.[54] Scott's most ardent defenders have countered that his clothing was perfectly logical considering his method for reaching the South Pole. Amundsen and his team relied on dog-driven sleds, as Peary had also done. While some of Amundsen's men drove the sleds laden with supplies, the others, unencumbered, skied alongside or in front. In contrast, Scott planned to have his men *manhaul*, or drag sledges carrying their supplies by themselves using harnesses attached to the sledges, for most of the journey to and from the Pole. Scott's defenders have pointed out that given these plans, fur clothing would have been far too warm and bulky for such strenuous activity.[55] Indeed, it is hard to find accounts of Amundsen and Scott's race to the South Pole that do not in some way touch on their clothes as part of their strengths or weaknesses as explorers.

In reality, Amundsen and Scott incorporated both fur and textile clothing into their expedition gear, but to very different degrees. Their clothing choices should not be interpreted as a wholesale appreciative adoption of, or prejudiced rejection of, Inuit material culture. Instead, their choices reflect the differing degree to which both men allowed their own personal experience in the polar regions, the images they wanted to project, as well as the sources they consulted while provisioning their expeditions, to influence their planning. These experiences and sources, in turn, are revealing of the many factors that buoyed exploration at the turn of the twentieth century.

Like Peary, Scott and Amundsen's South Pole treks were the result of cumulative polar experience. In addition to leading a 1902–1906 Arctic expedition on the ship *Gjøa*, the first to successfully traverse a Northwest Passage by water, Amundsen had served on ships in the North Atlantic as a civilian sailor, and had been part of the first expedition to overwinter in Antarctic waters, the *Belgica* expedition of 1897–1899. Scott was a British naval officer and had led a prior expedition to Antarctica, on the ship *Discovery* in 1901–1904, although he had no Arctic experience. This meant that unlike Amundsen, Scott had never had sustained contact with Inuit people, something that likely influenced his choice of garb for the field.

For Amundsen, polar exploration was approached with a kind of passionate meticulousness, for he saw himself as a professional explorer above all else. Indeed, almost his entire adult life was devoted to planning and leading polar expeditions, unlike Peary and Scott, who were also employed by their country's navy.[56] Amundsen's first experience with fur clothing came while serving on the *Belgica* expedition in Antarctica, alongside a Brooklyn doctor named Frederick Cook. Though he would later become Peary's rival claimant for the North Pole, Cook had previously served on Peary's 1891–1892 Greenland expedition, and had lived among an Inuit community there. From Cook, Amundsen became convinced of the superiority of Inuit garb, writing in his diary on February 6, 1898 that, "The Doctor had [brought Inuit] sealskin clothes, which proved very practical. They dry easily . . ."[57]

A few years later, Amundsen organized his own polar expedition, the attempt to sail the Northwest Passage on the *Gjøa*.[58] As the expedition's sole organizer, he had the freedom to seek what he considered the best possible supplies and confer with other explorers, both Norwegian and British, to determine what to bring. Primarily he relied on the advice of his mentor, Arctic explorer Fridtjof Nansen, who had worn fur clothing on his expeditions.[59] Amundsen's plans included making contact with an Inuit community and spending an extended amount of time with them to learn polar survival skills.

In the autumn of 1903 the *Gjøa* landed on King William Island in the central North American Arctic, in a harbor called Uqsuqtuuq (known today as Gjoa Haven), where he met a community of Netsilik Inuit. Amundsen and his crew spent two winters there. In a speech to the Royal Geographical Society in London on February 11, 1907, Amundsen described the local people as his "inseparable allies," and noted that, "In one thing there was a general consensus of opinion, namely, that Eskimo fur garments were the most suitable for the climate. We had, therefore, taken time by the forelock and bartered with the Eskimo for the lightest and finest reindeer-skin clothing we could get."[60]

Some historians have argued that Amundsen and other Scandinavian explorers were inherently less biased against native Arctic peoples than other Westerners. For example, Riffenburgh writes that, "They [Scandinavians] were not limited in outlook by nationalist superiority as were Britain or the U.S. From their very entrance into the Arctic, the Norwegians respected the native peoples of the north … [and] were willing to learn from them."[61] Amundsen might have been willing to learn from the Netsilingmiut, but he was not in Uqsuqtuuq to study them as an anthropologist. He wanted to learn from them specifically to improve his own polar survival skills for future expeditions. For example, he spent countless hours building dozens of igloos to perfect his technique, much to the amusement and frustration of his native instructor Teraiu.[62] Even Huntford, an admiring biographer, writes that though the Norwegian was friendly toward his local neighbors, "His motives at the start were wholly utilitarian."[63] Amundsen appreciated Inuit craftsmanship in clothes, later noting the "wonderful … artistic sense and fabricating skill evidenced by these garments."[64] Yet he was not above casting his relationship with the Netsilingmiut in the model of the powerful white man and the naïve, childlike native. Recalling his time at Gjoa Haven, he later wrote, "To all savages, the civilized white man has some of the attributes of the gods…. This superstitious fear is the strongest safeguard of the explorer."[65] Amundsen also did not hesitate to exercise this "safeguard" to serve his aims. In a later published account he boasted that when he discovered some local men had stolen provisions from the *Gjøa*, he gathered the entire community together and then used concealed dynamite to explode an empty igloo, a warning of what he could do when angered.[66]

The Northwest Passage successfully charted, Amundsen was in the midst of preparing for an attempt to reach the North Pole in 1909 when Peary and Cook both announced that they had separately attained that goal. (After years of public controversy, Peary emerged as the "official" conqueror of the North Pole, but his claim has been contested ever since.)[67] Realizing he could not hope to capture the public's imagination now that this honor had been taken,

Amundsen secretly changed his plans to attempt the South Pole, using much of the same gear he had already started to assemble.

Amundsen knew that good clothing was fundamental to reaching the South Pole and returning safely. As with the rest of his gear, he paid meticulous attention to it and obtained what he felt from his previous Arctic experience was the most appropriate for the conditions he anticipated in Antarctica. His use of metaphor when discussing his exploration strategy is telling; he explained to his crew onboard his ship *Fram* that, "If we are to win, not a trouser button must be missing."[68]

For the seven men, later reduced to four, who were to accompany him to the South Pole, Amundsen obtained "the richest assortment of reindeer-skin clothing; we had it specially thick, medium and quite light."[69] Two hundred fifty skins were sewn, by a tailor in Christiania (now Oslo), in the pattern of Netsilingmiut clothes as specified by Amundsen.[70] From Jens Daugaard-Jensen, the Danish colonial administrator for Greenland, Amundsen purchased Greenlandic Inuit-made ensembles: "14 complete Eskimo suits of sealskin, 20 prepared sealskins to repair the suits …"[71] But recognizing the bulkiness and intense insulation of fur, he also purchased fabric clothing to be worn in (relatively) warmer temperatures and during the hours of strenuous skiing: "thick woolen underclothing and … overalls of two different materials: Burberry 'gabardine' and the ordinary green kind [of wool] that is used in Norway in the winter…. Our Burberry wind-clothes were [custom] made in the form of [an Inuit] *anorak* (blouse) and trousers, both very roomy."[72] Gabardine is a tough, tightly woven fabric, made of worsted wool or cotton, patented by British clothier Thomas Burberry in 1888. In the early twentieth century it was often used for the manufacture of outer coats, as it is wind- and water-resistant.[73] As with other textiles, however, its wearer must prevent the gabardine from becoming damp with perspiration, which can freeze into the fibers at low temperatures, reducing the fabric's insulating properties.[74] By ordering the gabardine cut

to a roomy Inuit pattern, Amundsen ensured that his men could take advantage of the "venting effect" to mitigate the effects of perspiration.

At the Norwegian base camp on the Ross Ice Shelf, Amundsen and his men worked to tailor, repair, and improve their clothing as much as possible before the push for the Pole. The furs were kept outside under a tent, to avoid the skins drying out and cracking in the dry, stove-fed heat of their cabin.[75] They proved their worth; Amundsen and his team were able to start their trek on October 19, 1911, while Scott and his team left their base camp on November 1. They planted a flag at the South Pole on December 14, 1911, more than a month before the Britons, and returned to their base camp on January 25, 1912.[76]

**27**
Amundsen and his crew at their Antarctic base camp on the Ross Ice Shelf, making adjustments to their fur clothing. From left to right: Olav Bjaaland, Sverre Hassel, Oscar Wisting, Helmer Hanssen, Roald Amundsen, Hjalmar Johansen, Kristian Prestrud, and Jørgen Stuberrud

—

As much as he paid attention to clothes for utilitarian reasons in the field, Amundsen did use fur clothing as a publicity tool to some extent. Amundsen certainly understood the importance of securing media coverage from the *Gjøa* expedition.[77] On his Antarctic trek, while Amundsen waited at his base camp before making his start for the South Pole, his brother and business manager, Leon Amundsen, was hard at work in Europe arranging a lecture tour for him, with American engagements planned by the well-known agent Lee Keedick.[78] In a letter dated May 27, 1912, Keedick asked Leon if Roald could "make arrangements to bring with him to America the personal equipment he used in making the dash to the Pole, that is, his fur clothing, his skiis [*sic*], and one sledge." Keedick went on to note that when Peary lectured in New York, he had his Arctic gear with him on stage, and that, "Notice of this added feature was published in the papers and served to arouse much interest."[79]

There is no evidence that Amundsen used fur clothing on stage in the same spectacular way that Peary did. Amundsen did, however, pose for photographers in Norway several times in full Inuit-style fur ensembles several times, including once in 1899 after returning from the *Belgica* expedition. Later, in March of 1909, Amundsen posed for photographer Anders Beer Wilse at Bunnefjorden, near Christiania, in a fur ensemble and with skis. One of the photos from this session was apparently a favorite of Amundsen's, and he used it as the frontispiece for the second volume of his published account of the South Pole expedition.[80] Perhaps he did not feel the need to act as a swaggering frontiersman, because he lacked Peary's connection to the American history of "playing native" and "frontier cross-dressing." Yet he clearly saw furs as part of his desired identity as the consummate polar explorer. It seems that at the very least, he wanted his ability to choose clothing to be seen as one of the many skills that had made him incredibly successful at what he did.[81]

In contrast to Amundsen, when Robert F. Scott made his attempt for the South Pole he put his faith largely in English knitted and woven wool, and cotton clothes, rejecting fur except as mittens, outer boots to protect the body's extremities, and sleeping bags. Scott used outer garments of heavy cotton gabardine, in the form of pants and a sleeved smock referred to as an "overall," and worn on top of many wool and cotton layers. Knitted wool balaclavas, separate gabardine hoods, wool mufflers, and felt hats provided protection for the head.[82] Scott's team wore reindeer fur boots they called "finneskoes," imitations of the boots worn by the Sami. Though made of skins prepared by Sami people, they were fabricated especially for Scott's crew in Christiania, by the famed ski outfitter Hagen.[83]

Scott and his four companions on the South Pole trek dragged their heavily laden sleds behind them on ski and on foot, using canvas and rope harnesses. Manhauling was a particularly British mode of polar travel, honed in the Arctic through decades of government-backed expeditions. It was thought to be more noble and more of a true test of manly strength than "passive" dogsledding, and some British explorers were convinced that dogsledding was less reliable in rough terrain *and* cruel to dogs.[84] As Solomon and Fiennes have asserted, furs would have been too heavy for the strenuous work of manhauling, which caused the men to sweat profusely even in freezing Antarctic weather. Unfortunately, the textile clothing quickly became wet with perspiration, and after hours of manhauling the damp clothes began to freeze as soon as the men stopped to rest. It proved more difficult than Scott had likely anticipated to thaw and dry them out properly at the end of each day in their tent.[85] Like Amundsen's team, once Scott's men settled into their tent they attempted to dry out any damp garments and switch into a second pair of boots. Unfortunately, they had only minutes before the damp textile clothes froze, and if the men were not careful they froze into odd shapes and had to be laboriously thawed out and reshaped before they could be put on again.[86] The stiff, frozen layers were also undoubtedly difficult to adjust or remove while sweating heavily on the march.

The problems with the clothes were compounded on the return trip from the South Pole, starting in mid-January of

**28**
Helmer Hanssen, 1910 or 1911

1912. Scott and his men were starving and suffering from scurvy.[87] They were also hampered by injuries and low morale from their loss to Amundsen's team. Progressing more slowly than the Norwegians, the men were still struggling back toward base camp in their heavy, stiff, poorly insulating clothing in March 1912, as the Antarctic winter set in, and by the end of that month all five had perished.[88]

In the aftermath of Scott's death he was treated as a tragic hero by the British public and by historians. More recent accounts of his expedition have faulted him for his choices in planning, especially the linked shortcomings of textile clothing and manhauling.[89] Given that alternatives were available for polar conditions—as evidenced by Peary and Amundsen—why did Scott make the choices he did? The evidence suggests that he and his men did not explicitly reject Inuit models so much as champion entrenched traditions of British polar exploration, including its gear and strategy. Yet as the earlier nineteenth-century examples show, some British explorers had previously embraced furs in the field, so Scott's choices cannot be chalked up to nationality alone.

**29**
(above) Roald Amundsen (left) and Helmer Hanssen, taking navigational measurements at the South Pole and wearing gabardine ensembles, cut in Netsilingmiut style, with fur boots, December 14–17, 1911

**30**
(facing) One of Roald Amundsen's favorite photos of himself, which appeared in his published account *The South Pole*, taken near Bunnefjorden, Norway, March 1909, photograph by Anders Beer Wilse

Perhaps by the time Scott set out, Britain had something extra to prove. For the members and backers of Scott's second expedition, British national pride rested on the attainment of the South Pole. As historian Stephanie Barczewski has written, after Peary's alleged conquest of the North Pole in 1909, there was a groundswell of sentiment in Britain that the South Pole should go to a Briton, especially since Britain had dropped from the glory decades of the early and mid-nineteenth century, when it was the most active nation in polar exploration.[90] Fears at home of the British empire's decline in power and the increasing decadence of the nation's culture helped fuel popular feeling that the expedition needed to succeed to prove that Britons could still accomplish something great on the world stage.[91] While Peary countered the ills of over-civilization in front of his fellow Americans by "going native" in furs, Scott seems to have adopted the opposite tactic, becoming further entrenched in British modes of dress. As he told one newspaper reporter in 1910, "It will, of course, be an all-British expedition in every respect."[92]

Certainly, Scott tried to portray his endeavor to the public as the epitome of British spirit in the face of decline. In an article outlining his plans for reaching the Pole in the journal of the Royal Geographical Society, Scott claimed that his enterprise was "an outward visible sign that we are still a nation able and willing to undertake difficult enterprises, still capable of standing in the van of the army of progress."[93] He undoubtedly knew that he needed to play to popular national sentiment if he was to get his ship *Terra Nova* out of the docks at Cardiff. Though Scott was a naval officer, the expedition operated as a private venture, not as an official government undertaking as had been the case with earlier British polar expeditions. While Scott and his organizing committee had received a government grant of £20,000 (and the endorsement of the Admiralty, which freed a number of enlisted men to serve on the expedition's crew), they were expected to raise the remaining funds, initially estimated at another £20,000, from donations.[94]

Perhaps the dual needs to stoke British pride and save money helped contribute to Scott's choice of gear. British companies, from chocolate purveyors to soap manufacturers, rushed to help outfit the expedition—often offering donations or discounted contracts—hoping for good publicity should Scott succeed. "[The] advertisement to be derived from the supply of stores to an Expedition such as this is thought of very highly in this country [Great Britain]," Scott wrote to his business agent in New Zealand, "and thanks to this and a patriotic wish for our success, we are getting goods on extraordinarily favourable terms."[95] For clothing on Scott's earlier *Discovery* expedition in 1901, British manufacturers Burberry and Jaeger provided gabardine outerclothes and wool undergarments respectively.[96] After the *Discovery* returned, an exhibition of photographs and sketches made during the expedition, and gear used by the crew, was held in London in November 1904. A souvenir program featured advertisements from both of the clothing companies, including Scott's praise of their products.[97]

Interestingly, Scott had used furs to some extent on the *Discovery* expedition. In preparation for the voyage he had asked the expedition's surgeon, Dr. Reginald Koettlitz, for recommendations for fur clothing, and based on his suggestions had ordered reindeer and wolfskin suits, caps, mitts, and boots from a supplier called Möller in Drammen, Norway.[98] Yet overall he was not satisfied with how they performed in Antarctica. In his published account of the *Discovery* voyage, Scott wrote "We had never contemplated dressing in furs for our [sledge] journeys," but had ordered the reindeer suits intending to sleep in them. They found them to be unwieldy and difficult to get into at the end of each day inside their tents, and quickly converted them to conventional sleeping bags.[99] They continued to wear finneskoe boots, which Scott later praised.[100] Yet just as Peary described in *Secrets of Polar Travel*, the Britons would use a bad experience with fur garments to write off considering them for Antarctic trekking.[101]

In 1910, the crew of the *Terra Nova* were again kitted out in British clothing: Mandelberg gabardine garb and woolens from the Wolsey company.[102] A later article written by Mandelberg pattern designer G. H. Boroughs quotes

Boroughs's correspondence with Scott while developing the clothes, showing his interest in the details of the garments and his satisfaction with the finished products. According to Boroughs, Scott "improved, where improvement seemed desirable, on the construction of garments previously used for the same purpose" but that he "had no use for . . . animal wool or fur."[103] Scott was not *thoughtless* in choosing his expedition clothes—he gave consideration as to what to bring—but he was perhaps overly reliant on established British dress and too quick to dismiss Inuit technology. Choosing to wear the heavier, bulkier furs on the march

would have meant abandoning strenuous manhauling, something that seemed out of the question.

If Scott was prejudiced against the Inuit in general, whether consciously or not, it was likely because he was deeply influenced by the thinking of his mentor and patron, Sir Clements Markham. Markham, a naval veteran, had traveled to the Arctic in the mid-nineteenth century as part of a search party for the lost Franklin Expedition, before spending years championing the cause of British exploration and imperial expansion through the Royal Geographical Society. Though Markham had observed Inuit life firsthand,

**31**
Three members of the *Terra Nova* expedition, Thomas Clissold, Frederick Hooper, and Dmitri Gerov, in Wolsey woolen long underwear, with fur sleeping bags, February 7, 1911, photograph by Herbert Ponting. Wolsey used this photo in an advertisement in programs for lectures on Scott's expedition.

he did not believe there was anything to be learned from them that would be appropriate for white explorers. He justified this position with the reasoning that the cyclical travel Arctic natives undertook to exploit various food sources was fundamentally dissimilar to extended overland exploratory voyages, and so the skills needed for one could not be transferred to the other. While the two types of travel are certainly different, the idea that no knowledge could be applied from the former to the latter seems bizarre to the modern mind, especially since Markham was very much in favor of transferring one specific method developed in the Arctic—manhauling—to Antarctica.[104] Yet Markham was a product of the nineteenth-century British Royal Navy, and held the Navy sentiment that traditional British approaches to expeditions were the best ones.[105]

Scott also may have felt that an expedition on which a nation's pride rested required the most modern, technically sophisticated equipment available. Historian Dane Kennedy has explained that European exploration and modernity have always been linked, with explorers trumpeting the technological innovations that allowed them to reach remote areas of the globe, map their geographic coordinates, and engage in scientific fieldwork with advanced instruments.[106] Scott certainly saw the *Terra Nova* expedition as a scientific one and championed the work that would be done by the geologists, biologists, and meteorologists in his crew at base camp; he maintained that the trek to the South Pole was only one component of a larger program.[107] (In contrast, Amundsen wrote that on his trek for the South Pole, "science would have to look after itself.")[108] To admit to requiring Inuit technology—including full fur outfits—would have thus contradicted prevailing ideas about the superiority of civilized people and their material culture over that of "primitive" peoples.

The idea of modernity did surface in Antarctica, at Scott's base camp at McMurdo Sound. On September 2, 1911, Henry Robertson Bowers, whom Scott had placed in charge of looking after clothing, food, and other gear, delivered a long lecture on examples of clothing, both fur and textile, used by previous polar explorers. Bowers concluded by characterizing fur clothing as primitive and out-of-date for anything other than sleeping or riding on a sledge.[109] Textile clothes were presented as the most modern option for explorers.

The next day, Scott commented in his diary,

Last night Bowers lectured on Polar clothing.... The points in our clothing problems are too technical and too frequently discussed to need special notice at present, but as a result of a new study of Arctic precedents it is satisfactory to find it becomes more and more evident that our equipment is the best that has been devised for the purpose, always excepting the possible alternative of skins for spring journeys, an alternative we have no power to adopt. In spite of this we are making minor improvements all the time.[110]

Scott's team was "making minor improvements" to their gear, tailoring and repairing their clothing as Amundsen's men were. However, the ambivalence in this diary entry shows that Scott was having inklings of doubt about relying so much on textile clothing, even as he characterized it as the most sophisticated option. A month earlier he wrote:

One continues to wonder as to the possibilities of fur clothing as made by the Esquimaux, with a sneaking feeling that it may outclass our more civilised garb. For us this can only be a matter of speculation, as it would have been quite impossible to have obtained such articles. With the exception of this radically different alternative, I feel sure we are as near perfection as experience can direct.[111]

Importantly, Scott wrote this entry after Bowers, expedition scientist Edward A. Wilson, and another crew member, Apsley Cherry-Garrard, had just returned from a month-long scientific excursion to Cape Crozier to collect emperor penguin eggs. Scott also intended for this trip to test the expedition's clothing and other gear in preparation for the longer trip to the South Pole. Manhauling in their gabardine and woolens in the middle of the dark Antarctic winter, with blizzard-force winds and temperatures hovering around –40°F (–40°C) and often dropping even lower, Bowers, Wilson, and Cherry-Garrard nearly died. But miraculously they did manage to stumble back to base camp at McMurdo, leaving Scott to conclude, "At any rate we can now hold that our system of clothing has come through a severer test than any other, fur included."[112] The fact that Bowers, Wilson, and Cherry-Garrard *had* managed to survive in the British-style clothes, if only barely, seems to have reassured Scott that he made the right choice. At that point, though, it was too late to make any major changes.[113]

Perhaps most importantly, Scott seems to have been extremely conscious of how much the expedition would be on view to the British public and the wider world. He knew how important it was to project the "right" image to his audience back home, one that displayed national pride, traditions of British exploration, and scientific modernity. Professional photographer Herbert Ponting accompanied Scott to Antarctica. Though he did not go with Scott on the final journey to the Pole, he documented the South Pole preparations and scientific work at base camp on moving and still film. Scott wrote in his diary on September 11, 1911, that Ponting's "value as pictorial recorder of events becomes daily more apparent. No expedition has ever been illustrated so extensively."[114] Ponting's photographs of Scott's base camp included shots of the crew posing with items donated by sponsors, which Scott specifically requested.[115] Besides serving as documentation of the expedition, Scott must have understood that Ponting's striking photographs would be key for generating interest and income back in Britain.

Scott set out from base camp on November 1, 1911, and reached the South Pole on January 17, 1912. Even after his five-man team discovered a Norwegian flag flying there, Scott felt that he might be able to seize victory by beating Amundsen to the cablehead with a story for the news outlets. In his diary on Wednesday, January 17, 1912, Scott wrote, "The POLE Yes but under very different circumstances from those

expected.... Now for the run home and a desperate struggle to get the news through first. I wonder if we can do it."[116] As he, Bowers, and Wilson lay dying in their tent eight weeks later (their other two companions had already perished), Scott wrote a final entry in his diary entitled "Message to the Public," in the hope that the journal, along with his body, would eventually be recovered. In this message, Scott defends his choices, including gear, from hypothetical later critics, explaining that "Every detail of our food supplies, clothing and depots ... worked out to perfection."[117]

Scott could have obtained fur clothing for the *Terra Nova* expedition, even in Europe, and he would have been aware of earlier expeditions that used fur clothing successfully. Indeed, as part of his preparations Scott consulted with Amundsen's mentor, Nansen, in Norway.[118] Yet in his planning Scott seemed to rely primarily on the model of textile-based clothing taken to the field by earlier British expeditions, the shortsighted recommendations of his mentor Markham, and perhaps most of all the need to project an image of strong, modern, Britishness to the public at home through his dress.

Modern research has borne out the differences between Amundsen and Scott's ensembles. In 2006, two teams competed in a "replica" of Amundsen and Scott's race for a British television documentary entitled "Blizzard: Race to the South Pole," filmed in Greenland due to current prohibitions on dogs in Antarctica. Both teams wore clothing constructed to be as close to Scott and Amundsen's original ensembles as possible. In conjunction with the project, physiologist George Havenith compared the insulating properties of the replica outfits. Havenith found that Amundsen's fur-based ensemble was dramatically more insulating than Scott's textile one.[119] While he remarked that the extra exertion of manhauling might have been enough to keep the men warm despite the less insulating textiles, Havenith theorized that, as the textile clothing froze, it would have become very heavy and added to the men's burden even more. Indeed, the men on the replica

Scott team eventually lost between 12 and 25 percent of their body weight.[120]

## Conclusion: Appropriation, Appreciation, and Shades In Between

From a modern standpoint, it would be tempting to link the use or avoidance of Inuit fur clothing for polar exploration simply to openness or prejudice toward other cultures. Yet polar explorers' clothing was a reflection of many factors: prejudices about race, but also the need for publicity and sponsorship, feelings of nationalism, and views about masculinity. All of these forces shaped exploration at the turn of the twentieth century, and in turn shaped how individual explorers presented themselves and interpreted their own experiences. The case studies of Peary, Amundsen, and Scott demonstrate Nicholas Thomas's assertion that even when drawing upon the same group of people or objects, "indigenous references are diverse and typically contradictory in their effects."[121]

In contrast to popular portrayals of exploration that only emphasize its heroism and romance, polar exploration as it was practiced by men such as Peary, Amundsen, and Scott, particularly the quests for the poles themselves, was a particular kind of Western enterprise, a "seemingly arbitrary ambition [that] speaks to the … nature of exploration in the age of empire … the idea was to plant the flag of king and country on some remote extremity of no possible use … simply because it was there."[122] Exploration at the turn of the twentieth century was tightly intertwined with colonialism, often acting as a prologue for Western nations to bring even remote parts of the globe under their political, cultural, and economic influence.

The Arctic and Antarctic may have been more ambiguous as potential colonies due to their remoteness and environment.[123] However, there were still resources, furs, whales, and later oil and minerals, to be extracted from these regions. Though such resources did not extend as far as the poles, planting flags there could create powerful political and cultural capital for a Western nation. The chance to absorb these regions—and by extension, their resources and people—was a powerful motivating factor for exploration. The ambiguity of the polar regions might have freed some explorers from the constraints of Western modes of dress. Yet the case of Peary also illustrates Thomas's concept of appropriation through appreciation—Peary adopted local Arctic clothing for practical reasons, but also as a way of demonstrating America's absorption of the Arctic into its sphere of influence.

Thomas cautions that the use of indigenous objects does not necessarily create any association with indigenous identity, since "Artifacts can be significant as markers of other people with whom one does not identify."[124] As his writings make clear, Peary viewed himself as a man who, even clad completely in fur, could never be mistaken for a native Arctic person because he led, not followed. While the Inuit had perfected dressing for a polar climate, Peary saw his own genius as the ability to recognize the usefulness of these indigenous clothes and incorporate them into great expeditions to conquer the North Pole, something only a white man was fit to do. Perhaps paradoxically, by donning the garb of these supposedly uncivilized people, Peary's standing as a white, civilized man was not only maintained, but enhanced. Donning Inuit furs did not make him truly "go native," but made him into something *deeply Western*: a polar explorer.

Scott, in contrast, embodied the image of the civilized British explorer, so confident in his nation's traditions that no indigenous knowledge or material culture could be of great use. If British ways of doing things, particularly in the military, had already won his nation a great empire, why should Scott have considered Antarctica to be any different?[125] His adherence to established protocol is evidenced by the fact that even in Antarctica—a politically ambiguous continent, with no land resources to speak of and no indigenous people to subdue—Scott was still deeply conscious of the way the expedition would be portrayed at home, and the need to keep up appearances in the field.

While national pride may have been a factor for Amundsen (Norway gained independence from Sweden in 1905, early in Amundsen's career), he seems to have been more motivated by his own deep-seated interest in the polar regions and in achieving records for the sake of achieving them.[126] Though he was not free from prejudiced beliefs, Amundsen embraced Inuit clothing, unlike Scott, but did not engage in Peary's brand of frontiersman swagger. Like Peary, though, he considered learning and adapting from the Inuit to be an essential part of the polar explorer's skill set, and approached Inuit communities with a very specific goal in mind. While Amundsen considered the Netsilingmiut at Gjoa Haven excellent teachers of polar survival skills, for example, he did not consider bringing Netsilingmiut men with him on future expeditions, only fellow Norwegians.

As they were during Peary's, Scott's, and Amundsen's careers, the polar regions remain geopolitically ambiguous today. A 1959 international treaty established Antarctica as a "continent of science," open to all and devoid of national territorial claims. However, seven countries still claim sections of the continent.[127] While portions of the Arctic are claimed by five nations, international law marks the ends of these claims at 200 nautical miles from land, putting the ocean and ice around the North Pole out of any country's official grasp. However, permanent summer ice around the North Pole is expected to disappear within decades, potentially leaving lucrative shipping lanes (a long-sought Northwest Passage?) and perhaps undersea oil deposits open for contestation.[128] Already, at least one British MP has called for the United Kingdom to appoint an ambassador to the Arctic.[129] Numerous companies are now bringing tourists to the polar regions, a phenomenon which would have seemed unbelievable to the explorers like Peary, Amundsen, and Scott, who built their reputations on being hardy enough for these extreme places.

Perhaps these events are the beginning of a second polar craze, in which the Arctic and Antarctica again seize the attention and imagination of the Western public. At the turn of the twentieth century, Inuit clothing was taken up by some explorers and rejected by others, but always through a complicated set of culturally mediated negotiations. When images of these clothes filtered back to Western audiences they did so as markers of the greatness of these men, who had faced the hardships of the polar regions and symbolically claimed them for the West, not as markers of the Inuit themselves. How will current and future dialogues around climate change, resource extraction, polar tourism, and even the exploits of modern explorers include the people who first showed Southerners how to live in the polar regions? How might Inuit objects be mobilized by Southerners with various agendas, and what role will the Inuit play in current conversations surrounding appropriation in fashion and proper forms of use and compensation? However these issues unfold, any observers considering Inuit material culture, including clothing, must remember to engage in what J. C. H. King has called the "practice of separating use and meaning."[130] And any outsiders traveling to these regions must keep in mind that even at the limits of human survival, dress is important: as the Scandinavian saying goes, there's no such thing as bad weather, only bad clothing.

# 3
# Fashion from the Extreme

## THE POLES, HIGHEST PEAKS, AND BEYOND

Patricia Mears

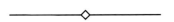

### The First Fashionable Expeditions

Travel to far-flung, exotic parts of the world began to attract an emerging class of well-heeled tourists as early as the late nineteenth century. Especially popular were safaris. Environmentally specific attire created for those treks to the wilds of Africa soon became easily recognizable to the general public, decades before expeditions to extreme environments would markedly influence high fashion. Although safari-specific garments and gear provided comfort in hot climates and improved mobility over challenging terrains, they were not absolutely essential to survival. However, they would inspire the creation and dissemination of extreme environmental wear in the following decades.

Safari enthusiasts were most often adventurous and wealthy Western Europeans and Americans. An entire industry catering to them arose in cities such as London and New York, including travel agencies and specialty retail firms. Before long, safari-specific clothing and accessories found their way into fashion. Sarah Pickman, in an unpublished paper entitled "Of Khaki and Hair Pins: Early Women's Safari Clothing,"[1] details how nineteenth-century uniforms

worn by British troops in countries such as India became safari essentials. These items, in turn, eventually were transformed into late twentieth-century fashion mainstays.

Pickman notes that garments that eventually became associated with safaris—hunting jackets, shirts, trousers, shorts, and even pith helmets, all made from khaki-colored cotton twill—were conceived just before the British Raj, or the colonial presence of the British Crown in the Indian subcontinent between 1858 and 1947. In 1848, a group of native Indian soldiers, the Corps of Guides, on the order of their commander, Lieutenant Harry Lumsden, were outfitted in cotton fabric that was dyed the now-familiar hue known as khaki, the Urdu word for "dusty." More comfortable than wool and a natural camouflage, khaki became the official uniform of the British colonial armies by the late 1860s, as English mills produced huge quantities of the fabric. The practical aspects of khaki cloth—cool, and easy to clean and dry—made it ideal for safari expeditions.

The golden age of the safari, however, was the interwar years of the twentieth century, especially for Americans. Even before the onset of World War I, the hunting exploits

**32**
*Vogue*, November 1, 1964,
photograph by John Cowan

of figures such as Teddy Roosevelt and taxidermist Carl Akeley were featured in newspapers and magazines across the country. Books such as Ernest Hemingway's *Green Hills of Africa* (1935) and *The Snows of Kilimanjaro* (1936) and Karen Blixen's *Out of Africa* (1937) were best sellers. The safari was further popularized and glamorized in Hollywood films such as *King Solomon's Mines* (1937) and *Tarzan the Ape Man* (1932), as well as in documentaries, such as *Congorilla* (1932), by the noted American explorers Martin and Osa Johnson.

Clothing for these adventures moved from battlefields to urban environments thanks to the rise of specialty retailers. One outstanding example was the New York firm of

Abercrombie & Fitch. Although it is impossible to correlate the company's elegant history with its current youth-oriented focus and decidedly sexy advertising campaign, the store was then America's premier retailer for the elite sportsman. From the outset, it was an upscale sporting-goods store founded by David Abercrombie in 1892, and located in lower Manhattan. Its status remained intact when the majority shares of the business were sold to one of its wealthy clients, Ezra Fitch, in 1900 (who later added his name to the establishment and became the sole proprietor), and as it moved progressively up the island of Manhattan.

As Abercrombie continued to move to increasingly larger spaces, he expanded the business to include women's clothing and produced thousands of copies of huge, top-rate catalogues that were mailed worldwide. In 1917, Abercrombie purchased its legendary, twelve-story building at the corner of Madison Avenue and East Forty-Fifth Street. The sprawling emporium included a shooting range and a rooftop fly- and bait-casting pool, where clients could take lessons from skilled instructors. In between, a breathtaking range of outdoor-sports clothing and gear, especially for hunting, was for sale. Abercrombie & Fitch even outfitted Charles Lindbergh for his historic 1927 flight across the Atlantic Ocean.

Like its British counterpart, Benjamin Edgington—and other purveyors in the United Kingdom including Holland & Holland, and Purdey, as well as the Italian firm Beretta—Abercrombie & Fitch played a key role in popularizing exotic travel, especially safaris. "Safari," the Swahili word meaning "voyage or "march," entailed overland travel with a focus on big-game hunting. British engineer William Cornwallis Harris is credited with leading the first safari in 1836. Departing from Cape Town, South Africa, he led a group that observed and hunted wildlife, and did so in great luxury.

Travelers were expected to bring along an array of khaki-colored wear for trekking through the Serengeti, of course, but safari-adventure culture also included social obligations that required at least one set of formal clothes

33
Osa Johnson, "Expedition Africa," 1929

for receptions and parties in cities such as Nairobi. Among the daytime wardrobe staples were hunting jackets and shirts, and a selection of bottoms, including pants, shorts, and culottes (fig. 34). Accessories included pith helmets (sometimes covered with veils), specially designed socks and boots, and other specialized items, from hunting rifles to tents and furniture. Finally, ladies packed floor-length evening dresses and gentlemen brought along full evening attire.

The exotic and glamorous allure of safari style proved irresistible, and it soon found its way onto the pages of leading fashion magazines. On the cover of the issue of *Vogue* for January 1, 1920, the celebrated French artist Georges Lepape created an image of a woman donning a pith helmet while standing amid the lush foliage of a jungle—with the figure of an indigenous person silhouetted in the background. Six years later, for the issue of January 15, 1926, *Vogue* again published an illustrated cover, this time by André E. Marty, of an elegant woman dressed in a long, green gown and veiled hat, riding a rearing zebra (fig. 35). Both the rider and her

ensemble remain coolly unruffled. Was this fashion illustration inspired by photographs of real explorers, such as Osa Johnson riding a zebra (fig. 34)? If so, Lepape clearly upped the fashion quotient: his rider eschewed the safari shirt and shorts worn by Johnson in favor of an haute couture garment. In addition to images, articles discussed safari wear. In 1935, for example, *Vogue* ran an article entitled "Vanity in the Jungle," by Alice La Varre.[2]

Decades later, in 1968, one of the twentieth century's greatest couturiers, Yves Saint Laurent, debuted his "Saharienne" collection. Key designs included his safari-style pantsuit and a khaki tunic. The latter was especially noteworthy. Not merely daring, the tunic was evocatively scandalous because it was both low-cut *and* barely long enough to be a dress, even in the era of the micro-mini-dress. Specially commissioned by *Vogue* Paris for the 1968 July/August issue, Franco Rubartelli photographed the tunic on the model Veruschka, with a gun slung across her shoulders as she stood on the African plains (fig. 36). It quickly became an "iconic" fashion image. On the eve of the 1970s, Yves

34
Osa Johnson riding a zebra near
Isiolo, Kenya, 1921

35
*Vogue* cover, January 15, 1926,
illustration by André E. Marty

**36**
Yves Saint Laurent, *Vogue* Paris, July/August 1968,
photograph by Franco Rubartelli

the "Safari" or "Mombasa" collection. Osa Johnson was the inspiration for collections by American Eagle Outfitters, Charlotte Olympia, and Kate Moss.

The firm Banana Republic took the safari theme one step further by creating an entire clothing company around this single concept. The company was founded by Mel and Patricia Ziegler in 1978, a couple who had a knack for acquiring interesting clothing items while traveling on business. They eventually opened a store in the Mill Valley area of Northern California, and became known for distinctive catalogues filled with hand-drawn images (by Patricia) accompanied by fictional traveler and explorer stories (by Mel), as well as their safari-themed retail locations.

## Fashions from the Arctic

While safaris were among the first "extreme" vacation destinations, one's very existence was not in immediate peril on the open plains of Africa, at least not to the extent that it was in places like the Arctic or atop the highest peaks on earth, where specialized survival gear and clothing were absolutely essential. The remoteness of the Arctic region is perhaps the main reason its indigenous cultures were the last to influence Western designers.

According to Sarah Pickman, aesthetic interest in the indigenous Arctic peoples, such as the Inuit and Eskimos of Greenland and North America, came about for several reasons. One factor was the popularity of star explorers to the North and South Poles in the early twentieth century. American Robert Peary, for example, not only lectured about his exploits to large audiences in New York and other cities during the 1910s, he did so in full Arctic regalia, with his sled and team of dogs in tow.

Thanks to the marketing efforts of Peary (among others), the glamour of polar expeditions captured the public's imagination. However, obvious Arctic influences on high-style clothing were not immediately evident. But fashion, like a number of cultural mediums, was already absorbing elements from this newly discovered part of the

Saint Laurent's transgressive, menswear-inspired garments propelled fashionable women into the new decade—yet with unabashed female sexuality on display.

In the coming decades, versions of the safari look would be created by an increasing number of high-end designers. One prominent example was Ralph Lauren's spring/summer 1984 *Out of Africa*-inspired collection, based on the film version of Karen Blixen's 1937 book, starring Meryl Streep (fig. 37). Tom Ford, who was the creative director of Yves Saint Laurent from 1999 to 2004, produced his reinterpretation of the "Saharienne" 1968 original in 2002, called

**37**
Meryl Streep in *Out of Africa*, 1985,
photograph by Frank Conner

world. Although there were probably several reasons for its ascent, the creation of the full-length fur coat coincides with the first high-profile expeditions to the poles. As Dr. Jonathan Faiers notes in his essay on fur, the fur coat began to appear in the last quarter of the nineteenth century, just as polar expeditions began in earnest during the middle of the nineteenth century, and the heroic age commenced around 1880. Prior to that time, fur was usually hidden and reserved for coat linings or garment trimmings. It should be noted that, fur coats aside, Parisian couture houses did not suddenly produce collections inspired by the early expedition pioneers.

Early twentieth-century fashion publications did indeed feature beautifully romantic imagery of the Arctic, although it was relatively rare. One dramatically captivating image was another *Vogue* cover created by Georges Lepape, depicting a feisty female hunter spearing a polar bear. One of the best fashion illustrators of the art moderne (or art deco) era, Lepape was among a group of top-rate artists who depicted not only fashion, but a wide variety of political and social events.

While Lepape drew his share of ultrafeminine images, he also specialized in portraying strong women driving fast cars and carrying guns while dressed in the latest styles. Clearly, he must have been aware of the up-to-the-minute trends in travel and exploration. Featured on the August 1917 cover of American *Vogue* (it also appeared on international editions), Lepape depicts a young woman (who could be a native of the Arctic region) spearing a polar bear on an ice field with a ship anchored in the distance (fig. 38; cf. fig. 10). Her ensemble did not resemble the prevailing fashions of the era. Instead, her short coat, thigh-high boots, and bulky head- and hand-coverings clearly reflect the clothing worn by denizens of Greenland, the primary region vital to Peary's expeditions.[3] Violent yet beautiful, both the bleak landscape and the woman's ensemble capture the brutal reality of the great North, and its reliance on furs and their careful construction for survival. But Lepape glamorizes the woman—with abundant swaths of white fur and boldly

striped red and blue insets—so that the brutality of life in the Arctic is softened.

Early twentieth-century fashions inspired by garments from the Arctic are rarities. A few unique but little known examples were produced in a collaboration between museum curators and fashion and textile designers in New York City. In the 2013 exhibition and accompanying publication entitled *An American Style*, curator Ann Marguerite Tartsinis scrupulously documented the unique alliance that arose at the onset of World War I, as the American importation of French couture and German dyestuffs was disrupted.[4] That phenomenon paralleled the desire on the part of some forward-thinking ethnographers, specializing in the study of indigenous Western Hemisphere cultures from the Arctic to the Andes, to spearhead a movement of uniquely American designs. Authentic museum objects were made available to an emerging group of designers in the field of textiles—such as Ruth Reeves, Hazel Burnham Slaughter, and Ilonka Karasz—and fashion—including Jessie Franklin Turner and Max Meyer.

Prominent figures at the American Museum of Natural History led the way. They included ethnographers Herbert J. Spinden; Clark Wissler, a curator of Peruvian art; Charles W. Mead; and especially Morris de Camp ("M. D. C.") Crawford, an amateur expert of Peruvian textiles and a prolific writer and editor at *Women's Wear Daily*, the fashion trade's leading newspaper. These curators proved to be instrumental in providing inspirational objects to the designers, later showcasing their work at the AMNH in the seminal and groundbreaking Exhibition of Industrial Art in Textiles and Costumes, held from November 1 to December 1, 1919. The event was publicized and reported to have been well attended (although exact figures are not known), and it was accompanied by an article replete with photographs in the museum's *Natural History Journal*. In addition, Crawford consistently promoted the designers' work in his articles published in leading fashion journals from the mid-1910s to the early 1920s.

Most of the early designs of this movement, from 1915 to 1919, focused on material from the Andes and the North

**38**
*Vogue* cover, August 1, 1917,
illustration by George Lepape

American plains. However, garments from the Arctic regions of Canada, Alaska, Greenland, and Siberia were also tapped. Tartsinis discovered long-forgotten images of these early designers modeling authentic garments including Eskimo and Koryak (Kamenskoye, Siberian) coats made from hide, fur, and sinew (figs 39, 40).

Thanks to Crawford, published articles displaying the fashions inspired by groups such as the Inuit and Koryak appeared in prominent publications such as *Women's Wear Daily* and *Vogue*. For the December 1, 1917, issue of *Vogue*, Crawford wrote an article titled "A New Source of Costume Inspiration." In it, three designs by Jessie Franklin Turner for Bonwit Teller & Co. were presented. One of them, a "negligee of rose duvetyn, kolinsky, and blue chiffon," was inspired by an "ancient Koryak garment" (fig. 41).

Max Meyer also created a range of original ensembles that adhered to the cutting-edge silhouettes of the day, but with embellishments that were closely based on the ornamentation on the fur and hide garments by the Koryak and the Reindeer Tungus.[5] His luscious and aesthetically refined high-fashion versions for the firm A. Beller & Co. demonstrate his range. They were on view at the AMNH's Exhibition of Industrial Art in Textiles and Costumes. One coat, seen on the far left of image (fig. 43), is clearly influenced by the one modeled by textile designer Ilonka Karasz (fig. 40), while a squirrel-fur-trimmed, blue silk, velvet opera coat is embellished with Koryak designs (fig. 42).

The collaborative efforts between the AMNH and the New York design community dwindled significantly after World War I. Crawford resigned his position at the

39
Model in "Eskimo" hide, fur,
and sinew coat, circa 1916

40
Ilonka Karasz in Reindeer Tungus (Evenk, Siberian)
hide, fur, and sinew coat, circa 1916

AMNH in 1921, then took his continued enthusiasm to the Brooklyn Museum. With Brooklyn's curator of ethnography, Stewart Culin, Crawford would go on to establish that museum's celebrated Edward C. Blum Design Laboratory, an important resource that served New York's fashion and textile-design community for decades to come. Designers such as Max Meyer continued to create Inuit-inspired works, this time culled from the collections of the Brooklyn Museum. But renewed access to Parisian haute couture for American buyers after World War I drastically curtailed his efforts.

One of the last mainstream fashion images illustrating the museums' cross-cultural efforts is a *Vogue* Paris cover illustrated by Harriet Meserole, a former *Women's Wear Daily* employee. Dating to January 15, 1921, the cover depicts two women walking in a winter landscape, away from the viewer (fig. 44). The figure on the right wears a gray coat ornamented with Ainu iconography.[6] While not strictly based in the Arctic Circle, the Ainu of northern Japan and far eastern Russia incorporated some of the traditions and iconography associated with the peoples of the Far North.

Although documentation illustrating the influence of polar gear on couturiers was not prolific during the early twentieth century, a sensation celebrating the cultures of the Arctic—the 1922 documentary *Nanook of the North*—was influential (fig. 45). More importantly, the film continued

41
*Vogue*, December 1, 1917, "Fashion: A New Source of Costume Inspiration"

42
Max Meyer for A. Beller & Co. Blue chiffon velvet evening wrap with squirrel-fur trim and beaded ornament based on Koryak fur coat, 1919, photograph by Julius Kirschner

to inspire fashion designers decades later, as the brutal beauty of life in the Arctic resonated on the runways and in the pages of leading fashion magazines. It was not until the post-World War II era that the impact of expedition-influenced fashions became widespread. In fact, the high point of the connection between indigenous fur garments (as well as moon and deep-sea innovations) and fashion was the 1960s.

Prominent images of those who had made a significant impact on culture—from artists to explorers—began appearing in fashion publications by the second half of the 1940s. This phenomenon, especially prevalent in *Vogue*, was part of midcentury fashion's expanding interest in world-altering events and people. *Vogue*'s star photographer, Irving Penn, for example, captured a compelling dual portrait of a couple that appeared in a 1945 issue: Peter Freuchen and his third wife, Dagmar Cohn (fig. 46).

Dressed in a coat made from a polar bear he supposedly killed, Freuchen was literally a larger-than-life figure, standing a daunting 6' 7" tall, who dwarfed his wife, demurely dressed and seated at his side. He was a celebrated Danish explorer, anthropologist, actor, and author who went on his first Arctic expedition in 1906 at the age of twenty. Traveling by boat and thousands of miles via dogsled, Freuchen discovered and immersed himself in Inuit culture. There he married his first wife, with whom he had two children. After her death in 1921, he continued his work in the Arctic, where he would lose a leg to frostbite (and even amputated several gangrenous toes himself), wrote on the indigenous cultures, and headed a film company specializing in Arctic-related scripts. In 1933, he starred as the villainous character in the film *Eskimo*, which went on to win an Oscar. During World War II, Freuchen, a Jew, joined the Danish Resistance, and was imprisoned and sentenced to death by the Nazis. He escaped and, in 1945, met Dagmar Cohn, a fashion illustrator. She is perhaps best known for her illustration of a Christian Dior "New Look" dress that was featured on the April 1947 cover of British *Vogue*.

While the dual portrait of the amazing and audacious explorer and his fashion-illustrator wife possesses a sense of power and confidence, Penn's 1951 image of another professional explorer, "Deep-Sea Diver," is more modest. Featured in Ariele Elia's essay, the photograph was part of a series of portraits of working people that Penn began in 1950 (fig. 128). Unlike the early twentieth-century photographs of August Sander, who took more naturalistic, anthropological

43
Max Meyer for A. Beller & Co. Installation
view, Exhibition of Industrial Art, 1919, photograph
by Kay C. Lenskjold

to the Museum at FIT. Probably made for après-ski, the outfit's styling is evocative of the furs, such as seal or wolf, that were routinely worn by the peoples of the Arctic. Laroche took the trend one step further by crafting an "after-ski" fur suit (fig. 48)—jacket, shorts, and headscarf—that would have looked more appropriate in an urban setting. But his choice of fur—the popular pet hamster—may have made potential wearers squeamish.

The influence of expeditions on 1960s fashion photography was celebrated brilliantly in the pages of leading magazines. *Harper's Bazaar*, for example, created an editorial

studies of German tradespeople and professionals in the settings where they worked, Penn's portraits, perhaps owing to his training as a painter and a fashion photographer, are more formal and personal.[7]

By the onset of the 1960s, as activewear was gaining worldwide popularity, venerated couturiers such as Madame Grès and Guy Laroche, for example, began producing their own versions of chic, Arctic-inspired garments. For example, deviating from her signature Grecian, pleated gowns, Grès created an ensemble consisting of voluminous, fur pants topped off with a thick, knitted-wool turtleneck. Photographed by Irving Penn on the model Verushka, the image appeared in *Vogue* (fig. 47). The ensemble was purchased by socialite Isabel Eberstadt and was later donated

44
*Vogue* Paris, cover, January 15, 1921,
illustration by Harriet Meserole

45
*Nanook of the North* movie poster, 1922

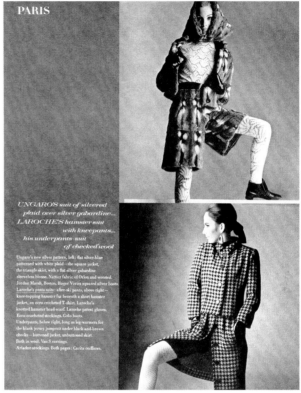

spread shot in a snowy landscape for the October 1962 issue.[8] Titled "Beautiful Barbarians" and captured by Richard Avedon, the model in the cover image (set on a vertical fold-out), as well as models shot on location and in studios, were swathed in furs such as civet, Mongolian lamb, and even Russian snow leopard (fig. 49). Editorial copy stated that Avedon "calls up the outer steppes of some unimagined frontier—and ambience of fearless, far-out, magnificence. Feathered, furred, leathered, or swathed in silks, his Beautiful Barbarians project is a proud, untamed, magnetism which all women may look to ..."[9] The lead model in the spread was China Machado. Of Portuguese and Chinese/Indian descent, her non-Western looks enhanced the "exotic" look of the "barbarian" images that, in turn,

articulated the period's racist view that indigenous peoples were less civilized than cultures south of the Arctic, an idea that continued decades after they were first denigrated by early European explorers.

Dramatic location shoots became a mainstay of *Vogue* magazine from 1963 to 1971, when Diana Vreeland was its editor-in-chief. Dynamic and highly creative, Vreeland consistently pushed the limits of fashion styling and photography throughout her decades-long career, and was among the first editors to oversee location shoots around the world while an editor at *Harper's Bazaar* during World War II. By the time she arrived at *Vogue*, Vreeland not only expanded the scope of travel to exotic locations, she amped up the glamour quotient and sense of daring.

46
(facing) Peter Freuchen and Dagmar Cohn, 1947,
photograph by Irving Penn

47
(above) main photo: Madame Grès, *Vogue*,
September 15, 1969, photograph by Irving Penn

48
upper photo: Guy Laroche hamster after-ski
pants and jacket, *Vogue*, September 15, 1966,
photograph by Irving Penn

**49**
China Machado, Russian Snow Leopard by James Terence
Brady of Bonwit Teller, St. Donat, Quebec, June 25, 1962,
photograph by Richard Avedon

—

Among Vreeland's most interesting ideas was an editorial shoot that appeared in the November 1964 issue, shortly after her *Vogue* appointment. She chose the British photographer John Cowan to capture her fantasy of high fashion among the icebergs (figs 32, 50, front cover). Cowan was an inspired choice: he was celebrated for a dynamic style that reflected the energetic atmosphere of 1960s "Swinging London." Cowan, together with his partner, model and photographer Jill Kennington, "sparked an exciting period of high-octane image-making for numerous magazines."[10] An inspiration for the main character in Michelangelo Antonioni's 1966 film, *Blow-Up*, Cowan's "energy and unconventional approach" inspired one of the film's most memorable scenes. According to Kennington, the "David Hemmings and Veruschka scene for *Blow-Up* was pure Cowan. Antonioni must have seen him working—I never saw anyone else take pictures quite that way. The shooting on the floor downwards, completely fluid, unhindered by tripods, etc., was typical Cowan."[11]

Fashion historian and journalist, Vogue.com staffer Laird Borrelli-Persson,[12] wrote that the fashion team comprised Cowan, Kennington, fellow model Antonia Bioeckesteyn, photography assistant Allan Ballard, and sittings editor Mary Kruming. That group, accompanied by the Canadian Royal Mounted Police, or Mounties, found their way north to Resolute Bay on Cornwallis Island in the Arctic Circle. According to Borrelli-Persson, they "had more than the cold to contend with; there was the unnerving silence, blinding brightness, and technical difficulties. 'The day started,' according to Cowan, 'when Mary Kruming said, "John, the sun's shining." The first problem we had was that both the Hasselblad cameras froze. We presume they froze as the shutters wouldn't work. Then we found that the film was bending and cracking because of the cold. Roughly, apart from one time when we really had a blast of fabulous sunshine (we had waited five or six days for it), we worked normal working hours, governed by the canteen food.'"[13]

The results are magnificent, but "for the girls, just wearing these thin clothes," as Cowan recounted in the magazine, "it was fantastically hard work."[14] He successfully captured both the poetry of the remote and icy landscape, and the otherworldly beauty of the models clad in white and silver. While the fashions were hardly appropriate in the frigid landscape, the images evoke the desolation and isolation of the Arctic, as well as that of the moon, "a glittering world" where "the very limit of cold" was "like the inside of a diamond."[15]

It was also during the 1960s that a unique Eskimo/Inuit invention—snow goggles (fig. 51)—found their way into haute couture. In her essay, Elizabeth Way discusses how designers such as André Courrèges created versions of this peculiar accessory to accompany their moon-inspired clothing (figs 108, 112). Courrèges's designs are made from white plastic (as are other earlier Western versions created for motorsports and skiing from the 1930s to the 1960s) and are similar, sometimes nearly identical, to those invented by the Eskimo and Inuit peoples. Indigenous Arctic goggles are carved with distinctive horizontal slits (either one long or two shorter slits) because the narrow openings limit the eye's exposure to the intense light of the snowy terrain, thus improving visual acuity. The Eskimo goggles were often off-white in color because the most readily available materials for making them were driftwood and animal bone (as well as walrus ivory and caribou antlers), which were usually lightly hued.

Vreeland's vibrant, imaginative style was short-lived, however. By the 1970s, fashion became less about haute creativity and more about a languid and earthy mix of sex and casualness. The mod era's approach to fantastical exotica and fanciful technology was being swept aside in favor of clothing that was simultaneously more functional and kinetic. As detailed in a later section of this essay—that alternates between the separate but intertwined histories of parkas and puffers—the 1970s was a period in which designers created numerous version of the parka: a utilitarian garment that became so polished it could be worn to work or to the disco.

By the end of the twentieth century, in keeping with fashion's cyclical nature, luxury and exoticism were back

**50**
(following) *Vogue*, November 1, 1964,
photograph by John Cowan

in full force. Opulent fashion shows and over-the-top garments dominated, as a new generation of designers began to find inspiration in the cultures of the Far North. Noteworthy among them were Jean Paul Gaultier's *Le Grand Voyage* and Isaac Mizrahi's so-called *Nanook of the North* collections. Both debuted during the fall/winter 1994 season.

Gaultier was one of fashion's leading figures during the 1990s. An equal balance of outrageousness and refinement, the Frenchman was a font of creativity who tapped themes ranging from Russian constructivism to illicit sex to Jewish rabbis, and dressed stars such as Madonna. His fall/winter 1994 *Le Grand Voyage* collection was aptly named as he assembled a mélange of non-Western clothing into ravishing ensembles. Chief among Gaultier's influences were fur coats, tunics, pants, and headwear appropriated from

Arctic and northern Asian peoples (Siberian, Mongolian, Himalayan). His heady blend of brocaded silks, embroidered skins, and furs (fig. 52) was so beautiful and received such glowing reviews that one of the runway shots appeared on the cover of *Women's Wear Daily*, March 4, 1994. The collection received extra coverage because Björk, the Icelandic artist/performer, made her one and only runway appearance in Gaultier's skin-and-fur-hooded jacket (emblazoned with his monogram, JPG) and red-silk brocaded pants (fig. 53).

Gaultier's collection gained popular-culture status thanks to the New York-based designer, Isaac Mizrahi. The 1995 hit documentary *Unzipped* is a behind-the-scenes glimpse into the fashion industry, specifically the making of Isaac Mizrahi's 1994 fall collection. In it, the designer finds

**51**
(above) Anavik at Banks Peninsula, Bathurst Inlet,
Northwest Territories (Nunavut), 1916, photograph
by Rudolph Martin Anderson

**52**
(facing) Jean Paul Gaultier, *Le Grand Voyage* collection,
fall/winter 1994, photograph by Patrice Stable

**53**
Björk modeling for Jean Paul Gaultier,
*Le Grand Voyage* collection, fall/winter 1994,
photograph by Patrice Stable

inspiration from seemingly incongruous sources—mainly Eskimos and a hit 1970s television series, *The Mary Tyler Moore Show*. Critic Janet Maslin, in her review for the *New York Times*, wrote that *Unzipped* was a "crafty valentine to the fashion world in general and this irrepressible designer in particular." She praised the film's tight structure, calling it "smart" and "spiky," and was particularly taken with Mizrahi's engaging personality.[16]

Mizrahi watched a number of films, from the 1935 MGM version of the Jack London novel *Call of the Wild* to the 1948

British production of the ballet-themed *The Red Shoes*, while beginning the creation of his fall 1994 collection. But it was his fascination with Arctic clothing in the groundbreaking 1922 documentary *Nanook of the North* that became that season's foundation. His modern versions of fuzzy parkas paired with vibrantly striped and voluminously cut evening skirts (figs 54, 55) became a cohesive aesthetic vision of winter luxury.

Among Mizrahi's many witty comments in the film, the most often quoted is: "All I want to do is fur pants, but

54
Isaac Mizrahi, fall/winter 1994,
photograph by Rose Hartman

55
Isaac Mizrahi, fall/winter 1994,
photograph by Ron Galella

I know, like if I do them, I will be stoned off of Seventh Avenue, like some wanton heretic or something. So there won't be any fur pants coming down my runway. It's about women not wanting to look like cows or something." Although the 1990s was a rather flamboyant period in modern fashion history, the more streamlined and functional aspect of American fashion may have eclipsed Mizrahi's full-blown creativity. And unlike Madame Grès in the 1960s, he never made fur pants.

One of the most dramatic scenes in *Unzipped* was the moment Mizrahi learned that Gaultier had also produced an Eskimo-inspired collection. One of Mizrahi's assistants brings him a copy of *Women's Wear Daily* in which a runway photo of an Asian model donning a fur-trimmed, hooded garment accompanies the headline: "Gaultier's Eskimo Chic." The cover also stated that "Nanook of the North has nothing on Jean Paul Gaultier, who's preparing an Eskimo-themed, Trans-Siberian collection . . ." Mizrahi's understandable outburst after seeing the paper resulted in his bright, ebullient take on Arctic chic, a collection that in no way mirrors that of Jean Paul Gaultier.

Arguably one of fashion's most beautiful and poetic renditions of indigenous Arctic and expedition clothing was created by Yohji Yamamoto for his fall/winter 2000 collection. Against a hypnotic soundtrack of central Asian and American Indian chants, Yamamoto, according to *Vogue* editor Hamish Bowles, "sent out a bravura collection that suggested a luxurious cocooning against an Arctic winter." The runway presentation was filled with models whom he described as "the brides of Mongolian or Tartar warriors ... swathed in fur—real fox and faux wolf" that encircled hoods and collars and bristled "from beneath the hems of padded crinoline skirts, as well as for such swaggering accessories as over-scaled Cossack hats, loop stoles, gauntlets and muffs" (figs 56, 57, 58).[17] Some of the models even wore goggles.

Inspiration for the collection came from the contemporary French photographer, Françoise Huguier. An avid world traveler, best known for her African images, Huguier

won the *Villa Médicis hors les murs* laureate in 1993 for her book *En route pour Behring* or *On the Road to Bering*, a photographic travel journal of her solo trip through Siberia. Images from the book were exhibited in numerous festivals and galleries, and she went on to win the World Press Photo prize that same year. Her depictions of Siberians dressed in an array of furs, and richly patterned textiles evocative of Oriental carpets, were gritty, engrossing, and lush.

Yamamoto took his cue from Huguier's subjects, all of whom wore or were set in a heady mix of Arctic furs and

56
Yohji Yamamoto, fall/winter 2000

central Asian woven textiles. The Japanese designer juxtaposed magnificently rich jacquard fabrics (some of which were commissioned for this collection) with panels of suede that were purposely cut to resemble the natural, ragged edges of animal skins. The sweepingly romantic collection balanced exorbitant volume and narrow silhouettes. The final looks were an Inuit-looking couple holding their baby, who was "enchantingly swaddled" in a manner that suggested "the sensuous pleasures of wrapping up against the cold."[18]

Yamamoto's runway presentation was one of the top hits of the fall/winter 2000 season. Select garments were also featured a few months later in leading fashion publications. One of the most memorable was an image styled by the great Grace Coddington and photographed by Arthur Elgort for *Vogue*'s September 2000 issue (fig. 59). Set in a barren, postapocalyptic landscape evocative of film *Mad Max*, the Inuit-inspired evening gown—made from pale-colored animal skins topping a voluminous, padded crinoline—became an otherworldly object of transcendent beauty.

57
Yohji Yamamoto, fall/winter 2000

58
Yohji Yamamoto, fall/winter 2000

A few avant-garde fashion designers increasingly incorporated skins with raw edges into their collections throughout the twenty-first century. It is ironic in this technologically driven era that cutting-edge creators are turning to this most ancient form of clothing construction. One of the pioneers is California native Rick Owens. Now residing in Paris, Owens referenced man's earliest clothing construction techniques, particularly when crafting his sensuous and moodily beautiful leather and fur garments while working for the venerated furrier, Revillon, beginning in 2006.

The decision to hire Owens may not at first have seemed logical. Revillon was a relatively staid producer of high-quality fur garments, and Owens was one of the edgiest designers in the world—one who embraced an earthy, if somewhat soiled, color palette; a gothic and moody sensibility; and a very lean and narrow silhouette, sometimes counterbalanced with sculptural jackets and coats with sharply angled hemlines. The American jolted the look of Revillon with his first collection, presented during the haute couture fall/winter 2006 season. First, Owens infused the garments with a slightly "deconstructed" aesthetic. Then, furs such as mink and fox were combined in his slew of vests, with tightly fitted backs and standing collars that fell into ruffles in front. All the fur and fur-trimmed pieces were paired with his louche, edgy, and intricately cut jersey-wrapped tops and lean trousers.

For all their edginess, the furs for Revillon and Owens's own line are constructed using contemporary fur methods, not those practiced by groups like the Inuit. This is true of all modern furs, including those by Gilles Mendel for his family-founded company, J. Mendel, and those by Pologeorgis for American couturier, Ralph Rucci. First, master furriers create a large expanse of fur, or a kind of base fabric, that is used to make the back of a coat or a sleeve. This base is made with long pieces or strips of fur that are, depending on quality, matched and then joined together. This technique of matching and sewing together assorted fur pelts is called plating. Rucci, for example, chooses whenever possible to

work with the finest pelts available, such as Barguzin sable and true broadtail. Most frequently, his furs are made using the "skin-on-skin" method: trimmed pelts are laid out and sewn together in large blocks. The advantage is that the fur has as few breaks in the pattern as possible. It is visually superior to the "let-out" method, in which narrow strips of fur are sliced along a diagonal, then sewn back together.

By the 2010s, fantastic and opulent renditions of life in the Arctic were being put on display in noteworthy fashion shows. One of the best was Karl Lagerfeld's breathtaking vision—using faux fur throughout—for the house of Chanel's fall/winter 2010 ready-to-wear collection (fig. 60). During a brutally cold March day in Paris, fashion journalist Sarah Mower wrote: "Freja Beha Erichsen and three bears on an ice floe. This was the arctic scene at Chanel, where giant chunks of bona fide iceberg, specially transported from Scandinavia, formed the frozen landscape around which models solemnly splashed through a sea of berg-melt in shaggy snow boots with ice-block heels." Interestingly, the collection had as many, if not more, "fur" or "fur"-trimmed garments than the real-fur collections Lagerfeld designed for the venerated Roman furrier and leather house Fendi. And it was so well executed that a number of viewers felt the ready-to-wear neared or even surpassed Chanel's couture collections.

Mower noted that while a few male and female models wore coats made from what seemed like polar-bear pelts, the women also wore garments in which fur "was woven into brown tweeds; formed deep pelmets on the lower half of leather jackets; became almost igloo-shaped capes, bonnets, even—for goodness' sake—furry trousers. Meanwhile, the suit and coat combinations also had a level of lavish elaboration usually reserved for haute evening wear. Fur-fringed embroideries and ice jewelry conspired to create intensely worked ruffled and beaded silhouettes that glinted with rock-crystal neckpieces and fistfuls of rings. Somewhere in there, a flash of translucent silver seemed to be a clutch in which the quilting of the CC classic bag had been frozen into the likeness of a refrigerator ice cube tray."[19]

**59**
Yohji Yamamoto, *Vogue*, September 2000,
photograph by Arthur Elgort

Three years later, Giambattista Valli for Moncler Gamme Rouge (the women's high-end collection of the French winter-sports company) created an equally opulent and compelling collection. "When fur-clad walkers led huskies onto the runway" in Paris, noted fashion journalist Tim Blanks, "it was all very *Game of Thrones.*"[20] While the inspiration for the collection was typical fashion whimsy—a love story between a snowflake and a polar bear—the clothes were a beautiful marriage of raw and refined (fig. 62). Blanks

also noted that the extreme performance elements inherent in Moncler's clothing were heightened thanks to Valli's "cinematic flair," in which "silvered, crystallized ice princesses were united with their ursine lovers. Enchanting!"[21]

Along with designers, fashion editors and photographers embraced and exaggerated the rugged allure of the Arctic culture. *Vogue* Korea, for example published a fourteen-page spread in its January 2012 issue. Photographed by Hong Jang Hyun, the editorial was entitled "Queen of Snow." A quartet

60

(above) Finale of the CHANEL fall/winter 2010
ready-to-wear show, photograph by Stephane Cardinale

61

(facing) "Queen of Snow," *Vogue* Korea, January 2012,
photograph by Hong Jang Hyun

of Korean models (Han Hye Jin, Song Kyung Ah, Jang Yoon Ju, and Jiah Yi) wear layers of furs, pelts, and knits, while sitting or standing alongside sleds and yurts, each with a towering and angular fur headdress strapped to her head (fig. 61).

## Parkas and Puffers

The increasing popularity of furs and Arctic-inspired clothing throughout the twentieth century also included the rise of the parka and the puffer. These two garments are related and have intertwined histories, but each style is distinctive and has its own story. This section traces those stories; the

text weaves back and forth along a general chronological trajectory while documenting their often parallel developments and influences on fashion, both high and low.

Staying warm and dry were primary goals of the early Arctic explorers, and the parka, or anorak, was key to successful polar expeditions. Credit for inventing the parka—a heavy, hooded jacket—goes to groups such as the Inuit and Eskimo. Meaning "skin" or "pelt," the parka was originally made from caribou and seal, but would later be crafted from woven fabrics, including synthetics that mimicked the insulating qualities of animal fur.

Throughout the twentieth century, the parka evolved to become an indispensable item of clothing worn by millions around the world. One of the paths this ubiquitous coat followed into the modern wardrobe was through sports, such as skiing. The modern ski era began during the interwar years: the first Winter Olympics was held in 1924 in Chamonix, France; twelve years later, the automated ski lift was invented. During this time, luxury ski resorts began to appear in the French, Swiss, Austrian, and Italian Alps, as well as in New England and the North American Rockies. The newly minted cadre of winter-sports enthusiasts began to purchase custom-made ski ensembles by couturiers such as Jean Patou, Jeanne Lanvin, and Elsa Schiaparelli. Some, like Gabrielle "Coco" Chanel, also participated and would frequent the tony resort St. Moritz. Touted in magazines such as *Vogue* and *Harper's Bazaar*, ski ensembles were made for style as much as for warmth. Most of these designs with their emphases on color and cut would not have been viable options for extreme cold-weather endeavors.

A garment specifically designed and made for extreme environments was the padded jacket filled with down feathers. The idea of sandwiching downy feathers between two layers of fabric is not new, but the creation of the short, semifitted, quilted jacket we know today as the "puffer," or down jacket, is a relatively recent invention. The genesis of the down jacket can be found in the rise of companies that made goods for lovers of the great outdoors. While

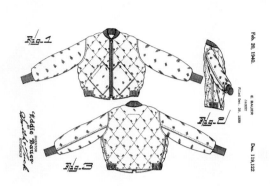

Abercrombie & Fitch catered to the client of means, Eddie Bauer (1899–1986) was among the first creators of clothing for the true explorer. The quilted down jacket was his groundbreaking innovation. Made for outdoorsmen, it was soon thereafter appropriated by armies and extreme explorers before becoming a global, wardrobe staple reinterpreted by leading high-fashion designers.

Born in a log cabin on Orcas Island, Washington, to Russian émigrés, Bauer was an avid outdoorsman and athlete. He began working at the only full-time sporting-goods shop in Seattle at the tender age of thirteen. In 1920, Bauer went into business for himself. By the early 1930s, he was importing feathers for fishing flies and badminton shuttlecocks, when it led him to a reacquaintance with goose down. Bauer learned of the material's insulating qualities from his uncle, a Cossack soldier who fought in Manchuria during the 1904 Russo-Japanese war. After nearly dying from hypothermia during a fishing excursion in 1928, Bauer designed and sewed the first prototype of the down jacket. By 1935, he held a patent for the jacket (fig. 63), and a monopoly that allowed him to put "money away ass over teakettle"[22] until America entered the war (fig. 64).

By the onset of World War II, the United States government began appropriating a wide range of raw materials, including goose down. Bauer was called upon to produce

twenty-five thousand of his flight suits, that were warm to 70 degrees below zero (fig. 65), and a quarter million sleeping bags. He could no longer manufacture down jackets for the general market during the early 1940s, but he did make a small quantity of coats from eiderdown (the eider

63
Patent illustration for Eddie Bauer
Skyliner jacket, 1940

64
Advertisement in *Outdoor Life* for
Eddie Bauer's first down jacket, 1939

is a now rare wild duck), a material that was not sanctioned. Like many American manufacturers who had to repurpose their production to meet military needs, Bauer was nearly bankrupt by the war's end. He rebounded thanks to two phenomena: one, the launch of his mail-order business; and two, increased sales thanks to GIs who wore Bauer products and spread the news via word of mouth.

Eiderdown was also the material of choice for the brilliant Anglo-American couturier Charles James, when he created, in 1937, one of his early masterpieces: the first high-fashion puffer (fig. 66). Like a duvet, it was made of two layers of white silk satin filled with down, then the satin layers were stitched together. But unlike the boxy shape of the Bauer model, James meticulously calculated the construction of his design around the human form and infused a degree of classicism by curling the silhouette so that it resembled the scrolled capital of an Ionic column. In 1975 he noted: "The stitching which held the shaped masses of eiderdown in place, being treated as scrolls or, as in the case of my coat as tapered arabesques, one within another. The stitching however had to be worked out with the cut. . . . This is done while the pattern lies in pieces after it has been first planned . . . The great problem in the development of this

concept was that it concerned the expansion of the silhouette by inflation with eiderdown which in some areas would be three inches thick at least."[23] In other words, the padded swells of satin were deflated around the shoulders, neckline, and armholes. Not only was the density of the down amended to enable ease of movement, it allowed James to achieve an aesthetic ideal.

While the meticulous engineering of this down jacket exemplifies James's working methodology, it is in many ways an anomaly when compared to his other important works. A milliner turned couturier, he adapted the process of hatmaking when creating his most celebrated designs during the 1940s and 1950s: evening dresses such as the "Four-leaf Clover," "Butterfly," "Swan," and "Tree." Layers of millinery materials—including buckram, horsehair, and covered wire—were used to mold and shape his three-dimensional, engineered gowns. These rigid understructures were then topped with materials—such as heavy duchess satin and silk velvet—that were draped but also twisted and torqued against their innate woven structure so that the bodies would sometimes rip and shred. Despite a few technical shortcomings, James's work in the mid-twentieth century reflected the overriding influence of the Belle Époque and the inherent rigidity of such fashion. Comparatively, his down jacket was much less cumbersome than his midcentury gowns because it reflected the languid and liberated look of pre–World War II fashions.

The modernist aesthetic of the 1930s steered James's creativity, making his evening jacket a design (though not a financial) success, and therefore a future fashion influence. This precursor to the contemporary puffer reflected that era's fusion of art and fashion: it was described by Salvador Dalí as the "first soft sculpture."[24] Likewise, it was a modern Western take on the exotic. *Harper's Bazaar* stated that the garment is the "newest, most deliciously feminine of evening jackets . . . quilted and padded like the jackets of Chinese Princesses."[25] George Hoyningen-Huene's accompanying black-and-white photograph of the garment further

65

Bauer's jackets and sleeping bags were highly prized by airmen during the World War II Aleutian Campaign, leading the US Army Air Forces to commission the military's first down-insulated flight suit, the B-9 Parka and A-8 Flight Pants.

66

Charles James, *Harper's Bazaar*, October 1938, photograph by George Hoyningen-Huene

**COMPANIONS IN ACHIEVEMENT**

Sir Edmund Hillary and Tensing Norkey, G.M., who together climbed Everest on Friday, May 29, 1953.

67
Sir Edmund Hillary (left) and Tenzing Norgay (right),
*The Times, Everest Colour Supplement,*
September 22, 1953

enhanced its beautiful and otherworldly artistic qualities.

This single object holds a coveted place in fashion history, but it was not the design that led to the universal ascension of the puffer coat. James incorrectly "suggested that his design inspired the Air Force quilted jackets of World War II, better known as the bombardier jackets."[26] It is clear that is untrue, at least in America, where the military wore Eddie Bauer's innovation.

The down-filled jacket continued to gain popularity thanks also to the growing interest in extreme mountain climbing, particularly after World War II. On May 29, 1953, Sir Edmund Hillary, a New Zealand beekeeper, and Tenzing Norgay, a Nepalese Sherpa (an indigenous group of the high southern slopes of the Himalayas), were the first successfully recorded humans to reach the summit of the world's highest peak (fig. 67). A joint venture between the Royal Geographical Society and the Alpine Club, the 1953 ascent brought about a dozen new designs including tents, sleeping bags, cookers, oxygen equipment, boots, and new windproof clothing.[27] Hillary and Norgay, like their predecessors, George Mallory and Andrew "Sandy" Irvine,

who may have reached the summit but perished in June 1924 (fig. 68), carefully calculated the clothing needed to endure this dangerous endeavor in the most unforgiving of environments.

Both the 1924 and 1953 expeditions relied on sensibly chosen base, middle, and outer layers of clothing. In both cases, the reliance on natural fibers—that were woven and knitted—was not a hindrance to survival. This did not turn out to be the case for the ill-fated Scott expedition to the South Pole.[28] Contemporary scientific research confirmed that Mallory and Irvine wore cotton leggings made with a tuck stitch, a honeycomb-like detail that trapped warm air and provided adequate insulation. Hillary, however, relied on synthetic long underwear, specifically Duofold's revolutionary fabric that was reported to "wick sweat better than coarse wool."[29]

On top of the base layer, Mallory and Irvine wore eight alternating layers of silk, cotton, and wool. Not only did silk provide windproofing, it easily glided over wool and gave the climbers greater range of movement. While Hillary wore a synthetic base layer, for his middle layer he opted for a Shetland wool "jumper suit" produced by T. M. Adie and Sons of Voe, Scotland. This natural wool, custom-made sweater reportedly offered great insulation as well as breathability.[30]

As for the outer layer, the 1924 climbers wore gabardine, specifically a worsted wool fabric used by Burberry for their original trench coat. Fabric made from both natural and manmade fibers was chosen by Hillary and Norgay for their outerwear coats: a thin, lightweight, and windproof material comprised of cotton and nylon.

Although the subject of waterproof garments was not addressed in the previous section on indigenous Arctic clothing, it was vitally important to the Inuit and Eskimo, as well as to later polar explorers and extreme mountain climbers. For example, the Inuit crafted ingenious waterproof coverings made from the intestines of whales and walruses, to wear while hunting in their kayaks. Initially, such waterproof clothing had no profound influence on high fashion.

**68**

British Mount Everest expedition, 1924. Back row (left to right) Andrew Irvine, George Mallory, Edward Norton, Noel Odell, and John Macdonald. Front row (left to right) Edward Shebbeare, Geoffrey Bruce, Howard Somervell, and Bentley Beetham; photograph by J. B. Noel

The creation of waterproof materials by companies such as Burberry, however, would go on to have a strong global impact on both high fashion and mass-produced clothing by the interwar years of the twentieth century.

Although many cultures produced water-resistant woven materials for centuries (such as the Chinese, who created oil-coated silk more than one thousand years ago), mass-manufactured cotton fabric coated in oil or rubber became a British specialty during the nineteenth century. Pioneering firms—such as Burberry, Barbour, Grenfell, and Jaeger—were leaders in creating windproof, waterproof, and breathable garments and outwear that were suitable for extreme work environments and sports. Their innovations were worn by seafarers, as well as polar explorers such as Amundsen, Shackleton, Scott, and Nansen. Although Burberry has become a top-rate high-fashion company, it is keenly aware of its expedition-based origins. It, and the other manufactures listed above, also paved the way for later waterproof fabrics, such as Ventile (which saved the lives of many British airmen who were thrown into the icy waters of the North Atlantic during World War II), and synthetic inventions, such as Gore-Tex. Thanks in part to the worldwide publicity generated by extreme explorers, water- and wind-resistant materials eventually became integral elements of mainstream fashion.

Scientists note that natural fibers have an advantage over synthetics because they do not accumulate body odor. And because Mallory's clothes were custom-made, he was able to move with greater ease and comfort than if he was wearing mass-produced climbing gear. Furthermore, some of the garments listed above were also lighter than contemporary examples. However, today's extreme climbing accessories, such as goggles, helmets (which were not worn until later in the twentieth century), ice axes, crampons, boots, backpacks, and sleeping gear are both lighter and stronger than ever. And those boots, backpacks, and even sleeping bags, also found their way into modern high fashion.

Equally important to extreme explorers have been their accessories. Among the indispensable items are boots. In

1953, members of the Hillary/Norgay expedition wore at least two types of boot. The most noted of them was a custom, high-altitude model made by the British Boot, Shoe and Allied Trades Research Association of Kettering, England.[31] This boot was revolutionary at the time, lightweight, with superior insulating properties. Both man-made and engineered materials were sandwiched inside a waterproof "envelope" to create what is known as insulation loft, or the ability to hold in heat at the extremities of the human body.

In 1953, the Hillary and Norgay team relied on rigid-frame backpacks made from lightweight aluminum frames. The backpack—also known as the knapsack, book bag, kitbag, or rucksack—is an ancient design. Cultures around

**69**
Prada nylon backpack, *Vogue*, August 1989,
photograph by Hans Feurer

the world have created many versions of this simple receptacle, made of animal skins or woven cloth, which is carried on one's back and secured with two shoulder straps. Hunters, soldiers, nomads, and later sportsmen, carried the backpack with regularity. Only recently has it become a fashion item.

Perhaps no version of the backpack gained greater style status than the black nylon version created by Miuccia Prada (fig. 69). Her grandfather, Mario, founded the company in 1913, and his first shop was in Milan's famed Galleria Vittorio Emanuele II. In 1977, Prada took over the family firm and formed a business partnership with Patrizio Bertelli, who later became her husband. Prada's first backpacks and totes debuted in the late 1970s. By the mid-1980s, Prada's most important technical innovation—a fine-twist, waterproof, nylon fabric called Pocone—was being used

to make both the classic Prada handbag and the brand's marquee item, its backpack.

Among the most important objects used by the Hillary/Norgay team was the sleeping bag. Based on earlier prototypes, such as the British models dating to the early 1920s, the New Zealand firm Fairydown constructed bags using nylon for the shell and down insulation for the filling. Their product kept the climbers alive on Everest's long, cold nights. The twentieth-century versions were modern incarnations of the *Euklisia* (Greek for "good sleeping place") rug patented by the Welsh mail-order pioneer, Pryce Pryce-Jones, in 1876. Reportedly made of carpet-like material that was folded and cut into a sleeping-bag shape, upward of sixty thousand Euklisias were sold to the Russian Army, as well as to missionaries in Africa and pioneers in the Australian outback.

70
Eddie Bauer Mount Everest climbing gear
from 1963 (left) and 2012 (right)

71
Pat Cleveland in Charles James
eiderdown coat, photograph by Juan Ramos

The down sleeping bag would later be reconfigured into an important and innovative fashion item.

American companies that were created to cater to extreme sports, such as REI, Patagonia, and The North Face, followed not only the rising popularity of such endeavors, but also the pioneering efforts of Eddie Bauer. Bauer's 1935 Blizzard Proof jacket (along with his later version called the Skyliner) and his pre-World War II down sleeping bags were improved for American climbing teams active in the Himalayas. The patented Kara Koram quilted down parka and pants, for example, were made for the 1953 American team that ascended K2.

In 1963, Bauer's company outfitted two American teams. Among them was the first US climber to summit Mount Everest, Jim Whittaker, and his Nepalese colleague, Sherpa Nawang Gombu. In 2012, the company began promoting the fiftieth anniversary of these two historic teams by documenting the clothing and equipment they used. While a photograph of the 2012 equipment is decidedly more modern, many of the elements look remarkably similar (fig. 70).

Perhaps it is no surprise that American-based designers began to create new fashion versions of the down jackets and coats during the 1970s, thanks in part to extensive media coverage of extreme sports, as well as the revived visibility of Charles James's 1937 satin evening jacket. Beginning in the early 1970s, wearing vintage fashion became a trend, and new designs were influenced by the art-moderne style

72
Giorgio di Saint'Angelo, *Vogue*, September 1976,
photograph by Arthur Elgort

73
Geoffrey Beene, *Vogue*, July 1978,
photograph by Arthur Elgort

of the interwar years. It was in this milieu that James's jacket became a celebrated object.

In 1968, James commissioned Antonio Lopez to illustrate several versions of the puffer. Lopez also photographed numerous shots of the jacket on model Pat Cleveland (fig. 71), one of which appeared in the May 1973 issue of *Esquire* magazine. It was one of several images of the jacket that surfaced, including one by Bill Cunningham for the *New York Times*. That photograph, set in James's Chelsea Hotel studio and depicting Lopez donning the jacket, illustrates the gender-bending flexibility of the design, as well as its relentless glamour amid the rumpled working environment.

The garment achieved cult status that spawned and later paralleled the contemporaneous trend for padded coats and jackets which had begun to appear regularly in fashion magazines. James wished to modernize his masterpiece. Near the end of his career, in 1975, he expressed a desire to revive it in different materials, from luxurious glove-leather to mass-market versions in nylon "stuffed with foam rubber, or better, KAPOK, or whatever has taken the place of KAPOK and 'marketed' for ski wear, use on motor bicycles etc., at a low price."[32] While the revised versions were never created, the ivory original continued to ignite interest in a new generation. Its presence in exhibitions, such as the Victoria and Albert's *Surreal Things* in 2007, and the Metropolitan Museum of Art's Charles James retrospective in 2014, kept this groundbreaking item in the public eye.

In 1975, the flamboyant New York-based designer Giorgio Sant'Angelo was producing his own quilted jacket: a photograph of it by Arthur Elgort appeared in the September 1976 edition of *Vogue* (fig. 72). The image featured model Lisa Taylor wearing Sant'Angelo's version, a hybrid of the parka and the down jacket, replete with a hood and drawstring waist.

By 1978, other American designers were producing even more variations on the parka. The July issue of *Vogue* featured a down-filled version made from "a luminous pale copper color" by Geoffrey Beene (fig. 73). Worn over a black

and lurex jumpsuit, the coat was described as: "The new dazzle ... the new impact. Totally unexpected—a quilted parka in 'satin'! Beene takes jackets to a whole new level!"[33] Clearly, the *Vogue* editor was excited about this contemporary version of an ancient garment. Later, in September 1978, *Vogue* presented a sportier version, this time by Perry Ellis. "Perfect for women who spend part of their lives in a car, or—just hacking around—the news of a jacket that's creamy cotton poplin filled with goose down. Short, warm, feather-weight."[34]

Arguably, the most famous version of the new, fashionable, down-filled outerwear garment was Norma Kamali's ankle-length, sleeping-bag coat (fig. 74). Designed for her

74
Norma Kamali, *Vogue*, September 1990,
photograph by Arthur Elgort

personal use, the sleeping-bag coat was one of the best and earliest creations to appropriate extreme wear for fashion. While her dresses and separates made from gray sweatshirt material that debuted in 1980 were groundbreaking, the sleeping-bag coat became one of her signature creations.

According to the designer, she came up with the idea in the early 1970s while on a camping trip. Kamali noted that "for a few years I continued to use actual sleeping bags," eventually creating "two coats, and stitching them together." Her best-known versions were sold with a matching drawstring pouch in which the coat, when rolled up, could be easily condensed and stowed. By the late 1970s and early 1980s, versions were appearing in major fashion

publications in the United States and in Europe. However, the parka's popularity also made gains beyond the realm of high fashion, as it become an important clothing item for cutting-edge, antiestablishment groups.

The descriptively named fishtail parka was designed with a longer, pointed back than a traditional parka. It was originally commissioned by the US Army at the onset of the Korean War, as protection against that country's brutally cold and severe winters (fig. 75). Versions of the fishtail parka were called the M-1948 (or M48) and M-1951 (or M51), thus denoting the specific year each was designed and manufactured. Several sources note that these parkas were made from the finest industrial-grade fabrics and were

75
Marines marching south from Koto-ri in the mountains
in sub-zero weather, Korean War (1950–1953)

constructed for durability as well as warmth. The range of materials included wind-resistant cotton sateen, mohair, and/or thick woolens, while the design details included drawstrings and a range of pockets and hoods. Fishtail parkas possessed the flexibility of a coat, but with better layering options than earlier, World War II versions. Even though the Eighth Army distributed huge numbers of the coats—331,000 for its final 1952–1953 winter campaign—demand outstripped supply.

Soon after the Korean conflict, many of the M-48 and M-51 parkas found their way into army surplus stores around the United States and overseas. It was during the

1960s in Britain that the fishtail parka was discovered and appropriated by the mods—which gave the coat a whole new life (fig. 76). The mods were young people who had limited income and were looking to make a statement against the immediate post-World War II era of conformity. So the fishtail parka—being cheap, warm, relatively waterproof, and hooded—became an ideal garment for a new generation of scooter-riding youth. It quickly became a staple of the emerging counterculture movement.

By the middle of the 1970s, the fishtail parka was to undergo yet another transformation. A far more aggressive youth group—the punks—took a turn integrating the coat into their distinctive look. Although the mods were considered revolutionary at the time, their suits and sleekly groomed hair were absolutely benign when compared to the punks. Donning an array of ripped and torn clothing ornamented with safety pins and spiky dog collars, Dr. Martens construction-style boots, and vibrantly dyed Mohawk hairstyles, the punks were often as aggressive as their appearance (fig. 77).

Simultaneous with the appropriation of vintage, military-style parkas by counterculture youth was the rise of performance outerwear. Companies like The North Face, founded in 1966 in San Francisco, and REI, founded in Seattle in 1938, became important sources for serious climbers, backpackers, and mountaineers in the mid-century. Similarly, the French firm Moncler (an abbreviation of Monestier-de-Clermont, a mountain village near Grenoble) was founded in 1952. Collectively, these firms did much to advance technology and the widespread popularity of extreme sports such as mountain climbing.

Moncler's popularity in fashion arose during the 1980s in Milan, the boom years of the Italian high-style clothing industry. A small subculture of young men began to appropriate work wear by companies such as Timberland and extreme environmental clothing by Moncler, along with select Italian labels such as Armani. These fashion mixologists were called the "Paninari" by the leading newspaper *La Stampa*, because they congregated at the Al Panino café.

76
Dutch mod band City Motions, 1960s,
photograph by Peter Wories

Their look not only had American roots (youth groups in the United States began wearing proletariat, or "prol," gear in the immediate post-World War II era), but they were the European counterpart to another, even more important and celebrated subculture, hip-hop.

Arguably, no musical movement has had more impact on contemporary culture and fashion—both high and low—than hip-hop. From its birth in America's black, inner-city neighborhoods during the 1970s, to its rapid global growth, hip-hop has embraced, created, promoted, and popularized fashion trends every step along the way. Two of its signature garments have been the down jacket and the parka. While numerous brands were worn and popularized by early hip-hop stars, none had more success than Tommy Hilfiger.

Hilfiger formed his brand in the 1980s. It quickly became a leading American company, specializing in what was dubbed "preppy style with a twist." By 1990, his brighter and bolder aesthetic was discovered by hip-hop stars. A fortuitous meeting in an airport between Hilfiger and rap star Grand Puba led to the designer's first alliance with the movement. The designer began to dress the singer gratis. Soon after, Hilfiger's initial product placement attracted stars such as Raekwon and Coolio, who wore the designer's clothes in hip-hop videos and on tour. Some of them even walked the runway for Hilfiger (fig. 78). They and their followers donned an array of neo-preppy items, including parkas. Some theorized that the bulky silhouette enhanced the human form, making it more massive and totemic, thus paralleling the overtly masculine and aggressive early hip-hop style.

The down jacket, also called the "puffer," became a rapper mainstay. While the exact origins of the term "puffer" are not known, some credit the hip-hop community with its popularization during the early 1990s, including a colloquial riff on the word, "puffa." Performers such as The Notorious B.I.G., on his 1993 *Party and Bullshit* release (he was called Biggie Smalls at the time), sang: "I used to have the trey deuce and a deuce deuce in my bubblegoose." He was clearly referring to the bubble-like exterior and goose-down insulation of his favorite style of jacket.

The female rapper, Missy Elliot, recontextualized what the puffer could be with her first hit, "The Rain," from the album and accompanying video *Supa Dupa Fly*. June Ambrose, the costume designer, was challenged to "sell" Elliot to mainstream America because she was, as Ambrose noted in interviews, "a full-figured girl," at a time dominated by slimmer female performers. The video director Hype Williams presented Ambrose with a concept in which Elliott was to be "blown up" like the "Michelin Man" (the tire company's oversized, puffy mascot). Ambrose designed a jumpsuit with a jet-black, patent-leather outer layer, and inner-tube material on the inside that was to be fully

77
Mod in parka, standing with punk

collection, the designer sent an array of models down a nearly pitch-black runway in long, glossy, black coats that were quilted and padded, with wide cone-like silhouettes topped with face-framing hoods, ruffs, or capelets (fig. 79). The overall effect was eerie and otherworldly, not unlike the far reaches of the planet. Interestingly, Watanabe's mentor, Rei Kawakubo, founder of the Comme des Garçons label, has been collaborating with Moncler and subtly redesigning the brand's down jackets for years.

In February 2011, Joseph Altuzarra, the young designer of French Basque and Chinese-American heritage, presented a fall/winter collection that was a sensuous ode to the parka. The ironic combination of grunge-inspired, printed chiffon dresses paired with mid-twentieth-century military outerwear was beautifully refined. Altuzarra stated that his collection was inspired by images from the 1990s of Kate Moss combining vintage military parkas (fig. 80) with decidedly feminine fashions. Hamish Bowles noted that Altuzarra "added his own high-voltage polish" to the parka because of his "ability to edit some great fashion moments of recent history and put together a sophisticated inspiration board." Bowles went on to state that Altuzarra "can make these the starting points for fashion adventures that are very much his own."[35]

While the references were evident, as was Altuzarra's ability to refine and burnish his counterculture references, the amount of work necessary to heighten the desirability of old military coats was compounded by "a lot of fittings" and much "trial and error."[36] Beginning with the simple premise of finding warm and functional outerwear for his clients, Altuzarra wanted a fresh approach. He found that performance wear—by companies from Moncler to REI—was an ideal starting point. The practicality of parkas further resonated with him, as they were also ideal for travel.

Altuzarra's big challenge was to make the utilitarian parka chic. Pushing the idea that such outerwear could also be fashion forward meant reworking the silhouette, making the collars and hood bigger, and reducing the volume around the torso. He added fur linings and chose the colors and

inflated, not unlike the early deep-sea suits described in Ariele Elia's essay. However, the suit leaked air. Perceived as a design flaw at the time, it actually turned out to be a happy accident, as the undulating layers of air and rubberized material made Elliot's movements more dynamic and visually compelling. Five years later, Elliot wore a decidedly feminine, pink version of the puffer on the cover of her 2002 studio album, *Under Construction*.

Throughout the 1990s, the parka and the puffer became fixtures in high fashion. Like members of the counterculture, designers from Ralph Lauren to Marc Jacobs were producing variations on these practical coats, recontextualizing and reconfiguring them for fashionable urban customers.

Fashion's cult of the parka reached its apex in the early twenty-first century. Some of the greatest versions were designed by Junya Watanabe. For his fall/winter 2009

78
Raekwon modeling in Tommy Hilfiger fashion show, 1994, photograph by Andy Hilfiger

79
(facing) Junya Watanabe, fall/winter 2009

patterns carefully (fig. 81). The result in the fall/winter 2011 collection was a parka that was recognizable but "turned on its head," so that it possessed a certain level of gravitas that ensured it was "not cartoonish."[37]

While the M-1948 and M-1951 American parkas repurposed for the grunge look inspired Altuzarra's 2011 collection, for his next fall/winter presentation he turned to the parkas of Arctic peoples. Among the most striking—and popular—objects sent down the runway in 2012 was his black-and-white patterned coat that looked similar to those worn by indigenous Arctic shamans. Aside from healthy

editorial coverage in fashion publications and online sites, this coat reappeared the following year on Jenna Lyons, president and creative director of J. Crew and a celebrated street-fashion star, as she donned the Altuzarra parka at New York fashion shows in February 2013. Images of Lyons wearing the parka in the falling snow were among the most poetic captured that season.

Other leading fashion houses recently presented collections in Paris that also reworked elements of the down jacket. Rick Owens had puffer gowns engulfing models' torsos, Acne chopped them up into duvet dresses and tiny

**80**
Kate Moss, 2000,
photograph by Richard Young

**81**
Joseph Altuzarra,
fall/winter 2011

cropped coats, and Stella McCartney made outsized vegan puffers crafted in jewel-toned velvets (as models strode to the tune "I'm vegan bitch!" from Snaxx's plantlife anthem *Get Yo Tofu On*). Outside of Paris, the down duvet was reworked by Sarah Burton as she fashioned lavish gowns out of puffers for the house of Alexander McQueen.

Arguably the most noteworthy recent version of the puffer appeared on a Paris runway during the autumn/winter 2016 season. For that collection, Demna Gvasalia, creative director at the house of Balenciaga, devised a new silhouette. Made in a vivid shade of red, the puffer looked as if it was casually sliding off the model, exposing the embellished shoulders of a crystal-encrusted turtleneck beneath (fig. 82). In actuality, it is purposely cut to look as if it is falling off, its collar loosely encircling the upper arms rather than the neck. This coat might initially seem at odds with the tradition in which the venerated house of Balenciaga is steeped. But its construction and inverted full-back silhouette, some argue, has moved high fashion forward just as Cristóbal Balenciaga's handcrafted innovations did decades earlier.[38] While Gvasalia is no craftsman and this point is debatable, there is no question that his version of the puffer jacket galvanized more interest and coverage than any other item that season.

Ironically, Gvasalia's disruptive influence stems from his antifashion philosophy. The designer—who named the brand that he formed with a tight collective of friends Vetements (the French word for clothes but spelled without the circumflex over the first "e")—is credited with recontextualizing the recent past as well as any designer in the world today. Just as Altuzarra looked to Kate Moss and the grunge movement, Gvasalia tapped 1990s fashion, both high and low. While growing up in Soviet Georgia, the oppressive uniformity of clothing experienced by many young people led Gvasalia and his friends to discover imagery beyond the borders of his relatively isolated, Communist country.[39] Specifically, it led him to the elusive avant-garde master, Belgium's Martin Margiela, for whom he apprenticed. Influences from that stint can be seen in Vetement's

remixing of Margiela's 1990s' and early 2000s' deconstructionist collections.

For example, Margiela created an array of body-engulfing clothing, one of the most famous being his "duvet" coat designed in 2000. Inspired by quilted, down-filled bed coverings, it was viewed as the latest evolutionary step in Margiela's long-held interest in deconstruction. Rather than unpicking the seams of garments and turning them inside out, as he did at the outset of his career, his "duvet" had detachable sleeves and was constructed to be folded into itself. The garment was lauded as a meditation on how far Margiela could push the philosophical boundaries of clothing design.

More simply, it can also be seen as a much later incarnation of Norma Kamali's sleeping bag coat (she was clearly the originator of the lofty, body-enveloping outer garment).

**82**
*T Magazine* cover, April 17, 2016,
photograph by Jackie Nickerson

Yet, no matter how the original Margiela duvet is to be interpreted, it was a top seller in 2012, when it was reproduced at a substantially lower price in the designer's collaboration with H&M, the huge Swedish firm specializing in "fast fashion." It joined the countless other puffers that conquered the global fashion landscape, including the many thousands sold by giant "fast fashion" retailers like the Japanese company, Uniqlo, as well as manufacturers of actual high performance wear such as REI, Patagonia, and The North Face.

## The Moon and the Ocean

As Elizabeth Way writes in her essay, outer-space exploration had a profound, if short-lived effect on high fashion. While Way probes the many ways in which the phenomenon defined 1960s couture, the roots of its creation began in the preceding decade. It could be argued that the wedge-shaped dresses made from double-faced fabrics grew out of the technical innovations of master couturier, Cristóbal Balenciaga (1895–1972).

After World War II, Balenciaga was the most revered figure in haute couture. For more than fifty years, he perfected his métier and was one of the few fashion designers capable of crafting a garment—beginning to end—with his own hands. Creating fashion in this manner became increasingly challenging for Balenciaga because the 1960s was an era dominated by the sudden "youthquake" movement and the steady rise of ready-to-wear in Europe. Although his work was antithetical to the prevailing trends, Balenciaga created his most abstract and conceptual designs during the final decade of his long career. These garments surpassed those of his contemporaries—from novice to veteran—in their purity, grandeur, monumentality, and beauty. His sculptural creations glided over the body, sometimes enhancing and occasionally eradicating the recognizable silhouette beneath, as the wearer and the garment fused into a single aesthetic vision.

Opting to use materials that he helped create with the Swiss textile firm, Abraham—gazar and zagar, which were stiff but simultaneously lightweight and flexible—Balenciaga crafted three otherworldly examples in 1967, shortly before his retirement. These were his "envelope," a black gazar cocktail dress shaped like an inverted pyramid, with each corner pinched in to create four large lobes; an evening dress topped off with a bias-cut gazar evening wrap molded into an explosion of fabric that framed the face like a giant cabbage rose (and aptly named "chou"); and his famous bridal gown, with a long, canted train that billowed into a perfect cone shape as the wearer moved, and air wafted and filled the skirt.

The wedding gown was an extreme version of a wedge-shaped dress Balenciaga initially developed about a decade earlier, in 1957. One of the first versions was sleeveless and was made of pale silk gazar, enlivened with three-dimensional embroidery rendered in an eye-popping array of vibrant colors (fig. 83). This garment not only served as the basis for his later innovations, it would provide inspiration for younger couturiers inspired by the midcentury space race.

Several designers who defined the space-age look, such as André Courrèges and Emanuel Ungaro, apprenticed at the house of Balenciaga and clearly appropriated the master's prowess for geometrically shaped garments. Their work influenced others, including another Parisian-based couturier, Michel Goma. One of the Museum at FIT's stellar 1960s garments is a wedge-shaped evening dress designed by Goma and dating to circa 1968 (fig. 84). While working as the chief designer for the venerated house of Patou, Goma crafted this dress out of black-and-white silk. The density of the fabric allows the garment's wide hemline to retain a cone-like silhouette, one that resembles the shape of NASA space capsules. The shape is further accented with a large, triangular ribbon of white silk. The biomorphic-shaped inset also reflects the popularity of op art.

Along with fashion, other mediums that incorporated clothing or costumes, such as film and even classical ballet, were influenced by space exploration. In an ode to the ultramodern, leotard-clad, "black-and-white" ballets by

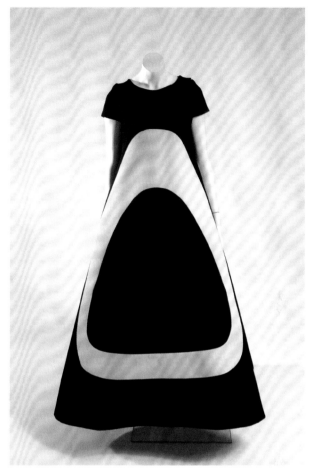

the preeminent choreographer, George Balanchine, that began to take hold in the 1950s, Frederick Ashton of the Royal Ballet choreographed *Monotones* in 1965. ("Black-and-white" refers to the dancers' costume of black leotards, very pale pink tights, and white T-shirts for the males.) Set to the music of Erik Satie, the pas de trois for two men and one woman (and a second work added later for two women and one man) was a hit.

Like Balenciaga, Ashton was in his sixties when he debuted his decidedly modern trio of dancers, all clad in body-hugging leotards (fig. 85). Although he was a noted classicist, Ashton understood that fashions had changed dramatically since his heyday, the 1930s to the 1950s. And his hometown, London, was leading the 1960s' unisex trend: long hair for men and androgynous clothing for both genders. Star dancer Rudolf Nureyev, who devoted most of his time to the Royal Ballet, was invigorating male roles in traditional ballets, a phenomenon that was nicknamed "Princes' Lib." Ashton caught and rode this unisex, modernist wave. Both trios in *Monotones* moved with the slowness that evoked recent film imagery of astronauts walking in outer space. Although men had not yet walked on the moon,

83
Balenciaga, 1958

84
Michael Goma, evening dress, silk,
1967–1969, Paris, The Museum at FIT

*Monotones* anticipated the event so well that within a few years, Ashton supposedly told an interviewer that his choreography was influenced "when you Americans were all landing on the moon."

Travel to outer space was always understood to be a Herculean human effort. Just as challenging (and by some accounts, more) has been travel to the deeps of the earth's oceans. According to Graham Hawkes, a submarine engineer, the deep sea is a richer environment than space, filled with unexplored oceans, and its mysteries are more compelling. The watery bottom of the earth is more challenging, and its life-forms are far more bizarre than anything yet seen in outer space.[40] While there have certainly been noted deep-sea expeditions, no part of the globe remains more unexplored than the depths of the great oceans. The

Mariana Trench in the western Pacific is home to a valley that dips to more than 36,000 feet below the surface—the deepest point known on earth. Divers in deep-sea submersibles reached the bottom of its depths in 1960 and 2012, but most of the trench is still an elusive mystery.

Expeditions to the oceans' depths have resulted in the discovery of amazing animals that expand our understanding of bioluminescence—the production and emission of light by a living organism. A few nonmarine bioluminescent species exist, such as fireflies and glowworms, but the vast majority live in the open ocean, including scaled fish, jellyfish, crustaceans, and mollusks. The most diverse and spectacular examples live in the deepest oceans. Scientists estimate that between 80 and 90 percent of all deep-sea creatures are bioluminescent. Squids, comb jellies, and amorphous creatures

85
Edward Watson, Marianela Nunez, and Federico
Bonelli in *Monotones II* by Frederick Ashton,
photograph by Tristram Kenton

—

emit blue- and green-spectrum light that often twinkles and flashes. Such wildlife has come to inspire the fantastic creations of designers such as Alexander McQueen and Iris van Herpen.

## Conclusion

It is fitting that newly discovered oceanic life-forms have come to be compelling sources of inspiration to fashion's most artistic and conceptual designers. Finding such treasures confirms the continuing argument that, for all the efforts of golden-age polar explorers, much has yet to be revealed in the nether reaches of our world. Cavers, for example, believe they are in the middle of their own golden age, as the deepest and largest underground grottoes remain unknown to humans. In the infamous, nightmarish subterranean labyrinths of Mexico's Yucatán, known as "cenotes" (Spanish for natural pits or sinkholes that result from collapsed, limestone bedrock that exposes groundwater underneath), the best cave divers are exploring the most dangerous terrestrial environments in the world.

Likewise, some of the world's most unnavigable rivers await human exploration. For example, the headwaters of China's Heilongjiang and Songhua Rivers and the Tua and Purari Rivers in Papua New Guinea remain untouched. While much has been written about the ascents of Everest, mountaineers have not yet scaled equally challenging peaks in Alaska, Greenland, and western China. The world's highest unclimbed peak, the 24,830-foot Gangkhar Puensum, is protected by Bhutan's ban on climbing the country's sacred mountains.

While some explorers sought to stake claims for their countries or to engage in scientific discovery, the overriding impetus that drove most to the edge of survival was the unquenchable urge to discover what was there. Fashion's greatest designers have likewise continued to pursue the outer limits of their own creativity as they seek inspiration from the extreme.

# 4

# Fur

## THE FINAL FRONTIER

Jonathan Faiers

---◇---

Looking into the inside, she saw several coats hanging up—mostly long fur coats. There was nothing Lucy liked so much as the smell and feel of fur. She immediately got in among the coats and rubbed her face against them, leaving the door open, of course, because she knew it was very foolish to shut oneself into any wardrobe.[1]

In the November 1977 issue of American *Vogue*, the season's latest fur coats were featured in a photo spread accompanied by the robots from the hit movie *Star Wars*, which premiered that year (fig. 87). The article, entitled "The 'Force' of Fur," featured top models of the time, including Jerry Hall, wearing a full-length, wraparound mink coat "with a big pull-up sable collar that puts fur where it's most appealing—all around the face!"[2]—a sensation echoing Lucy's sensory pleasure described above, as she pushes her way through the fur coats and on into the adventures she will find in C. S. Lewis's *The Lion, the Witch and the Wardrobe*.

The contrast between the gold, metallic sheen of C-3PO or the space-age whiteness of R2-D2 with the "pale-honey beige fox," "Russian golden sable," and "chestnut brown

mink" furs featured in the *Vogue* spread can, on one level, be understood as a cynical marketing ploy, forging an uneasy alliance between that year's box-office hit and, by the 1970s, traditional fur's dwindling relevance to contemporary fashion.

Leaving aside the relative "fashionabilty" of the coats featured in the spread, what "The 'Force' of Fur" article does signal, with startling clarity, is the central role that the fashionable fur trade has played in our understanding of global economic history, and specifically how this history has been one of exploration, border crossings, and transition. The desire for fur, its sensory appeal and unparalleled ability to act as a visual signifier of wealth and privilege, is reflected both in its fashionable history and our collective cultural psyches. The tactile frisson Lucy experiences in the wardrobe ripples down through the ages, is central to Western artistic and literary traditions, and continues further back into universal myth and creation legends. Similarly, the pioneering spirit celebrated in the *Star Wars* films and their central appeal to "feel the force" encapsulate the magnetic allure of fur, both sensory and economic,

**86**
Amy Johnson wearing a leopard-skin coat kisses her husband, aviator Jim Mollison, goodbye, as he embarks on a new world-record flight, 1936.

making the *Vogue* spread simultaneously visually disconcerting and conceptually apposite.

What this essay will attempt to explore briefly is how the way that fur has been worn—in the West primarily as a fashionable material—can also be used as a form of vestimentary map that charts fur's various journeys. These explorations include those to the outer limits of fashion; the round trips back and forth from acceptability and approbation to disrepute and in some cases illegality; as well as its psychological and economic traversing of borders from inner, private pleasure to external, public display. The history of where and what type of fur has been worn on the body, and how it has been incorporated into fashionable

garments and represented in words and images, provides us with an extensive and varied logbook of fur's numerous expeditions. As Phillippe Perrot so effectively reminds us: "Clothing displays obvious signs, attenuated markings or residual traces of struggles, cross-cultural contacts, borrowings, exchanges between economic regions or cultural areas as well as among groups within a single society."[3]

Fur's numerous expeditions, although typically embarked on for mercantile and economic reasons, are, at a deeper level of understanding, also explorations into our desire to discover and become something else. The instinctual, physical response we all have to the touch of fur (whether living or in the form of garments) is undeniable and makes our

87
"The 'Force' of Fur," *Vogue*, November
1977, photograph by Eisuke Ishimuro

reaction to fur clothing, regardless of possible ethical and moral disgust, unique. The essential dichotomy inherent in the idea of fashionable fur, where fur, that most basic and essential of materials, is translated into fashion—a system commonly criticized as artificial and unnecessary—is what also makes fur's fashionable journeys explorations of constant and surprising discovery, telling of lands distant, fabled yet essentially familiar.

Naturally such a complex subject as fur's incorporation into fashion history would require a much longer discussion than this essay can accommodate; however, the theme of the exhibition *Expedition: Fashion from the Extreme*, which this book accompanies, can provide a useful set of coordinates with which to discover some of fashion's most exciting forays into the terrain of fur. Fashion, like our understanding of the expedition, is of course inseparable from the concept of space, whether that be the physical space of the body it covers, protects, and adorns; the spaces of garment construction that generate a specific discourse of volumes, silhouettes, and excess; or the geographical and temporal spaces of fashion production: the where, when, by whom, and from what fashion is made. Christopher Breward so aptly expressed this when discussing fashion's relationship to the city, suggesting that "fashion is a bounded thing, fixed and experienced in space—an amalgamation of seams and textiles, an interface between the body and its environment."[4]

The word "expedition" carries with it not only ideas concerning the exploration of space, of travel and journeying, but also of discovery, the negotiation of thresholds, and the breaking down of barriers. It is in this sense that any history of fashionable fur must be approached. There are, of course, the cultural and ethical barriers that make fur both attractive and repulsive, admired and reviled. Similarly, the barriers between human and animal, between the exterior and interior of the body, between the hidden and the seen are also automatically negotiated, however remotely, every time animal skins are used as fashion. The sensitive nature of the subject has meant that, in recent times, fur has been off-limits to reasoned, critical discussion. Yet despite the continued headline-grabbing activities of animal rights organizations, and heated debates concerning the relative merits of the sustainable fur industry versus the polluting by-products created in the production of fake fur, it seems fur is undergoing a fashionable renaissance. In order to comprehend the complexity of fashionable fur, we perhaps need to turn to the philosophies of an earlier era to fully understand our intricate relationship to it, and why it can arouse such polarized responses.

Fur invokes sensations of limitlessness. Structurally, it is composed of thousands of individual hairs, too fine and numerous to comprehend, which in combination produce furry landscapes of lustrous beauty and tactile sensuousness, apparently having no distinct edge. Similarly, fur resonates with the ferocity, primitivism, and carnality of the natural world, a world at once seductive and terrifying. The economic and cultural legacy of fur charts yet another vast, almost incomprehensible, terrain of wealth, power, and sensuality. Together these boundless planes make our experience of fur akin to that of the sublime. As Kant formulated when grappling with our reactions to the grandeur of landscape, "the mind feels set in motion in the representation of the sublime in nature,"[5] and if we understand fur as a quintessentially natural object, his understanding of the mental struggle involved in comprehending the awe-inspiring in nature can similarly help us understand our responses to fur. For, even though fashioned and manipulated into garments, the natural awesomeness of fur remains, and our response echoes Kant's mental movement, which, "especially in its inception, may be compared with a vibration, i.e. a rapidly alternating repulsion and attraction produced by one and the same object."[6] What else but the sublime is Lucy experiencing as she inhales and revels in her journey through fur in the wardrobe? And surely Jerry Hall's ecstatic expression is the result of a sublime moment of contemplation preceding her envelopment in her sable "pull-up collar"?

To provide some reassuring coordinates during our expedition into the limitless terrains of fur, we can perhaps understand the complex history of fashionable fur as a series of passages, or, more precisely, as transitions—spatial, economic, and cultural. The most important of these transitions when considering any history of fur is how, for the majority of its fashionable life, it has been used as either a lining or as a decorative edging. The modern-day fur coat where the actual hair of the animal skin being used is worn externally to form a complete garment, is a comparatively recent phenomenon. Fashion historians will debate the exact date of the appearance of the contemporary full-length fur coat, but most agree that it begins to be recorded in the last quarter of the nineteenth century. Before that period, with a very few exceptions, the history of Western fashion's utilization of fur has been primarily practical, hence its use as a lining, or ceremonially with fur edges and trimmings used symbolically to signify professional or institutional affiliation and merit. We would need to go very far back into history, certainly before the principally Western notion of fashionable clothing has any relevance, to find examples of fur being worn externally. Favorite ancient or fabled accounts of fur-wearing encompass those found in the Bible, including God, arguably the first furrier, creating what presumably were fur garments for Adam and Eve: "Unto Adam also and to his wife did the LORD God make coats of skins, and clothed them," and John the Baptist's: "raiment of camel's hair."[7] Among the ancient visual representations of fur are the various prehistoric rock and cave paintings depicting scenes of hunting, gathering, and the wearing of animal skins, often by what are thought to be shaman-like figures, and Egyptian tomb paintings of priests and pharaohs wearing leopard skins, both ancient examples of the hierarchical significance of wearing fur.

Leaving ancient, fabled furs and moving forward to the Middle Ages, into fashionable fur's more recent history, we witness the first and most lasting of its spatial transitions. While the ceremonial and social significance of fur is retained throughout this period, fur's practical benefit of providing a layer of warmth next to the skin meant that fur, to a large degree, disappeared from view, taking the form of thermal linings to garments made of other materials such as wool. This, of course, was a necessity during a time when people, certainly in northern climes and regardless of their station in life, lived in cold, inadequately heated dwellings. Fur was used extensively both for lining clothes but also for interiors. During the Middle Ages and into the early modern period in Europe, in addition to the use of indigenous species of fur-bearing animals, much of what we might understand as the nascent fur trade was centred on Constantinople (Istanbul). This was superseded in the fifteenth century by Venice and Genoa, which became important centers for the international trade in furs along with London, principally as a result of that city's becoming a foreign trading post of the Hanseatic League in 1303. The League, a powerful mercantile confederation, dominated Baltic maritime trade along the coast of Northern Europe, and furs, especially from Russia, were a principal source of revenue for its traders. The League's influence declined as the regions where its members were located, such as Britain, Holland, and Scandinavia, saw the rise of powerful trading nations, with fur remaining a vital component of their mercantile success.

Fur in the Middle Ages was regarded as both a necessity and a luxury. A series of sumptuary laws instituted between 1300 and 1600 set out strict controls for its use. This extract from an early French law is typical: "No bourgeois man or woman will wear vair [gray fur, generally squirrel], gris, or ermine fur, and they shall surrender all they have a year from next Easter."[8] Fur was used, as with much fashion, to demarcate and segregate society. Only nobility and the clergy were permitted to wear the most costly of furs such as ermine, sable, squirrel, lynx, and marten, while the poor could only wear sheepskin, goat, wolf, cony (rabbit), and cat. What becomes immediately apparent when considering these prohibitions connected with fur is that they formed the basis of what remained a constant factor in fur's fashionable regard up to the twentieth century. That is, rougher, "shaggier," coarser furs are considered of less value and therefore "lower class," while softer and smoother skins are more expensive, desirable, and by extension, aspirational.

During this period, when fur was visible, it was at the edges of garments, their furry linings revealed at cuff, collar, or hem, or as decorative borders that had a ceremonial and status-affirming function. The clergy were the first institutional wearers of fur, with ermine being the most widely used to line and edge vestments. Nobility and clergy alike during the Middle Ages and on into the sixteenth century spent vast sums on fur, incurring equal amounts of censure as they did admiration. Fur frequently was regarded as immoral, decadent, and a sign of profligacy, a contradictory reaction to fur that remains today and underlies the controversies between pro- and anti-fur lobbies.

Fur's journey from outer to inner, from exterior to interior, provides an insistent metaphor for our collective response to, and understanding of, fur. It is a metaphor that evokes concepts concerning the relationship between the inner and outer layers of the body (human or animal), the expeditions into the interiors of uncharted territories fundamental both to the history of the fur trade and to the exhibition this publication accompanies, and the outward display of wealth and power that has determined so much of the development of fur as a fashionable material. The tension between fur as both a thermal lining and a sign of wealth and status is clearly seen in the portrait of Edward VI of England circa 1547, attributed to William Scrots (fig. 88). The young king wears a sumptuous, richly decorated, russet silk cloak, embroidered with gold thread and velvet, made thermally effective by its lining of lynx; a substantial garment in terms of its sheer bulk, but also, of course, it is significant as a clear vestimentary signal of its wearer's preeminent position. The tension that exists between the inner and outer layers of any structure, the inherent violence associated with the skinning and wearing of animals, and the economic demarcation of society expressed by the ability to own and wear fur are palpable when we start to journey through fashionable fur's seductive surfaces. The negotiation of this tension between inner and outer is in

fact the history of vestimentary fur, and resonates with the same poetic allure that Gaston Bachelard found in his masterful exploration of space: "Outside and inside are both intimate—they are always ready to be reversed, to exchange their hostility. If there exists a borderline surface between such an inside and outside, this surface is painful on both sides."[9]

By the late sixteenth century, the demand for fur had diminished due to a number of factors. Its thermal properties were of increasingly less importance owing to the improvements in living conditions, certainly among the more affluent members of society: window glass was being used more widely in buildings, the development of chimney architecture was making fires more effective, and tapestries were being used to line and insulate walls. Of more

88

Portrait of Edward VI of England, attributed to William Scrots, circa 1547 importance was the gradual replacement of fur's socioeconomic function to signal its wearers' wealth, status, and taste by newer techniques of personal display. The period's growing "culture of appearances" hankered after "fashionable," often imported goods, such as silks, velvets, and fine woolens, which were made into layered, padded, and ever more voluminous styles, thus increasing the inherent thermal qualities of fashion at the time. Accompanying this, exotic gems from the East fueled the invention and artistic creativity of goldsmiths, who produced ever more elaborate and ostentatious jewels. Simultaneously, European stocks of suitable fur-bearing animals began to dwindle as a result of the previous demand for fur, which in turn led to imported furs becoming even more costly, with the highly prized Russian sable regularly topping the list of most welcomed diplomatic gifts. All of which meant that fur's former dominant role as a signifier of status was eclipsed by other, newer, and more fashionable means of self-aggrandisement. An exception to the decline in fur's popularity at this time was ermine's increased use in official dress. Joining its already established function as a border and lining on royal ceremonial robes and ecclesiastical vestments was its deployment as a signifier of status and power on academic and legal robes, a function of course that ermine retains today.

Ermine is in fact the name given to the white winter coat of the northern species of stoat with a characteristic black-tipped tail. Compared to its coarser, sandy-brown summer coat, the winter coat is very dense and silky, making it one of the most highly prized of all pelts in the fur trade. The transformation of its coat, a physiological reaction triggered by seasonal changes in the length of day and night, makes it an especially pertinent fur to consider in the context of this essay. The popular perception of fur as a material that has the capacity to transform its wearers, bestowing in vestimentary form the characteristics of animals, evokes the larger economic, national, and cultural transformations the history of the fur trade has facilitated.

Not all ermine is ermine, however, and due to the seasonal availability of the fur, what could be considered the first sustained example of fake fur was introduced. Miniver, the white underbelly of the squirrel, was a common and less expensive substitute, with the characteristic black tips of the ermine faked by dotting the miniver with other pieces of fur, such as black sheepskin. The history of faking cheaper furs to resemble more expensive skins provides an interesting counterpoint to the contemporary fashionable trend to dye real fur in a dazzling range of unnatural colours. James Laver, writing of early twentieth-century furs in his seminal *Taste and Fashion*, also notes: "The new use of synthetic dyes made it possible to employ a variety of furs which would have been despised—particularly rabbit, which, under the name of cony (generally dyed cony), is now an important part of the fur industry. Marmot could be dyed to represent mink, and musquash to resemble sealskin. A whole new chapter of the fur industry was opened."[10] What Laver would have made of today's purple, green, and pink furs we can only speculate, but the current trend not only displays the level of technical skill fashionable fur has reached, but also may assist its wearers in avoiding attacks from the anti-fur lobbies, who might understandably think these brilliantly hued real furs are in fact synthetic.

As a sign of wealth and status, exotic fur linings and trimmings continued to be popular throughout the succeeding centuries, even while fashions in fur fluctuated. The spotted fur lining, the spectacular yellow "jack," as these Dutch, short, fur-trimmed jackets are known, depicted in Vermeer's *Young Woman with a Pearl Necklace* of 1662 (fig. 89), may be genuine ermine or possibly a cheaper fur masquerading as ermine, but nevertheless signals the comfortable bourgeois lifestyle associated with these representations of Holland in the seventeenth century. The jack became, in fact, a form of vestimentary shorthand for the affluent Dutch Republic at this time, a garment at once practical and domestic. The jacket's fur lining and hood were often detachable for the summer months or for wearing indoors, yet ostentatious enough to befit a woman enjoying the benefits the wealth accrued by a mercantile society, in which the fur trade played a vital part, brought her.

The migrations of fur from ancient outerwear, to medieval and early modern inner wear, as linings and decorative edgings, continued. During this period, fur detaches itself entirely from fashionable garments and takes the form of accessories that would become staples of the furriers' art on into the mid-twentieth century. Fur collars, popular on dresses in the sixteenth and seventeenth centuries, eventually become separate items and developed into the tippet, or what today we would understand as a scarf or stole. It is in the form of the tippet that the trend for wearing the complete skin of an animal—including the head, paws, and claws, often embellished with gold and precious stones set as eyes—emerged; it remained fashionable, reaching a peak in the late nineteenth and twentieth centuries. Similarly, the deep, fur cuffs of dresses journeyed out and away from the actual body of the garment, and merged to become a separate item: the muff, which first appeared in the 1560s. Rarely seen today,

the muff remained a principal indicator of fur's fashionable status, worn by both men and women, often reaching extravagant dimensions, especially in the late eighteenth and early nineteenth centuries, and was embellished with a variety of animal parts. It has also acted as a nexus of the erotic relationship between fur, touch, and sexuality. The first recorded use of muff as a slang reference to the female genitalia is from the 1690s, a sexualization of fur that Wenceslaus Hollar, in his famous etching depicting winter fashions of 1643 (fig. 90), seems to predict. The scene of a masked, luxuriously furred woman wearing a tippet and carrying a large muff is accompanied by an erotic verse, which synthesizes many of the issues concerning the erotics of fur that have exercised the imaginations of writers and artist for centuries:

> Winter
> The cold, not cruelty makes her weare
> In Winter, furrs and Wild beasts haire
> For a smoother skinn at night
> Embraceth her with more delight.

Although the muff today may have become obsolete as a fashion item, it is perhaps an indication of fur's recent dramatic reappearance on the fashion stage that it became the vehicle through which Rick Owens seemed to ponder fur's migrations, through, away, and back again into fashion history. As part of his spring/summer 2017 ready-to-wear collection, he featured garments that spoke of the peripatetic and possibly dysfunctional use of fur in fashion, with his characteristic draped dresses featuring one semi-detached fur cuff, and what resembles atrophied muffs attached to the bodice (fig. 91).

The visceral act of plunging one's hands deep into a fur muff, or enveloping the neck with the complete pelt of an animal, echoes the belief held by many ancient civilizations that it is possible to assume the characteristics of an animal by wearing its skin. While this may seem remote from the concept of Western fashion history, this "becoming animal" remains a vestigial promise when considering fur's relationship to fashion. It is perhaps in the latter half

*The cold, not cruelty makes her weare*
*In Winter, furrs and Wild beastshaire*
**Winter**
*For a smoother skinn at night*
*Embraceth her with more delight.*

been explored. It is hardly surprising, therefore, that two of fashion history's most radical designers, Elsa Schiaparelli and Cristóbal Balenciaga, should have been responsible for many of fur's most fashionably conceptual expeditions. Schiaparelli's wool, jersey sweater engulfed by monkey fur from 1948 (fig. 93) is shocking in today's eyes ("shocking" being a description that Schiaparelli turned into her own brand identification), and revisits her earlier use of monkey fur in the 1930s. Loaded with cultural and sexual symbolism, the garment transforms its wearer into a chic simian, referencing popular culture's fascination with the "primitive" at that period, replete with cinematic echoes ranging from King Kong to Marlene Dietrich's appearance as the intensely eroticized gorilla in the "Hot Voodoo" number from *Blonde Venus* (Dietrich was one of Schiaparelli's most devoted clients). The garment also crystallizes many of the strategies Schiaparelli derived from the surrealist artists, whom she admired and worked with, particularly that of displacement, here expressed by the relocation of African primitivism to the world of Parisian couture, and indeed the reassignment of gender, constructing via its use of fur the figure of a hairy-chested, soigné woman about the urban jungle.

Balenciaga's play on, and with, fur, takes a typically more historicist approach in his spectacular, ermine-tailed-and-bustled, velvet evening dress of circa 1964 (fig. 92). The transformative properties represented by ermine and its ability to change the color of its fur is referenced here by Balenciaga, alongside ermine's historical religious and regal significance. The optical power of black spots on white that ermine traditionally radiates is here reversed by placing the white part of the tail on the black ground of the garment's nineteenth-century bustle, which in turn produces the effect of a peacock's or similar exotic bird's tail. Its wearer is thus transformed into an ermine/bird hybrid.

The previous discussion concerning the importance of accessories such as muffs and tippets to the fur industry, which in the form of the twentieth-century stole and today's fur scarves remain for many their first entrée into the world

of the nineteenth century that this zoomorphic belief in the power of fur, and the wearing of dead animals, gave furriers and taxidermists alike their greatest opportunities. The 1880s and 1890s saw a bewildering array of animal skins used to edge and line clothes: stoles of fox and other species with heads, feet, and claws intact draped around the most fashionable shoulders, while packs of small mammals were utilized by milliners to transform late nineteenth-century heads into portable menageries (fig. 94).

It is perhaps in twentieth-century fashion that fur's full animalistic, transformative, and libidinous potential has

**90**
(above) *Winter*,
Wenceslaus Hollar, 1643

**91**
(facing) Rick Owens, spring/summer 2017,
photograph by Valerio Mezzanotti

**92**
(facing) Cristóbal Balenciaga, evening gown of black velvet,
with bustle trimmed in ermine tails, circa 1964, courtesy of
the Texas Fashion Collection, photograph by Neal Barr

**93**
(above) Elsa Schiaparelli, woman's sweater,
wool jersey, monkey fur, spring/summer 1948,
Philadelphia Museum of Art

—

of fur-wearing, brings us to probably the most economically and geographically far-reaching use of fur in the history of fashion, the beaver hat. The beaver hat can justifiably be considered one of the most enduring items in men's fashion history. There are references to beaver hats as far back as the Middle Ages (Chaucer famously refers to a merchant's "Flaundrish bever hat" in the General Prologue to *The Canterbury Tales*). Continuing to find favor on the male head, it reached a peak of popularity in the 1600s (fig. 95), as we can tell from that most sartorially obsessed observer, Samuel Pepys, who in 1663 notes: "This day at Mrs. Holden's I found my new low crowned beaver according to the present fashion made, and will be sent home to-morrow."[11] In order to produce a beaver hat, the longer, coarser guard hairs of the animal are separated from the shorter downy hairs, and it is these softer hairs that are needed for the felting process used to make the finished hat.

By the end of the seventeenth century, supplies of domestic European beaver had been exhausted due to the demand of the hatmaking industry. This demise coincided with the increase in expeditions to the New World, initiated by adventurers in search of the Northwest Passage, as well as European fishermen working the seas of North America, who were quick to exploit the vast stocks of longer-haired American beaver, along with other fur-bearing animals they encountered on their expeditions. The importance of fur to the development of trade in the New World cannot be overestimated. It led to the formation of the Hudson's Bay Company, which would to a large degree determine the course of fur's subsequent fashionable history. The longer-haired American beaver's impact on fashion history can be gauged by the stylistic transformation in men's hats. These developed from the characteristic early seventeenth century, duller, felted, broad-brimmed styles, to what today we would understand as the typical, straighter, crowned "stove-pipe," or "chimney"-shaped, top hat, made from the longer beaver fur (fig. 96), which first appeared at the end of the eighteenth century, and remained the dominant form of male headwear for the next hundred years, beaver gradually being replaced from the 1850s onward by shinier silk plush.

The appearance of the full-length fur coat we recognize today concludes this brief and necessarily partial history of the journeys of fashionable fur. The last leg of fur's journey from outer to inner, inner to margin, and back again to the exterior of the fashionable garment, is once again inspired by an idea of progression, a progression brought about by technological advancement similar to those advancements that transformed the way fur was worn in the sixteenth and subsequent centuries. The rapid development of nineteenth-century transportation, leisure, and media technologies irrevocably changed the way people perceived, desired, and wore fur. This general process of modernization was accompanied by similar technological advancements in the fur industry itself that meant that

**94**
Toque, labeled Mme Heitz-Boyer, Paris. Fox fur, silk charmeuse, silk velvet, lace, and glass beads, 1890s, photograph by Brian Sanderson, courtesy of the FIDM Museum, Los Angeles

furs, of increasing varieties, were obtained, dressed, and fashioned into complex garments that hitherto would have been inconceivable.

The first fashionable full-length fur coats appeared around the 1880s, typically of sealskin, often trimmed with sable. As the century drew to a close, a number of other factors influenced the wearing of fur, including the mass migration of Eastern Europeans to America and elsewhere, bringing with it not only skilled workers in fur who would revolutionize the garment industry, but also a general artistic and cultural influence that made all things Russian, such as the wearing of full-length furs, and varieties such as astrakhan, become de rigueur. These fashionable shifts in the attitude to wearing fur generally, were accompanied by similar shifts in the taste for specific varieties of fur and animal skins; fur at this period, in fact, becomes truly fashionable in the modern, seasonally changing sense of the word. This process continued throughout the twentieth century, until becoming relatively static again with the rise of mink to a position of preeminence.

The advent of the automobile in the early 1900s gave rise to the need, and fashion, for motoring coats made of warm, protective fur. Coats of previously little-used, longer-haired, shaggy varieties of fur such as bear, raccoon, wolf, and sheepskin, as well as lynx, fox, and opossum appeared. Tastes in fashionable fur from the sleek, silky, and shorter-haired varieties popular at the end of the nineteenth century changed in the early twentieth century to a more overtly animalistic wearing of fur. Fashionable people now increasingly demanded their fur be as primal, natural, and "wild" as possible, a psychological shift that accompanied society's general sexual, moral, and aesthetic liberation. The American craze for the raccoon coat, for example (fig. 97), as worn by college students, symbolized this new, emotionally expressive self-fashioning via the wearing of fur, that now joined its established practical and status-affirming functions.

Swiftly following the development of the automobile, air travel in the twentieth century meant that increasing numbers of people were traveling greater distances. The concept

95
Hat, beaver fur, felted, blocked,
English, 1590–1670, copyright the
Victoria and Albert Museum, London

96
Hat, beaver wool trimmed with grosgrain ribbon,
English, circa 1830–1840, copyright the
Victoria and Albert Museum, London

of the tour or the voyage of discovery typified by the aviator, polar explorer, and big-game hunter alike became part of popular culture, facilitated by the advent of cinema and newsreels. The concept of travel and the trappings of luxury associated with it, spurred on by the fashionable and exciting lifestyles promoted by Hollywood, made fur, and the fur coat especially, throughout the first half of the twentieth century the preeminent sartorial expression of this newly discovered sense of adventure. The craze for coats made from exotic and patterned furs such as leopard, cheetah, and monkey, with tiger and zebra skins for interior decorative schemes, enabled the "untamed," the "wilderness," and the "jungle" to be experienced sartorially, without the unnecessary hardship associated with an actual expedition. The 1936 photograph of the pioneering aviation duo, Amy Johnson and her husband, Jim Mollison, with Johnson wearing a leopard-skin coat, perfectly encapsulates this prewar spirit of fashionable adventure (fig. 86).

Armchair traveling in the form of cinematic narratives of derring-do influenced twentieth-century fashionable fur not only in its familiarization with, and desire for, exotic species, but also by what might be understood as an essentially cinematic representation of fur as glamorous, aspirational, and erotic. The high-contrast, black-and-white cinematography of the classic Hollywood film was achieved through dramatic lighting and glistening surfaces, making boldly patterned, white, or pale furs especially cinematic. Hollywood had a direct influence on high-fashion fur, with varieties such as silver and Arctic fox, white mink, and ermine becoming especially popular during this period (fig. 98).

Another November edition of American *Vogue* will conclude this brief exploration of fashionable fur. Again it teams fur with new technology, in this instance not the fantasy of science fiction, as in "The 'Force' of Fur" spread, but state-of-the-art automotive technology in John Rawlings's marvelous 1957 image of mink-clad models accessorized with pink-and-metallic-gray Cadillacs (fig. 99). The model in the foreground wears a classic midcentury mink coat,

**98**
Actress Irene Dunn wearing white fur, circa 1935,
photograph by John Kobal

—

**99**
"Fur Coats and Cadillacs,"
*Vogue*, November 15, 1957,
photograph by John Rawlings

full sleeved, voluminous, and eminently desirable, the ultimate coat for the aspiring woman, who has the car, the man, and now the mink to complete her American dream. This dream, as we can tell from the later *Vogue* spread, remained quintessential for many fashionable women, despite the rise of fake furs in the 1960s, and the growing tide of prohibition against fur that would reach a peak during the 1980s.

Besides their obvious aspirational glamour, both of these representations of fur can be understood as visually condensing some of the deeper historical and hypothetical considerations of fur this essay has attempted to detail. The relationship between fur and technological progress, as with the historical advancements in domestic architecture and transport that directly altered how we wore fur, and in the fur production industry itself that led to an ever more sophisticated and varied use of fur, makes the coupling of the most ancient of materials with state-of-the-art technology, whether automobiles or robots, entirely fitting. The idea of progress, of travel, of expedition, represented by the speed of a Cadillac or the galaxy-hopping fantasies of *Star Wars*, mirrors the actual journeys of fur, be that on a vestimentary level traveling back and forth across the fashionable garment, its mercantile voyages of exploration that would shape the economic future of nations, or the psychological journeys the wearer of fur embarks upon while traveling deep into the sensate, sexual landscape of our most animalistic desires. The models in the 1957 advertisement clad in their transcendent furs look out at some distant horizon, beyond midcentury America, beyond a "galaxy far, far away," as far as the touch of fur and our imaginations can take us, even perhaps to the land Lucy discovered once she had journeyed through the time- and space-defying thresholds of fur:

Soon she went further in and found that there was a second row of coats hanging up behind the first one. It was almost quite dark in there and she kept her arms stretched out in front of her so as not to bump her face into the back of the wardrobe. She took a step further in—then two or three steps—always expecting to feel woodwork against the tips of her fingers. But she could not feel it.[12]

# 5

# Looking Back at the Future

## SPACE SUITS AND SPACE AGE FASHION

### Elizabeth Way

———————◇———————

The April 1965 issue of *Harper's Bazaar* was photographed entirely by Richard Avedon, the most prominent fashion and commercial photographer of the time. Avedon was guest-editing this special issue to commemorate his twenty-year tenure at *Bazaar*, and he wanted it to capture the most significant forces in contemporary culture. Avedon chose Jean Shrimpton, the current it-girl model, for the cover, included photographs of two of the Beatles, and produced profiles and portraits of artists Roy Lichtenstein, Claes Oldenburg, and Jasper Johns. He also photographed physicist George Oster and, despite much controversy among advertisers and subscribers, black model Donyale Luna. He also included an essay by Tom Wolfe. Writing in *Vanity Fair* in 2009, David Michaelis discussed the Avedon issue, stating that Avedon had sought to create "a harmonious and cinematic whole flowing from cover to cover to convey in words and pictures everything current and future in art, fashion, intellect, and music."[1] Added Michaelis, "After nearly two decades of re-inventing the form, he knew exactly what he was after, and he knew how to get it. He wanted the moon."[2]

Michaelis meant that literally. In 1965, only one motif could capture the newness that Avedon sought: the Space Age, which represented everything current and about to arrive. The Space Age proved to be the perfect mise-en-scène for Avedon's vision of the exciting present and future possibility. He pulled the thrilling reality of the space race into the optimism and fun of Space Age fashion by combining the real artifact (a Project Mercury space suit) with culturally constructed images of space (a comic-book background, bubble-helmeted ladies, new futuristic fashions) and positioned the most significant figures in music, literature, science, and fine art among them to create a two-dimensional environment of cutting-edge culture.

The cover is a tight shot of Shrimpton's face, enveloped in a hot pink "nouveau space helmet" by milliner Mr. John, with one blue eye winking at the reader through the application of a holographic strip.[3] Avedon also photographed model Naty Abascal and Shrimpton for a beauty editorial, both wearing an authentic, silvery Mercury space suit, complete with helmet and NASA badge (on loan from the space agency) (fig. 100). Shrimpton posed as Ultima, a

**100**
Naty Abascal, space suit by NASA, New York,
December 21, 1964, photograph by Richard Avedon

—

**101**
The Apollo Lunar Module, 1969

fictional first woman in space, set against an interplanetary battle in a cartoon by Lichtenstein, as she extolled the virtues of her futuristic makeup. Paul McCartney sat for his portrait wearing the same NASA space suit. This was not the first time a real space suit had graced the pages of *Bazaar*. Avedon photographed the astronauts Alan Shepard, Gus Grissom, and John Glenn in their Mercury suits for his "Avedon: Observation on Heroes" spread in June 1961. The photos appeared a month after the Mercury *Freedom 7* mission made Alan Shepard the first American in space. However, Shrimpton and Abascal wore the space suit as if it were a chic jumpsuit, the ultimate in futuristic fashion.

Throughout Avedon's self-commemorative issue, the Space Age represents all that is fashionable, thrilling, and young. One editorial, "Galactic Girls," featured models in clean-lined sportswear and clear-bubble headpieces, posing on the moon by the Sea of Tranquility (actually a construction company's quarry in Fort Lauderdale). Avedon included illustrations of a woman standing among "the craters of Archimedes—one of the moon's chicest new resort regions" in a graphic blue and yellow shift dress fit "to catch the eye of circling astronauts."[4] He revisited Shrimpton as "the Mercury Blond" in a dynamic portrait printed in pure silver, and he featured models in op-art mini-dresses with matching helmets by Mr. John.

In two spreads, he highlighted the work of André Courrèges, who was known as the Space Age couturier. One was a series of photographs in which a model jubilantly undressed from her Courrèges ensemble. She started in a buttoned-up coat and ended in a sleeveless top and short shorts; however, she kept on her cowboy hat, white gloves, high socks, and white patent Mary Janes to fully convey Courrèges's "space cowboy" look.

The Space Age, beginning with the launch of *Sputnik* by the Soviet Union in 1957 and ending in 1972 with NASA's last mission to the moon, was a period of unprecedented technological achievement in the aeronautical field. It was also a manifestation of Cold War brinksmanship between the United States and the Soviet Union and, at its peak during the mid-to-late 1960s, it was a revolutionary period in fashion. The Avedon issue of *Harper's Bazaar* was released between NASA's Gemini 3 and Gemini 4 earth-orbiting missions (during the latter, in June 1965, Ed White became the first American to walk in space).

Space exploration has always piqued human curiosity, and since at least the nineteenth century, writers and artists have speculated on what humans would wear in space and in the future. Yet during the 1960s, as space missions and space suits became a reality, Space Age fashion served as a powerful metaphor for a rapidly changing Western world. Space Age fashion was not inspired by historical modes; it was modernist and sleek, with pared-down geometric shapes and metallic details, and acted as a vehicle for new and controversial ideas about clothing, such as miniskirts, trousers for women, and body-revealing styles. Space Age fashion turned away from the sophisticated New Look lady of the previous decade, signifying the ascendance of youth culture, the confidence of modernity, and in many cases, the evolving position of women in Western society. Ruth Ansel, who as a young art director worked with Avedon, said that "it was considered a joke to see a woman in an astronaut suit." Yet, in hindsight, Michaelis saw it as portentous: "American women had rising ambitions, even if such ambitions were still being brushed aside. Avedon playing prophet, wasn't just saying, The Moon Next Time. He was saying, Feel the Joy. This isn't anarchy we're seeing in the streets, it's youthful vitality."[5] Space Age fashion represented the assertion of this joy and willful naïveté in the face of the frustration, disappointment, and rage at society's failures, which became ever more evident as the 1960s wore on. Like the space race itself, Space Age fashion was a bubble that held out against the impending doom of the nuclear arms race, the violence of the American Civil Rights Movement, the horrors of the war in Vietnam, and the social inequities that led to the student riots in Paris.

Both the aesthetic fantasy and the real artifacts of the 1960s' Space Age that Avedon referenced followed decades of precedent. Technological progress marks every age, but it

seemed especially rapid during the twentieth century—the first airplane flew in 1903 and a mere fifty-eight years later man had broken the barrier to outer space. Western literature had been rife with conceptions of the future and space technology since the second half of the nineteenth century. Jules Verne wrote *From the Earth to the Moon* in 1865, followed by *Around the Moon* in 1870. Although Verne makes no mention of space suits (his explorers wear their everyday garments inside a projectile shot to the moon from an enormous cannon), he accurately predicts not only many of the logistics and conditions of space travel, but also that the United States would be a dominant force in space exploration, and this subject would capture the entire world's fascination. Two other visionary French writers, Georges Le Faure and Henry de Graffigny, wrote *Extraordinary Adventures of a Russian Scientist* in 1888. In the first volume, the characters again travel to the moon in earthly attire—though they also wore "respirols," which:

> allow[ed] their wearers to venture with impunity in the most unbreathable and rarefied atmospheres; they consisted of a sort of rubber hood falling down to below the chest and buttoned tightly under the arm: two glasses placed before the eyes allowed them to see as clearly as if they were wearing a pince-nez, and in front of the mouthpiece was an opening controlled by a valve that vented outwards to allow the evacuation of pulmonary combustion gases.... In a side pocket was a steel cylinder, a quarter of a liter in capacity, containing liquefied oxygen; opening a tap released this gas and it came through a pipe to the rubber bag, which inflated without the gas escaping.[6]

J. Cayron's, Henriot's, and L. Vallet's illustrations of the characters show the odd juxtaposition of nineteenth-century fashion with the futuristic breathing apparatus, particularly on Selena, the scientist's daughter, who wears her gas mask while fully corseted in flowing skirts (fig. 102). In the second installation, when the characters travel to Venus, the authors introduce space suits:

**102**

Illustration of Selena wearing a space helmet and late nineteenth-century fashionable dress in *Aventures extraordinaires d'un savant russe* (1888)

... in a trice they had donned their space suits. These were a kind of clothing made of an elastic rubber-like material, so that the limbs and torso were completely and hermetically constrained; the fabric itself was supported by a network of metal springs of extreme delicacy and remarkable elasticity, in order to resist the expansion of the gases contained in the travelers' living tissue. The head was protected by a sort of egg-shaped selenium helmet like the respirols which Ossipoff and his companions had already used to explore the visible hemisphere of the Moon.[7]

Science fiction increased in popularity during the 1920s and 1930s, especially through the many comic books that focused on space. By the 1950s, movies set in space were common entertainment. These works exposed a cultural ambivalence about advancing technology that vacillated between excitement and fear. Cultural historian Emily Rosenberg stated, "In films, comics, and literature of the pre-Sputnik 1950s, space travel had provided an ideal venue for elaborating various utopian and dystopian visions of a technological future directed by techno-scientific and political elites."[8] The collective visual and written images in these works also built a body of shared ideas of what space suits and futuristic clothing should look like. Often space suits were depicted to fit slimly on the body in a streamlined, sleek silhouette, mirroring the clean lines of rockets. Buck Rogers cartoons of the 1930s offer such a look. Movies such as *Destination Moon* from 1950 and *Project Moonbase* from 1953, written by the noted science fiction writer Robert A. Heinlein, offered more realistic space suits: bulkier and enveloping with columnar or round-bubble helmets. In 1955, Disney hypothesized space-suit requirements in its *Disneyland* television episode, "Man in Space." The narrator outlined the hazards of zero gravity and cosmic radiation, noting that a flexible, airtight space suit would be needed. It is illustrated with a cartoon astronaut in a somewhat abstract, linear suit that is color-blocked in black and purple with a triangular yoke. It appears to be smooth, with convoluted joints, and is completed with a bubble helmet, mini-rocket-propulsion system,

and antenna. Another animation in the episode depicts a similar suit, more realistically rendered and designed in optical white, with a large numeral on the chest like a sports jersey.

Fictional shipboard ensembles tended toward uniformity and body-conscious sportswear separates. The *Disneyland* cartoon astronaut, for example, wore a slim, gray jumpsuit with a pointy, black collar, while the space cadets in *Project Moonbase* wore uniforms of tight T-shirts, short pants, boots, and fitted caps that came to a point at the forehead. Metallic accents played a large role and, for women, high hemlines signaled the future. All of these images contributed to cultural constructs of the sartorial future of the Space Age. Movies and cartoons released after men had successfully traveled to space, such as *The Jetsons* (1962–1963), *Star Trek* (original series, 1966–1969), *2001: A Space Odyssey* (1968), and *Barbarella* (as a cartoon in 1962 and film in 1968), further explored the aesthetic role of metal, streamlined or geometric shapes, uniformity, and female-body revelation in futuristic fashion, serving to reinforce these ideas in the public mind. When American engineers and technologists invented and designed functional space suits, these shared preconceptions played a role in determining what actual astronauts should look like. The technological demands of real space suits, in turn, guided the evolution of fictional and fashionable space attire alike.

## Space-Suit Technology and History

Space suits are not meant to be clothing. They are marvels of technology that surround an astronaut's body, creating a personal environment to protect the wearer in the airless, heatless vacuum of space. The image of the shiny, sleek space suit, popularized in some science fiction, depicted both armor and machine. However, space suits are closer to clothing than aerospace engineers might like to admit, and they are indisputably fashion-conscious. Architect and urban-design theorist Nicholas de Monchaux argues that the materiality of the space suit that ultimately traversed the lunar surface in 1969 had more in common with New Look couture garments than armored machines. The technology and craftsmanship that created the foundation of the New Look—layers of fabric and rubber that encased and reshaped bodies into ultrafeminine proportions—also produced the all-fabric, multilayered, handmade, custom-fit Apollo A7L space suits that kept Neil Armstrong and Buzz Aldrin alive on the moon.

The high-altitude pressure suits from which space suits evolved were first developed for pilots, whose bodies could not withstand conditions inside increasingly faster and higher-flying airplanes. The invention of supercharged engines during the 1920s allowed aircraft to venture higher than 20,000 feet above sea level. Not only does oxygen become scarce and the temperature inhospitably cold, the decreasing air pressure allows liquid to boil at lowered temperatures. For a human, dizziness and unconsciousness occur, and at approximately 63,000 feet, liquid at 98 degrees Fahrenheit—the temperature of blood in the body—vaporizes and expands. Pressure is needed to counteract these effects, either within a closed aircraft or a suit.[9]

Mark Edward Ridge, an American balloon pilot, tested the first high-attitude pressure suit in 1933, designed especially for him by Dr. J. S. Haldane of Oxford University and Sir Robert H. Davis of Siebe, Gorman & Co., a British deep-sea equipment manufacturer. It successfully protected Ridge in a low-pressure chamber simulating an altitude of 90,000 feet. To maintain his body temperature, Ridge designed an insulating garment to wear underneath the Haldane-Davis suit, made from layers of aluminum foil and cotton cloth. Over the next seven years, Ridge approached the US Navy and the US Army Air Corps, as well as the British and possibly German governments, seeking funding for a live balloon-test of his suit. Although reliable high-altitude pressure suits would have beneficial military applications, he was rejected by all parties and was never able to wear his suit in an open balloon.[10]

In the meantime, another American, the record-breaking pilot Wiley Post, successfully tested his own pressure suit in an open-air cockpit airplane. Post correctly theorized that he could fly faster at higher altitudes by taking advantage of the jet stream in the stratosphere, located at an altitude of 30,000 to 50,000 feet. Airplanes with pressurized, closed cockpits were too heavy to gain the speed he needed to break world records, so he devised a pressure suit to protect his body. Post worked with fabricators from the B. F. Goodrich Company in 1934 to create a suit composed of rubberized, bias-cut parachute silk. He also had an aluminum helmet, rubber boots, and pigskin gloves. The first version of his suit was patterned by a professional tailor to custom-fit Post's body. Post would test two more versions while working with Russell S. Colley of Goodrich's experimental division. The third and final version had dual layering to combat the effects of internal air pressure, such as ballooning (the suit overfilling with air and distorting) and rigidity leading to immobility. In 1934 and 1935, Post successfully flew up to 50,000 feet above sea level without physiological harm. His suit would provide the basis for the suits worn by the Mercury astronauts.[11]

Post introduced the aesthetics of his space suit to the American public in 1935. Cameoing in the film *Air Hawks*, he wore his white-and-silver suit of metal, cotton, and latex, complete with columnar metal helmet. This look was a significant break from previous pilots' clothing. Charles Lindbergh, for example, cultivated an adventurer's persona in jodhpurs and fur-trimmed leather jackets, and when Post flew around the world in 1933, he wore a gray suit with a shirt and tie. Yet now, as early as 1935, Post had created a space explorer's look that previously had existed only in fiction. In *Spacesuit: Fashioning Apollo*, de Monchaux calls Post's pressure suit, "symbolic and transformative attire ... the pressure suit did not hide the body of the aviator, but instead, by wrapping it in shining fabric and aluminum, revealed the futuristic fantasy with which his body became imbued."[12]

Leading up to and throughout World War II, the United States and several other countries researched and developed prototypes for pressure suits, attempting to adapt the human body to advancing aircraft technology. A functional design for full-pressure suits frustrated experimenters. The current technology produced suits that stretched to hazardous proportions when inflated; joints became so rigid that pilots could not move their arms or legs. The most common materials in these early high-pressure suits were fashion fabrics—silk, cotton, linen, and nylon—that were rubberized and treated to be airtight, and worn with metal and plastic or glass helmets. Like the United States, the Soviet Union was devoting significant resources to developing effective pressure suits as early as 1934. As the Cold War intensified, these suits became critical to pilots flying new planes, such as the B-52 bomber and U-2 surveillance plane, designed in the early 1950s to fly at altitudes of 50,000 to 70,000 feet.[13]

The US Air Force and Navy led American research programs, recruiting commercial and industrial companies to create experimental prototypes. These companies included rubber manufacturers like Goodrich and Goodyear, as well as aircraft corporations, such as Boeing Aircraft Corporation, Bell Aircraft Corporation, and Hamilton Standard, but also included undergarment producers, such as the Berger Brothers Company, owner of the Spenser Corset Company. The three biggest companies to emerge as space-suit researchers and producers for NASA were Hamilton Standard, the David Clark Company, and International Latex Corporation Industries (ILC).[14] The David Clark Company, which began as a knitted-textile manufacturer making undergarments, started producing pressure suits by the early 1940s, and later took that experience to manufacturing brassieres. Company founder David Clark explained, "We began making bras in 1947, after we had been in the g-suit and pressure suit business for some eight years. Designing bras was fairly easy. It's another g problem, a weight supporting problem, that's all."[15] It was no coincidence that they began making bras in 1947—the New Look silhouette made padded, highly structured undergarments a necessity for fashionable women everywhere. ILC was most popularly known for its trademark Playtex bras and girdles. The company was the largest postwar producer of foundation garments in the United States, marketing their girdles in shiny, futuristic, metal tubes.[16]

From 1959 to 1968, the X-15 flight research program experimenting with rocket-powered airplanes, jointly supervised by NASA (which was created in 1958), the Air Force, and the Navy, was an important component of the American space program. X-15 pilots broke previous altitude and speed records, and several earned Astronaut Wings by flying higher than 250,000 feet. The David Clark Company supplied the essential X-15 pressure suits, which featured a breakthrough technology that Clark initially prototyped by hand with knitting needles. This lightweight "link-net" layer was a loosely knitted, nylon layer worn over the rubberized, inner-bladder layer of the pressure suit. It controlled ballooning, while maintaining flexibility when the suit was inflated. The suit glowed futuristic silver thanks to an aluminum-powder coating on the outer layer. The X-15 suit was also an important breakthrough aesthetically.

David Clark learned the value of aesthetics in 1953 when *Collier's* magazine featured B. F. Goodrich's full-pressure suit on its cover, instead of the more technically advanced David Clark suit, because "the 'khaki-colored' Clark suit appeared far less futuristic to the magazine's editors."[17] Urged by his friend, former Navy test pilot Scott Crossfield, Clark applied a new silver lamé-like fabric to the 1956 X-15 pressure-suit prototypes. Crossfield advised, "A coverall of this material would look real good, like a space suit should—photogenic. To justify it technically we can tell them this silver material is specifically designed to radiate heat or something."[18] Clark added black boots and gloves for an appealing contrast.[19] This suit better met visual expectations for futuristic flight gear, and was featured on the cover of *Life* in January 1958 (fig. 103). It also influenced future space-suit design. B. F. Goodrich created a gold-coated pressure suit for the Navy in 1957–1958, and utilized shiny, aluminum coating on the Mercury suits for NASA's first manned space missions. These suits were developed from the Navy's olive drab Mark

**103**
Scott Crossfield in the X-15 full pressure suit made
by David Clark Company, *Life* cover, January 6, 1958

IV pressure suits, the silver coating serving to repurpose the battle gear for civilian space missions.[20]

B. F. Goodrich's "dazzling aluminum-coated nylon-and-rubber creation"[21] for the Mercury program looked like a futuristic piece of technological innovation. However, according to de Monchaux, "the silvery, machine aesthetic of the Mercury spacesuit was only a surface, sprayed onto, and hiding, a much more natural interior."[22] The suit incorporated an inner bladder of natural latex, worn over a cotton long-john garment. Its outer layer was made of nylon, by the early 1960s a readily available consumer fabric. While modifications had been made from the Navy Mark IV suit, the Mercury space suits were basically high-pressure suits that protected the astronauts in case of life-support failure inside their capsules. The later Gemini and Apollo suits were true space suits that acted as the only barrier between the astronaut and space during extravehicular activities (EVAs), such as spacewalks.[23]

Lloyd Mallan, author of *Suiting Up For Space*, wrote that the Mercury suits' "colorful" aluminum coating "served the double purpose of a heat buffer and a radiation shield ... the suit coating would act like a mirror to reflect heat away from the astronaut's body ... [and] could to some extent absorb and decelerate particles of nuclear and electromagnetic radiation."[24] Whether ultimately serving more protective or aesthetic purposes, the silver-colored coating was eliminated by the time of Ed White's space walk in 1965—his David Clark suit featured an equally futuristic white, high-temperature-nylon outer layer that "did not run the risk of the astronaut dazzling himself with his clothing while facing unfiltered sunlight."[25] More utilitarian silver-colored fabric reappeared on the space suit made for Gemini 9 astronaut Gene Cernan. The bottom half of his outer layer was coated in Chromel-R fabric, made from stainless steel, protecting his body from temperatures of up to 1,200 degrees Fahrenheit. However, this fabric was quickly restricted to small areas that needed extra protection because it cost "hundreds of dollars per square inch" and was difficult to manipulate.[26]

De Monchaux notes that the silver pressure suits and space suits, though short-lived, created a public conception of the nationalism and heroism of space-suit technology:

These early silver prototypes dominated public perception of space-age attire throughout the 1940s and 1950s. It was only really with the white-suited spacewalks of the Gemini era, and the first televised images of an American silhouetted against stars and the planet, that a paradigmatic shift in perception took place, and the aesthetics and presentation of manned, government-funded spaceflight eclipsed a prior narrative of the "space age." From this moment, the mythic quality of spaceflight ceases to follow science fiction, and instead is extended, incredibly, by science fact.[27]

The silver suits had a large impact on fashion's conception of the Space Age, evidenced by their prominence in Richard Avedon's April 1965 *Harper's Bazaar* issue, though white would also be adopted into fashion as a symbol of futuristic modernity.

The Gemini and Apollo suits were marvels of technological achievement, but they were made the old-fashioned way—on sewing machines—not surprisingly, considering they were manufactured by the lingerie companies David Clark and ILC. Earlier pressure-suit prototypes further reveal structural relationships to undergarment manufacture and design. For example, Mallan discussed a 1941 partial-pressure suit in his book, showing that it "applied counterpressure by brute force, with a tight corset and tightly laced puttees" on the legs.[28] Scott Crossfield, who had been working with David Clark on pressure-suit development since 1951, noted that the earliest prototypes were run up on Mrs. Clark's sewing machine.[29] David Clark's 1953 pressure suit that Lt. Colonel Marion E. Carl wore to the edge of space (83,235 feet) shows "brassiere-making influence" in its reinforced seams.[30] These suits proved to be as hot and sweaty as the rubber girdles worn under the concurrent New Look fashions. The effort of moving in a pressurized suit caused Gene Cernan to sweat so profusely during his Gemini 9 EVA

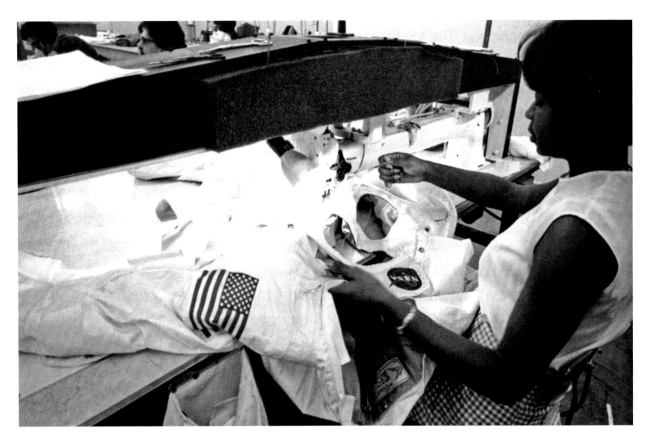

that his helmet visor fogged and then froze over, prompting improved ventilation on later suits, and, drawing on experiences of girdle discomfort, David Clark added "a layer of fuzzy girdle liner" into the inner bladder layer.[31]

The Gemini and Apollo space suits were sewn to painstaking specifications—exceeding the quality control on commercial lingerie, and even on couture garments. The ILC technicians sewing Apollo suits—women pulled from Playtex bra and girdle manufacture—were charged with stitching each seam line to an accuracy of one sixty-fourth of an inch (fig. 104). They were discouraged from pinning the fabric to hold it in place, and many technicians slowed the pace of their Singer machines to one stitch per footfall.

De Monchaux noted, "For the hundreds of feet of seams in each suit, this meant venturing stitch by tiny stitch across the length of a football field, with a single misstep leading to a discarded suit."[32] Other Playtex craftspeople applied their knowledge of dipping nylon tricot fabric (the same used in bras) into latex to create the airtight, flexible convolutes that provided astronauts with mobility. Like *les petites mains*, "the little hands" that meticulously sew haute couture garments in Paris, these women were essential, their intricate skills necessary to produce garments custom-fit to each astronaut. During the 1960s, when many women were undervalued in the workplace, these technicians trained male engineers and applied their specialized knowledge to

104
(above) Hazel Fellows, ILC group leader, assembling the shell, liner, and insulation of a Thermal Micrometeoroid Garment cover layer

105
(facing) NASA-Ames AX hard-bodied space suit, photograph by Mark Avino, Smithsonian National Air and Space Museum

—

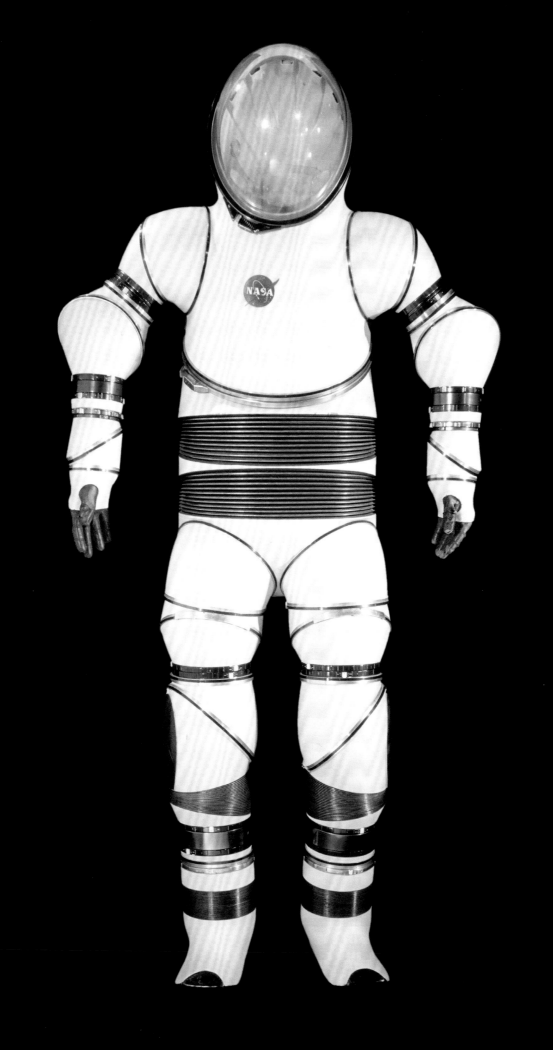

improve the space-suit manufacturing process—making a significant contribution to ultimately landing men on the moon.[33]

The soft, fabric Apollo space suits did not directly translate into high fashion. Space Age couturiers were more inspired by a rigid, smooth, metallic aesthetic, analogous more to spacecraft than to functional space suits. Yet hard-bodied suits, favored by popular culture, did exist, and were among the first space suits to be covered by the press, as early as the late 1950s. The vacuum-tube company Litton Industries, and later the NASA Ames Research Center working with the aerospace-technology company Garrett Corporation's AiResearch Division, began developing hard suits in earnest after President Kennedy's 1961

challenge to reach the moon before 1970. Rigid suits had technical advantages: they did not change volume when inflated—thereby performing at higher pressures—and did not rest on the body, conserving the astronaut's energy when moving in space. Hard suits were also preferred by many engineers, who thought of fabric suits constructed from patterns on a sewing machine as old-fashioned and low-tech, too close to the banal everydayness of clothing. Hard suits severely limited mobility in early prototypes, but were ultimately rejected because the rigid components took up too much space in the Apollo capsule. Nonetheless, the hard suits continued to embody what the public imagined a Space Age aesthetic to be, because they drew from accepted ideas of the futuristic (fig. 105). According to de

**106**
André Courrèges, *Elle*, March 1965,
photograph by Peter Knapp

Monchaux, "the Litton suits proved enduringly successful ... in becoming a popular image of space-wear. Their hard gleaming surfaces fulfilled a science fiction fantasy of spaceflight; sleek, efficient, functional, and firm."[34] This image and others inspired by the space race had a dramatic, if short-lived, influence on fashion in the mid-to-late 1960s, as well as on longer movements in architecture, interior design, and the decorative arts. Rosenberg describes this midcentury modern style as "emphasiz[ing] eclecticism, mixing retro primitivism with futuristic styles. It juxtaposed calm, planet-shaped curvatures with abrupt, space-ship-style thrust. If the science of space penetration suggested sleek exactitude, the wonder of the cosmos encouraged unpredictable pastiche."[35] This spirit was carried directly onto the body through the designs of the Space Age couturiers: André Courrèges, Pierre Cardin, and Paco Rabanne.

## Space Age Fashion

Space Age style was one of many varied modes of fashion that found traction during the tumultuous 1960s. In Paris, Gabrielle "Coco" Chanel, Madame Grès, and Cristóbal Balenciaga, all old masters of couture's golden age, still ruled their ateliers. The houses of Lanvin, Balmain, Givenchy, and Christian Dior (under Marc Bohan's leadership since 1960), were also popular, creating a range of styles. Yves Saint Laurent emerged as a rising talent when he opened his own couture house in 1961. Only a handful of Parisian couturiers embraced the startling new fashions inspired by space suits, spaceships, and other ephemera of science fiction made real. The Space Age aesthetic in high fashion was at its strongest from 1964 to 1969, when André Courrèges, Paco Rabanne, and Pierre Cardin created a dramatic break in French haute couture, one that embraced futuristic design inspired by the ebullient spirit of the space race, encompassing technology, new materials, and modernism. Their designs were the Parisian answer to the emergence of an influential youth culture worldwide, a movement that was barely acknowledged by other French couturiers. Valerie Steele explains, "In the 1960s, the French had no youth culture the way the English and Americans did—no Beatles, no Rolling Stones. Confronted with London Youthquake fashions, the French couture was frozen. Then Courrèges used the idea of futurism as a metaphor for youth—all his moon girl outfits, silver trousers, etc. That was really pivotal."[36]

For Courrèges, Cardin, and Rabanne, Space Age design was the future meeting the present. It represented the promise of technology, youth, and women's expanding freedoms at a time of social upheaval, struggle, and violence. Although these are the three designers most often associated with Space Age fashion, they were not alone in creating the style. Emanuel Ungaro and Rudi Gernreich were both innovative within the genre, and many other designers riffed on the most extreme Space Age designs, usually tamping down the outré accessories and styling to contribute to a Space Age fashion aesthetic that was widely publicized by the fashion press. Balenciaga also played a large role in introducing the Space Age aesthetic. He trained Courrèges and Ungaro, who each took elements of the master's signature style—welted seams, structural fabrics, volume standing away from the body—to build the Space Age look. Although Space Age designs were highly directional, they effectively trickled down to the masses, either as watered-down versions of the originals or as lasting and powerful images in fashion magazines.

*Using past dress as inspiration is as ridiculous as trying to perfect a spaceship by studying the steam engine.*[37]

—André Courrèges

André Courrèges was most closely associated with the Space Age aesthetic and was among the most influential and innovative fashion designers of the 1960s. Upon his death, the *Telegraph* wrote that Courrèges's own "'new look' swept the world in 1964 almost as dramatically as had that of Dior in 1947, but, unlike Dior, whose clothes evoked the opulence of a bygone age, Courrèges's highly distinctive designs owed virtually nothing to tradition, instead they

**107**
André Courrèges, *Vogue*, March 1, 1964,
photograph by William Klein

**108**
André Courrèges, *Vogue*, March 1, 1965,
photograph by William Klein

—

embraced the 'Space Age.'"[38] Physically active from a young age, Courrèges admired women who were strong and vigorous. He approached modern fashion with a desire to liberate the female body. He rejected tight and body-manipulating undergarments and stripped his designs down to their architecture, removing surface decoration and ornamentation. He stated:

> To me it is the woman who is important, not the dress— what she does, how she moves, how she lives. Her clothes should not be chic abstractions. They must be rational and logical. . . . My aim is to dress women to permit them to live and to live with a piece of clothing, to take into consideration their real needs, which are indivisibly functional and aesthetic. The purely functional can be very ugly. But the functional must be the soul of dress, its composition, its interior rhythm, and its sense. Aesthetics is the envelope.[39]

Courrèges was born in 1923 in the French Pyrenees. He studied engineering before serving as a pilot in the French Air Force during World War II, and then settled in Paris in 1945. He worked briefly for designer Jeanne Lafaurie before obtaining an entry-level position in Cristóbal Balenciaga's atelier in 1950. Training under one of haute couture's most talented and technically rigorous designers for a decade armed Courrèges with the skills to open his own maison in 1961. He left his position with not only Balenciaga's blessing, but also one of the master's other employees, Coqueline Barrière. Courrèges and Barrière worked as partners in design and business. Although she eschewed the spotlight, she was his muse (fig. 113). They would later marry, remaining together for forty-nine years, until his death in 2016.

The house of Courrèges was immediately popular among couture clients, though his early work, noted for its precision and proportion, largely reflected his training with Balenciaga. His experience in engineering and aeronautics, as well as his lifelong love of modern architecture, most likely contributed to the strict, straight-lined tailoring that Diana Vreeland described as "precise as a Swiss watch."[40]

Courrèges himself likened his design process to that of a technician or an architect, and described his atelier as his laboratory. He experimented with new consumer fibers— such as DuPont's Qiana—plastics, PVC, and materials intended for aviation, sports gear, and the army.[41]

As he grew into his own style, Courrèges introduced more daring designs. He was credited with inventing the miniskirt in the mid-1960s (also attributed to British designers Mary Quant and John Bates), as well as other silhouettes that encouraged freedom of movement, such as knitted, ribbed body stockings. Courrèges was an early promoter of women in trousers and showed designs of slim-pant ensembles as formal wear in the early 1960s. A particularly daring 1964 design—that also reflects his Space Age aesthetic— featured silver-sequined trousers worn under a gleaming white, full-length evening coat, held precariously together at the bust with a single tie. The trousers sat low on the hips, revealing the model's tanned midriff.

Courrèges's designs, in their androgyny and body revelation, embodied the changing position of women in Western society during the 1960s. Although his designs were criticized for their emphasis on youth—to the extreme that they looked like children's clothing—they played an important role in normalizing the idea that women should be able to move through their days and nights as unencumbered as men.

Courrèges's Space Age details permeated his collections of 1964 and 1965, exemplified in William Klein's 1964 photograph for *Vogue* (fig. 107). The model wears a clean, white tunic with welted seams and pockets, perfectly cut, slim, white trousers, and a matching space-capsule hat, kid gloves, and flat boots. She blithely reclines on the floor, her fingers flashing the peace sign. As the caption attests, everything about this ensemble and the young woman wearing it "leaps into the future."[42] The double welted seams, machine-sewn to appear as hermetically airtight as a space suit, and Courrèges's use of structured, luminous, optical white fabrics convey what was popularly understood as a futuristic, technological look. Further emphasizing Courrèges's

Space Age style, *Vogue* featured his baby-doll-bonnet hat on its cover in November 1964. The round, enveloping shape and silver-sequin-ball trim resemble an astronaut's helmet. The next year, Courrèges showed his models as space cowboys in sporty trouser suits trimmed in navy stripes; mini-dresses with pastel-plaid, hip-length jackets; and skirts with built-in braces (fig. 106). Likewise inspired by menswear, Courrèges also gave his models the tough, easy look of men in undress, dressing them in white T-shirt tops with round necklines, and tank tops with deep arm-holes (fig. 108). He continued to style his ensembles with white kid gloves, and in spring 1965 his boots featured slit toes. He further accessorized with goggle-like sunglasses and squared-off cowboy hats (figs 110, 111, 112). More than any other collection, the spring 1965 show, presented in his atelier with the models dancing energetically to jazz music, embraced the Space Age and America's leadership in the race to the moon.

Optimism defined the Courrèges look. Reflecting on their 1960s designs in 2001, Coqueline Courrèges stated, "We were inspired by the generation of the year 2000. What we imagined would come in the future and what we would encounter. The first confirmation of our vision was when man walked on the moon in 1969" (fig. 109).[43] *Women's Wear Daily* wrote of Courrèges in 2016, "The designer often said he felt more American than French. 'I love America, I love the American spirit. The spirit of going to the moon. The American way of life. The grandeur of American space.'"[44] This attitude was evident in the cowboy hats he paired with his Space Age ensembles—a light-hearted pastiche that recalls midcentury modern design. Although the history of the space race is typically centered on the US and the USSR, it is important to note that the French space agency, Centre National d'Études Spatiales (CNES) was established in 1961, and in November 1965, France became the third space power by launching the *Astérix* satellite.[45] Courrèges's celebration of both space technology and the United States was mirrored in the close collaboration between CNES and NASA in its early years. France went on to become a leader

within the developing European Space Agency (then called the European Space Research Organisation).[46]

Courrèges's designs were met with mixed reviews—some thought his ideas to be outlandish and unwearable, while others were elated by his vision of the woman of the future. French journalist Françoise Giraud, writing for the *New York Times* in September 1965, explored both sides. She noted Coco Chanel's horror at the short, sleeveless dresses revealing "everything that is most ugly on a woman."[47] (However, Chanel had to concede to the precise cut of Courrèges's trousers, admitting, "He knows his business."[48]) Giraud also described a surreal review by *Vogue* reporter Violette Leduc, for whom the spring 1965 collection inspired happy childhood memories. Leduc compared

**109**
André Courrèges, dress, wool, circa 1968,
Paris, The Museum at FIT

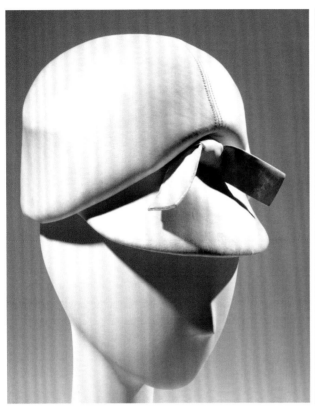

the Courrèges woman to an "apricot with a mental life."[49] Seeking her own opinion and bracing herself with a scotch for courage, Giraud tried on a Courrèges dress made up for her at his atelier. She assessed:

> A dress by Courrèges is like nothing else one has been in. It is something white (because white, he says, is joy) and difficult to keep clean—hence a sign of luxury. It is a very pure white and rigorously smooth, with seams placed in such a way that nothing is tightly fitted, nothing hinders you. It is something which completely modifies the balance of the body because it is impossible to wear it with high heels. It is something which gives you the feeling of being vigorous, healthy, clean, of looking like a sculpture by Brancusi or a building by Corbusier. It is something that makes both women and men alike turn around immediately and ask you: "Is it a Courrèges?" Finally, it is something which, alas, makes you disgusted with all your other clothes.[50]

Although Giraud was won over by the balance and simplicity of the Courrèges look, her article focused on the unstable state of haute couture. Courrèges's spring 1965 show had been a massive success—though not for him. His chic, easy-to-duplicate dresses were a huge hit for manufacturers who copied his designs and sold them on the mass market. In this way, the Courrèges look had a large impact on women in Europe and the United States, and came to be a defining look of the mid-1960s. Even his white boots (later rebranded as go-go boots) and cowboy hats were seen

**110, 111, 112**
(above clockwise) André Courrèges, hat, leather, 1963,
Paris; boots, kid leather, 1964, Paris; sunglasses, plastic,
spring/summer 1965, Paris, The Museum at FIT

everywhere. Only the precision of his trousers proved hard to emulate. Courrèges was angered by this blatant copying and refused to show a fall 1965 collection—though his ideas were all over other designers' runways.[51] By the time Giraud visited the atelier to write her story, Courrèges was taking orders from only a few private clients. Then he closed his doors—temporarily, until the spring of 1967. Coqueline and André Courrèges used that time to modernize their business, establishing their own manufacturing so that the house could add ready-to-wear to the couture offerings.[52]

Courrèges's signature style, which he maintained and developed throughout his career, had made a tremendous impact on fashion culture. Yves Saint Laurent, for example, said, in 1966, "Things have never been the same since Courrèges had his explosion.... It was a necessary and healthy happening in the fashion world."[53] He added, "I found it difficult to break away from traditional elegance and Courrèges changed that."[54]

*The clothes that I prefer are those I invent for a life that doesn't exist yet—the world of tomorrow.*[55]        —Pierre Cardin

Pierre Cardin, a couturier famous for modernizing and diversifying his business—he may be better known today as a brand than as a designer—was also an early enthusiast of Space Age design, not only in clothing, but also in furniture and architecture. Born in Italy in 1922, Cardin immigrated to France with his parents when he was two years old. He began a tailoring apprenticeship at fourteen and moved to Vichy to train at a couture house four years later. Arriving in Paris in 1945, he worked at the houses of Paquin, Schiaparelli, and Christian Dior, where he assisted with the 1947 New Look collection. In 1950, he opened his own maison, developing a style that focused on elegant silhouettes, often incorporating one or two dramatic details, such as oversized collars.[56] In 1959, he introduced a ready-to-wear collection that resulted in banishment from the couture federation. Undaunted, Cardin began significant expansion into licensed products, paving the way for modern branding.

Cardin's biographer, Jean-Pascal Hesse, described the designer as deeply interested in the Space Age: "He was a lunar Pierrot, obsessed with the cosmos, technology, lasers, and the progress of the space program. He designed satellite dresses, tubular forms in the shape of rockets, wheeled pants, kinetic dresses, and jackets with metal breast cones."[57] Cardin's engagement with space technology began in the late 1950s, when he incorporated sleek, modern forms into his accessories' designs. In 1966, he introduced his Cosmos line (figs 114, 115), echoing much of the feeling for bodily movement and functionality in clothing that Courrèges had also embraced. Like Courrèges, Cardin was copied. Curator Valerie Mendes wrote of Cosmos:

Every member of the family was accommodated. The basic outfit was practical and unisex consisting of a short tunic or pinafore over body fitting, jersey rib sweater and tights or trousers. A domed felt hat echoing cosmonaut's helmets completed a female Cosmos and a peaked

**113**
Coqueline Courrèges wearing André Courrèges in a battery-powered car prototype by André Courrèges, *Vogue*, November 1, 1969

**114**
(following) Pierre Cardin, Cosmocorps collection, 1967, photograph by Yoshi Takata

cap resembling NASA off-duty attire was worn by men. In fact, a Cardin Cosmos was functionally dressed for comfort and mobility, but the complete ensemble was far too adventurous for general consumption. However, the pinafore without its space-like accessories was copied by mass manufacturers and rushed into high street shops.[58]

The streamlined shapes for men included exposed zippers with large, round pulls, and large, round, padded collars that resembled the rigid neckline of a space suit without its helmet. Women's dresses and jumpers had geometric cutouts and inserts, worn with round, planet-like caps or space-capsule helmets that dropped over the head. Vinyl

or silver inserts and thigh-high vinyl boots added to the futuristic feeling. These ensembles brought the contemporary science fiction of living in space into reality. For example, *The Jetsons* were animated in similarly geometric dresses, jumpers, and pared-down separates in bright colors. Cardin's designs also bear resemblance to the costumes in the original *Star Trek* series, especially in their uniform details, such as block coloring, epaulets, and Mao collars—as well as to its later iterations on television and film.

From the mid-1960s, Cardin regularly incorporated vinyl, plastic, and metal into his designs (fig. 116), but he also pushed the technology of Space Age fashion fabrications forward by creating his own synthetic fabric, Cardine.

**115**
Pierre Cardin, dress, doubleface
wool jersey, 1967, Paris, The Museum at FIT

**116**
Pierre Cardin, dress, wool and vinyl,
1969, Paris, The Museum at FIT

Developed in collaboration with Union Carbide in 1968, the seamless Cardine mini-dresses he designed for his haute couture collection were molded into sharp pyramids and high-relief circles, and were worn with vinyl, baby-bonnet headdresses. Despite the sharply defined, three-dimensional details, Cardine was pliable. *Vogue* enthused, "From Paris, Pierre Cardin's moulded dress, made of the exciting new fabric everybody's talking about.... You can wash it, pack it—it never crushes, never loses its shape—and wear it straight away."[59] Like many of Cardin's designs for women, the Cardine dress featured a miniskirt hemline (fig. 117). Cardin and the other Space Age couturiers found modernity and freedom in revealing legs, and short hems seemed to herald a more contemporary way of living. Journalist Suzy Menkes quoted Cardin, "My way was to draw something of the future—to be young, to see that a woman could be free.... I wanted to give women in the 1960s a chance to work, to sit, to take the car and drive in my dresses."[60] Cardin's Space Age designs are sometimes described as androgynous, yet he sought to emphasize the female body: "My cosmonaut models for women remain feminine ... they are slimming ... the ribbed sweater moulds the bust and a woman remains a woman."[61] Although he covered miniskirted legs with tights, creating an encapsulated look, some of Cardin's designs drew attention to the breasts with inserted design elements or silver-lined cutouts.

**117**
Pierre Cardin, dress, fuchsia Dynel (Cardine),
1968, Paris, The Museum at FIT

**118**
Pierre Cardin, dress, wool crepe and polished
steel plates, 1968, Paris, The Museum at FIT

**119**
Penelope Tree, dress by Pierre Cardin, Paris,
January 24, 1968, photograph by Richard Avedon

Cardin's space-cadet looks related to Courrèges's space cowboys in their short lengths and giddy enthusiasm, and these looks created a distinct dialog with science-fiction costuming. Cardin also created evening gowns in 1968 and 1969 that captured the futuristic in a more elegant, sensual way: he utilized silver collars and insets to graceful effect in otherwise simple columnar gowns. Although Cardin's metal details employed a common element of Space Age design, seemingly referring to spacecraft and equipment, the photographers at *Harper's Bazaar* and *Vogue* interpreted models in Cardin's stark gowns as otherworldly creatures straight from science fiction. Penelope Tree's large, downward-lashed eyes stared ethereally into the camera in Avedon's 1968 *Vogue* image of Cardin's black wool and metal-harness dress (fig. 119). The solid, gleaming collar forms a square around her neck and drops into a round amulet at her chest, finished with a diamond bulb. The metal harness shines blurrily in the image, suggesting motion in the otherwise still Tree. On the facing page, Tree wears a white version, "One of the most spectacular evening ideas in Paris fashion now. White wool crèpe . . . hangs from wide-set polished steel straps on a sculptural band—pure, unadorned, absolute in its sensuousness."[62] Her hair is sculpted into a flat circle on her forehead, lending an alien look. The black harness dress was also photographed by Bill King in *Bazaar*, described as "a space age hanger for a straight drop of black crepe. . . . Cardin's lucky stone—a diamond—like a rocket's headlight, centered in the motif."[63] Here the model's hair is arranged in tentacle-like loops around her head. In December 1969, *Bazaar* featured the photographer Silano's image of Cardin's silver-ribbed, black mini-dress (fig. 118) in profile, set against a lunar collage landscape. The model's head is encapsulated by a tight mesh cap of shining, silver roundels. The byline states, "Reflections of a modern age throwing off highlights into an ultra luscent landscape."[64]

Concurrently with Courrèges, Cardin tapped into the needs of active, young women and gave them clothing to express their longing for the future within the context of their growing sexual liberation. He also gave men new options that broke with the formality of traditional menswear. Although not young himself, Cardin acknowledged the power of youth culture by specifically targeting his Space Age designs to the young, "What I try to do is create a style . . . a style which is contemporary, modern. But I would like everyone to understand that it is a style for young people and not middle-agers. At 44, I would never dream of dressing myself up as a cosmonaut."[65] Cardin was not exclusive to the Space Age aesthetic during the period from the mid-1960s to the early 1970s, but at the peak of his Space Age period, he designed some of the style's most memorable and unconventional silhouettes: wheeled trousers that ended at the cuff in flat disks; tunics that fell from outstretched arms to reveal swaths of cut-out fabric; and a variety of playful, geometric sunglasses. He took inspiration from astronaut apparel but focused on a streamlined look that had more in common with the idealized, hard space suits—as he explained in 1969, "The real astronaut's suit is 'very fascinating' but too bulky."[66] His designs could range from outlandish to sophisticated, but both extremes had an impact on the fashion and costume design of the period.

Cardin continued his career well past the Space Age craze in Parisian fashion. By 1972, he had shifted toward softer, draped styles. His later fashion designs occasionally resurrected futuristic aspects, but he also channeled his interest in futuristic forms and technology into environmental design. Cardin opened a dedicated studio in 1970, and designed Space Age products that ranged from furniture to bicycles, alarm clocks, computers, and wallpaper.[67]

> *My dresses are statements . . . like manifestos in literature. Some experiences have to be pushed to the limits to make minds react. I use my metal and plastic dresses to cleanse women's eyes.*[68] —Paco Rabanne

Paco Rabanne is unique among fashion designers and even among the Space Age couturiers for his rebellion against traditional fashion materials. Also, he was not an haute couturier in the late 1960s; he began by making (handmade) ready-to-wear clothing and was invited to join the couture federation only in 1971.[69] Rabanne's designs were shockingly new, body-revealing, and completely in line with futuristic aesthetics, yet he did not claim the Space Age directly as his inspiration. While Courrèges embraced the optimism of the American spirit in the race to the moon, and Cardin designed for life in the future, Rabanne devoted his energy to materials research and development. Courrèges and Cardin created new, streamlined, and abbreviated silhouettes with smooth, moldable fabrics, but Rabanne was indifferent to the lines of clothing, stating "I am only interested in the research for new, contemporary materials.... Shapes do nothing for me. Why would I want to compete with people who are so good at cutting outfits? ... No one can beat Balenciaga anyway, when it comes to shape."[70] Rabanne approached the future of fashion by rejecting the traditional cut-and-sew ways of making clothing with fabric, and instead used plastics, metals, paper, leather, and other materials. He invented and patented unique ways to link together rigid parts so as to fit smoothly over a three-dimensional body, using pliers instead of needles and thread to build new "fabrics."

Born in 1934 in Spain, Rabanne and his mother escaped the Spanish Civil War as refugees in 1939, settling in France. Although his mother had previously worked as a *première main* for Balenciaga, Rabanne had little interest in fashion, enrolling at the École des Beaux Arts in Paris to study architecture in 1951. He only began sketching designs for *Women's Wear Daily* in 1959 to supplement his income. During the early 1960s, he progressed into accessories design for Roger Model, a couture leather-goods supplier, and then for the shoe designer Charles Jourdan. His accessories work tended toward clean lines and geometric shapes, foretelling his future clothing designs. Rabanne also worked as a couture craftsman for such houses as Balenciaga, Givenchy, Courrèges, and Cardin, designing and producing specialty buttons, and introducing a new method for attaching embroidery with rivets, saving both time and money.

During the mid-1960s, Rabanne gained popularity with his colorful, Rhodoid, plastic accessories and Space Age sunglasses and visors, created for the burgeoning French ready-to-wear designers, Christiane Bailly, Michèle Rosier,

and Emmanuelle Khanh. Rabanne described these women as "full of new ideas, madly imaginative ... they gave a shock, excitement to dull conventional [ready-to-wear]. They reflect the young modern spirit in fashion, not too serious. They dare and I like that."[71] Khanh's husband, environmental designer Nguyen Manh Khanh, was also a close friend. His inflatable furniture and house designs for his Paris firm Quasar were inspired by the inflatable components used in satellites and EVA suits; they also inspired Rabanne's rejection of traditional materials.[72] By 1965, Rabanne's accessories work—especially his large, bright, geometric earrings—featured frequently in the fashion press.[73] His philosophy was to create fun, colorful accessories that would amuse in the short term, "Young people don't wear jewels anymore.... Get a gadget-jewel very often, quickly change the color, the form ... that's the new feeling of the young."[74] His accessories tapped into the same optimistic, youthful attitude as did the designs of Courrèges and Cardin.

In April 1966, *Vogue* described Rabanne as "the *accessoriste* whose wild and witty sunglasses, visors, earrings, spangles and other bijoux—all plastic, of course—have been Paris raves for several seasons."[75] He was heavily featured in the magazine; the next month, for example, *Vogue* showed his designs in several editorials, including a thick, plastic, rectangular visor with round, inset lenses in a sportswear story, and large, multicolor, op-art earrings complementing a patterned peasant skirt.[76] In both cases, his accessories were the highlight of the fashion image, stealing the spotlight from the clothing. Gaining increasing exposure for his couture craftsmanship, *Vogue* also credited his embellishment work in July on Philippe Venet's "sleeveless sweeping evening fantasy in thick white cotton satin, appliquéd with huge gleaming plastic geometries (these and the plastic earrings, by Paco Rabanne)."[77]

In February 1966, Rabanne presented his first clothing collection, which he described as "unwearable dresses made of contemporary materials."[78] *Vogue* pronounced the showing of twelve slim, colorful sheaths of linked Rhodoid disks "a sensational collection of modern clothes," while

**120**
Donyale Luna, dress and sandals by
Paco Rabanne, New York, December 6, 1966,
photograph by Richard Avedon

—

**121**

Paco Rabanne, dress, plastic and metal,
circa 1966, Paris, The Museum at FIT

Like Cardin, Rabanne experimented with his own synthetic fabrications, releasing his Griffo raincoat prototype in 1968 after three years of development. The coats were made from a plastic solution sprayed into a mold. The process was invented by manufacturer Louis Griffard and plastics specialist Jean Fougeray, who approached Rabanne with the idea to design clothing using their product. Remarkably, Rabanne designed the Griffo coat with all the components attached, so that the entire garment could be made from a single mold, eliminating the approximately five hundred separate processes used to make a traditional raincoat. Each shiny, liquid-looking Griffo coat could be produced in one minute. Although not a commercial success, the Griffo was truly a futuristic design with a production process to match.[84]

Throughout the 1960s and beyond, Rabanne investigated industrial and commercial materials and products, such as metal-linked butcher's aprons, industrial aerospace material, and rubber bands, to create innovative fashion. He also treated natural materials in new ways, combining feathers and fur with plastic and metal, or cutting expensive fur pelts into strips and knitting them into warm, lightweight coats.[85] Kamitsis noted, "Paco Rabanne took to all materials insofar as they brought new sensations and forced people to revise their traditional guidelines."[86]

Although his work was criticized as fashion extremity (the film *Who Are You Polly Maggoo?*, released in October 1966, satirizes a designer who immobilizes his models in metal sheets), Kamitsis argues that Rabanne's work was, in fact, wearable thanks to the detailed research the designer put into the materials and how they relate to the body.[87] Furthermore, the outrageousness of his manifestos fit the mercurial nature of the times. Fashion editor Polly Mellen recalled, "The first time I went to one of his shows, I remember saying: 'What is going on here? I don't believe it! It's so beautiful and different! Gladiator dresses, a suit of armor, a warrior, the new male!'"[88] Beyond the strong aesthetics, Mellen also vouched for the clothing's wearabilty: "The clothes themselves were at first quite heavy, but when you got them on—and I had to try them on—they were balanced in a

**122**
Paco Rabanne, wedding dress, plastic and metal, circa 1968, Paris, The Museum at FIT

very beautiful way, in a very engineered way. He was able to work metal on a woman's body, where curves were needed. And the sounds these dresses made—I was fascinated."[89]

Rabanne created some of the longest-lasting fashionable impressions of the Space Age with his designs for the film *Barbarella*. He costumed Jane Fonda as a futuristic space-ship captain, sent to another planet to retrieve a dangerous weapon and its inventor. In the opening scene, Barbarella enters her ship from outer space and, floating in zero gravity, removes her bulky silver space suit, piece by piece, revealing her naked body. Throughout the film, Barbarella is dressed (and undressed) as a futuristic sex symbol, an astronaut, a fighter, and a sexually liberated woman. Rabanne's costumes were bold statements of futuristic femininity in plastic and molded-metal armor, tight body suits, high boots, and chain-mail capes. Everything was designed to reveal or emphasize Fonda's body, but also her individuality and confidence. The film is deliberately camp, but it expressed a real urgency in women at the time. Rabanne stated, "In France during the 60s, we had a similar women's liberation movement as in America. At the same time I was doing the costumes for the movie 'Barbarella.' So it was a moment when women emerged to be warriors because they needed to affirm their desire of emancipation, freedom and liberty. The armor was necessary."[90]

Although not directly referencing the Space Age and rejecting the title of "futurist," Rabanne created the most committed examples of futuristic fashion, pushing the limits of what could be clothing. Throughout his career, he continued to utilize novel materials for his fashion, even circling back to fabric, which was fresh to his design philosophy. But Rabanne did not choose materials arbitrarily. Kamitsis states, "He mastered matter by making conscious choices. Paco Rabanne did not set out to work with all unused materials for the sake of contradiction alone, although he was not indifferent to that side of the adventure. He sought provocation by using 'vile' materials to make clothes that were supposed to beautify the person who wore them."[91] As a modern designer, he disparaged haute couture as old-fashioned, but Kamitsis also ascertains that because

of his compulsion to innovate, especially during the late 1960s and early 1970s, "he was the only one in the business who could claim to be, not a couturier, but the custodian of the traditional values of Haute Couture."[92]

Using ultramodern aesthetics, Courrèges, Cardin, and Rabanne engaged the world around them with their designs, expanding beyond the contemporary confines of Parisian haute couture. They advanced the couture business model, embracing ready-to-wear, branching out into furniture and product design, transforming fashion shows into spectacles, and including racially diverse models. They helped bring Paris into a fashion conversation that the youth cultures in England and the United States were dominating during the mid-1960s and early 1970s. This dialogue appealed especially to young women, whose lives were expanding with new technologies and new freedoms. With the release of the birth control pill in 1960, women could take control of their sexuality and their lives in unprecedented new ways; body-revealing clothing to the point of skintight silhouettes or even partial nudity tested and celebrated this freedom. Aesthetically, the clothing looked more toward sleek space-ships and rockets than actual space suits, yet the fashion mimicked space suits' functionalism. After all, the space suit is essentially a tiny spacecraft, whittled down to encapsulate just the astronaut's body. Space Age fashion also jettisoned extra details—no unnecessary high heels, long skirts, or elaborate ornamentation. This was a rejection of the historical references so evident in conservative 1950s fashion. Courrèges, Cardin, Rabanne, and others used Space Age design as a vehicle toward a more logical and progressive lifestyle; Courrèges summed up the philosophy of the group, telling *Life* magazine in 1965, "Women of today are archaic in their appearance.... What I want is to help them coincide with their time."[93]

The collective look they created has come to represent the futuristic, recognizable even fifty years later, in both fashion and science-fiction costuming. The Space Age looks designed in the 1960s have been consistently referenced since that time, but the concept has also evolved. Hussein Chalayan, for example, shares Rabanne's experimental focus on materials

**123**
Alberta Tiburzi in Paco Rabanne, Cartagena,
Colombia 1966, photograph by Hiro

research, clearly seen in his spring 2000 collection. That season, Chalayan created an airplane dress from the same smooth, white, rigid material used to construct aircraft (fig. 124). The dress transformed by remote control, lifting its skirt panels to reveal a tulle petticoat. Chalayan's design is an extraordinary example of the continuation of the Space Age couturiers' emphasis on provocation, new silhouettes, and scientific inspiration into the twenty-first century.

Research in space suits also forges ahead, as NASA prepares to send astronauts to Mars. The space agency, an organization dependent on the public's interest for government funding, is as conscious of aesthetics as it was during the 1960s. Utilizing crowdsourcing, NASA held an online vote in 2014 to select a design for the newest model in its Z-series space suits, to be used for Mars mission training. For the Z-2 suit, produced by ILC, the public chose from three designs. The "Biomimicry" design was described as "mirroring the bioluminescent qualities of aquatic creatures found at incredible depths, and the scaly skin of fish and reptiles found across the globe." The "Trends in Society" model was "reflective of what everyday clothes may look like in the not too distant future ... [using] electroluminescent wire and a bright color scheme to mimic the appearance of sportswear and the emerging world of wearable technologies." The winning prototype, the "Technology" style, paid "homage to spacesuit achievements of the past while, incorporating subtle elements of the future."[94] The ultimate appeal of a design that references past space suits reveals how deeply the images of the 1960s' Space Age are held in the public imagination.

Private space companies are even more invested in creating fashionably appealing space suits. Elon Musk, founder of the SpaceX rocket company, seriously considered aesthetics in the design of his new space suit: "If we're to inspire the next generation to want to go beyond Earth ... they have to think they want to wear that suit one day."[95] He noted that the SpaceX suit will look more like the smooth, idealized space suits from films, again drawing from the repository of space images built up over the twentieth century. Echoing Cardin's criticisms of existing space suits, Musk commented, "One of the more embarrassing things about space suits is that the backside kind of pooches out pretty bad.... So we wanted to have something which would not do that."[96] Musk secured the vision of Jose Fernandez, a costume designer and sculptor, known for designing superhero costumes in films such as *Tron: Legacy, The Avengers,* and *Batman v. Superman.* Fernandez's design for a helmet won Musk's approval, and the two worked together to design a space suit that would later be reverse-engineered to function in space. Fernandez noted of the process, "He [Musk] wanted it to look stylish. It had to be practical but also needed to look great. It's pretty badass ... when people put this space suit on, he wants them to look better than they did without it.... You look heroic in it. It's an iconic thing to be a part of."[97]

Virgin Galactic also turned directly to designers, announcing its partnership in January 2016 with Y-3, the high-fashion sportswear line by Yohji Yamamoto for Adidas. Adam Wells, the head of design, said, "Together with the incredibly talented team at Y-3, we will explore the potential to create innovative apparel and accessories—both for our staff and for our pioneering customers—that is appropriately functional and fit-for-purpose, is thoughtfully and elegantly crafted, and is fulfilling and fun to wear and use."[98]

Functionalism remains the barrier to the idealized streamlined space suit. NASA's Z-series suits, while better performing, are as bulky, if not more so, than their precursors. Dava Newman, Deputy Administrator of NASA, and Aeronautics and Astronautics and Engineering Systems professor at the Massachusetts Institute of Technology, is developing an inventive solution in her BioSuit. Like partial-pressure suits of the 1940s that apply mechanical force to counteract depressurization, the BioSuit would compress at the skin's surface instead of encapsulating the body in pressurized gas. The sleek and body-fitting space suit utilizes tiny coils (perhaps inspired by Faure and Graffigny's nineteenth-century conception?) that can be activated to produce pressure. Prototyped in optical white, crisscrossed with graphic black and red lines, the suit would increase an astronaut's range of motion while decreasing the energy expended. Perhaps as important, it would finally bring the culturally prized image of the Space Age into reality.

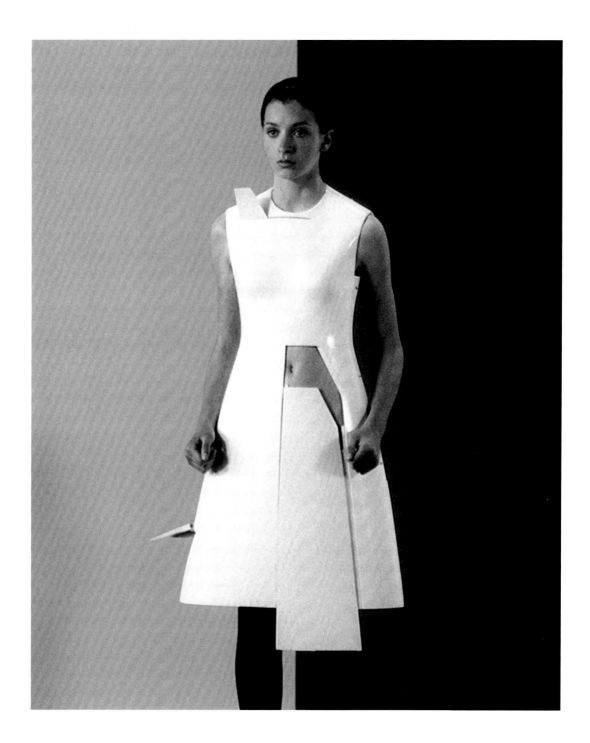

124
Hussein Chalayan, airplane dress,
spring/summer 2000, still from *Aeroplane Dress*,
film by Marcus Tomlinson

# 6

# Ocean Exploration

## FASHIONS FROM THE DEEP

Ariele Elia

———◇———

In the October 2010 issue of *Vogue*, the magazine featured a letter from one of its readers who expressed concern about discrepancies in a photoshoot for the article "Turning the Tide" (fig. 125).[1] The reader explained:

> Though Miranda Kerr looks lovely decked out in scuba-diving gear ... I noticed several errors in your image. There is no regulator strap attached to the valve, she isn't wearing a wet suit, and she lacks a dive buddy and other safety measures and equipment. Though scuba diving is a relatively safe activity, it places women and men in a hostile environment not to be trifled with.[2]

It is amusing that *Vogue* decided to publish this reader's comment. The photograph was not intended to accurately portray a scuba diver, but to create the fantasy of one. Legendary fashion editor for *Harper's Bazaar* and *Vogue* Diana Vreeland described the objective of a fashion magazine as, "You've got to give people what they can't get at home. You've got to take them somewhere."

Drawing on the growing popularity of scuba diving, beginning in the late 1950s, fashion magazines constructed romanticized scenes that transported their readers into a fantasy world far below sea level. "Ocean Exploration: Fashions from the Deep" will explore fashion's curiosity with deep sea, and how it has inspired fashion editorials and designers. It will also look at how diving was introduced into magazines, and at the transition away from the practical aspects of surviving underwater through fashion styling. Before "diving" into this topic, it is essential to understand the actual equipment used in deep-sea diving, and how it has evolved. This will help provide context to what fashion references, and how it is interpreted or subverted.

### Atmospheric Diving Suits

Atmospheric diving suits used to explore the deepest depths of the ocean are engineering marvels. There are many factors developers must take into consideration when creating such a suit. One of the most important challenges is to design a structure that can hold its shape under extreme pressure, while being light enough to move underwater. Also, an internal environment that is equivalent

**125**
"Turning the Tide," *Vogue*, July 2010, photograph
by Patrick Demachelier, model Miranda Kerr

**126**
Deep-sea atmospheric diving suit designed
by Alphonse and Théodore Carmagnolle,
circa 1882, photograph by Myrabella

—

to the atmospheric pressure in the open air on dry land must be maintained, in order to protect the diver from the physiological effects of decompression sickness. Another challenge is mobility. Breathable air supplied to the diver through a long hose from the surface limited the diving radius. While suits are large and bulky, their joints have to be flexible enough for the diver to have a range of motion sufficient to collect scientific data.[3] These joints also need to be properly sealed to prevent leaking.

While development of the atmospheric diving suit began in the 1710s, it took two centuries for a successful suit to be developed. In 1882, the Carmagnolle brothers, living in Marseilles, France, constructed an atmospheric diving suit that mimicked the structure of the human body, complete with twenty-two joints in the torso, arms, and legs (fig. 126). This was a dramatic improvement from the barrel-shape of

earlier designs. The helmet was composed of twenty-five, two-inch glass ports for the diver to look through. While this was a huge technological step forward, its weight—830 pounds—and complications arising from problems with waterproofing, rendered it unusable.

In 1930, British diving engineer Joseph Salim Peress unveiled his atmospheric diving suit, Tritonia. It was described as "looking like a metallic science fiction creation—Jules Verne come true"[4]—and it overcame the engineering challenges previously mentioned. Significant advancements included a reduction in weight by replacing steel with cast magnesium, and improvements in the strength and mobility of the joints by placing cushions of oil between them. The refined joints also helped to waterproof the suit. On October 26, 1935, British diver Jim Jarrett used the Tritonia to explore the wreckage of RMS *Lusitania*, 300

**127**
Tritonia atmospheric diving suit (left) and the standard
diving suit (right) on ship deck before diving to explore
the wreckage of the RMS *Lusitania*, 1935

feet (90 meters) below the ocean's surface. An image taken on the ship's deck just before the launch of this expedition showcases the Tritonia on the left (fig. 127). Although the Tritonia suit claimed to have a diving depth of 1,200 feet (370 meters) and sustain pressures of up to 35 atmospheres, the suit fell out of favor with the Royal Navy, which only required divers to reach a depth of 300 feet (90 meters). As Tony Loftas, journalist for *New Scientist*, explains, "The [Tritonia] suit, probably the most advanced armoured diving suit of its time, faded into obscurity."[5]

## Standard Diving Suit

The development of the standard diving suit has an equally long history. The original creation of this suit dates back to the 1820s, when Charles and John Deane designed a copper helmet that prevented firefighters from inhaling smoke. Their design was executed by the British engineer Augustus Siebe. The Deane brothers soon thought to apply their design to deep-sea diving. Shortly after, Siebe improved the design by adding a valve to the helmet, which prevented water from seeping into the suit when the diver moved horizontally. He later attached the helmet to a waterproof canvas suit. Over the course of the nineteenth century he continued to modify his design, which eventually evolved into the standard diving suit of the early twentieth century.

A photograph from 1880—mentioned in the Introduction by Patricia Mears—features French actress Sarah Bernhardt posing as the "Ocean Empress," wearing a standard diving suit (fig. 5). The late nineteenth-century design differs little from a version of the standard diving suit known as the Mark V, which was adopted by the US Navy from 1916 to 1984. By the 1930s, the standard diving suit eclipsed the atmospheric diving suit, and it became the focus of technological advancement. Instead of isolating the diver from the atmospheric pressures, developers worked on solutions to manage the physiological effects of decompression sickness. The 1935 photograph taken on the ship deck (fig. 127)

features a diver in a standard diving suit (right), holding the robotic hand of the diver in the Tritonia atmospheric diving suit. The sharp contrast between the two suits is evident as the Tritonia dangles from a cable in anticipation of being hoisted into the water, while the diver in the standard diving suit was able to simply jump in.

Irving Penn was well known for his glamorous fashion photographs in the pages of magazines. However, in 1951, *Vogue* commissioned Penn to photograph city workers in Paris, London, and New York, wearing their uniforms for a number of editorials. Entitled the "Small Trades" photography series, Penn captured the pride and personalities of the various laborers—and a deep-sea diver was among them. A full-page photograph of Penn's deep-sea diver was featured in the July 1951 issue of *Vogue*. This is one of the earliest sightings of a diver in a fashion magazine. All the elements of a standard diving suit are on display in the Penn photograph (fig. 128). The copper helmet (55 pounds) resting on the floor has four glass ports for viewing, each protected with brass grilles to prevent objects from piercing and breaking the glass. The copper chest-plate supports the helmet's weight and fastens it, creating an airtight seal. A vulcanized rubber and twill-canvas diving suit (30 pounds) is attached to the chest-plate, and was available in different thicknesses depending on the temperature of the water. The lead-sole boots (17½ pounds each) have brass toe caps that allow the diver to walk on the ocean floor. The belt (84 pounds) is filled with lead blocks to prevent him from floating upward with each breath. Lastly, there is the knife, which is used not as a weapon, but as a tool to pry, hammer, or cut obstacles while underwater. In total, a standard diving suit can weigh over 176 pounds. This weight creates a negative buoyancy that allows the diver to sink and work on the ocean floor at depths up to 600 feet (180 meters). Later we will see Penn's infatuation with the deep-sea diver in his fashion photographs for *Vogue*.

Although the standard diving suit was less cumbersome and offered more flexibility than an atmospheric diving suit, one of its drawbacks was the time needed to decompress

**128**
Deep-sea diver, New York, *Vogue*, July 1, 1951,
photograph by Irving Penn

the diver's body after use. As an example, after diving to a depth of 300 feet (90 meters) for sixty minutes, a diver would have to spend seven hours and thirty-eight minutes in a decompression chamber.[6] Also, the standard diving suit did not have the capacity to explore the extreme depths the way the atmospheric diving suit did.

## Scuba

Until the late nineteenth century, divers relied on an air supply from a hose that extended from the water's surface to the diver's helmet. This system not only limited mobility, it also posed several dangers. For example, if the line was severed, the surrounding external pressure could crush the diver's skull. By 1925, the first successful self-contained underwater-breathing apparatus—now known by the acronym "scuba"—was introduced by Yves Le Prieur in France. Cylinders of compressed air allowed divers to move around freely without the restrictions imposed by a hose. Unfortunately, there was not a high demand for the product, and the technology did not reach the commercial market.

During the World War II German occupation of France, Émile Gagnan engineered a gas regulator to aid with gas shortages. In 1942, he teamed up with naval lieutenant Jacques Cousteau to apply this technology to diving apparatus and released an improved version of the scuba design. Known as the Aqua-Lung, it extended the duration of dives and became the most popular breathing apparatus worldwide. By 1949, commercial scuba equipment had reached the United States through outlets such as Rene's Sporting Goods in Westwood, California.

## The Early Pioneers of the Wet Suit

The need for a warmer diving suit came about during World War II, when US Navy combat divers complained of insulation issues during cold-water dives. Their two-piece

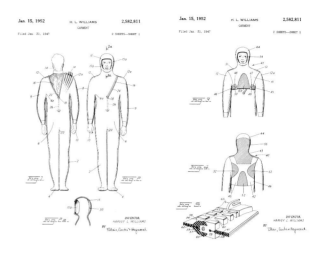

dry suits were made of thin layers of rubber, and the divers relied on wool underwear for warmth. To create a waterproof seal, divers would tie the top and bottom together in a knot at the waist, and seal the ankles and wrists.

University of California, Berkeley, physicist Dr. Hugh Bradner, who had been part of the Manhattan Project—which developed and produced the first nuclear weapons during World War II—specialized in the effects of absorption on unicellular materials. Bradner became interested in finding a solution to the US Navy's cold-water problem. In 1949, he began working on a suit made of neoprene, a synthetic rubber foam that contains trapped air bubbles. A year later, he tested his design in the icy waters of Lake Tahoe. The test was deemed a success as it kept Bradner warm in the freezing temperatures. The suit was also sent to Bradner's colleagues at Scripps Institution of Oceanography in La Jolla, California, for testing, and it received positive feedback about its functionality. Bradner formally introduced his design in the fall of 1951. John S. Foster can be seen wearing one of Bradner's early suits at Scripps around the same time (fig. 130).

Bradner's suit differed from previously patented designs, such as Harvey L. Williams's 1947 waterproof suit made of

**129**
(above right) 1947 patent registration for Harvey L. Williams's waterproof diving suit

**130**
(facing) John S. Foster in an early wet suit created by Hugh Bradner, circa 1951–1952

rubber, which required an additional vest to provide insulation to the diver (fig. 129). Bradner's revolutionary idea was that the diver did not have to stay dry to be warm; his use of neoprene provided insulation.[7] When the diver enters the cold water, a small amount of water penetrates the suit, and the diver's body temperature warms that thin layer of water between the neoprene and the body.

Bradner partnered with engineers at UC, Berkeley, to form the Engineering Development Corporation (EDCO) to market and manufacture the wet suit. In 1954, EDCO placed advertisements for their completed design, the EDCO Sub-Mariner, in diving magazines. When presented to the US Navy, they ultimately determined that Bradner's design was novel, but not useful to them because the air bubbles made the divers more detectable through sonar.[8]

Bradner passed the wet-suit patent application on to the University of California attorneys. However, the application was abandoned after Bradner indicated, "I see no large commercial application . . . there were only a few hundred divers and surfers in the world at that time."[9] In Bradner's correspondence with the Committee on Undersea Warfare and the National Research Council, Walter A. Hahn insightfully writes, "I do not really understand your complete resistance to benefit financially from the production of these suits, particularly when it is obvious someone will."[10] Bradner recalled that his focus was on being an inventor and a consultant to the US Navy. He later stated, "I found out I wasn't much of a businessman. I didn't think there was a good market for them."[11] Left unpatented, his technology created an opportunity for others.

One such person was Bev Morgan, an avid surfer and diver living in Manhattan Beach, California. During his spare time, he conducted research at the Scripps Institution of Oceanography library.[12] In the early 1950s, a librarian at Scripps recommended that Morgan read Bradner's report and correspondence about his wet-suit invention.[13] In 1953, Morgan opened his Dive N' Surf store in Redondo Beach, and soon invited surfing-and-diving twin brothers Bob and Bill Meistrell to join him as partners. Morgan began working with the Meistrells to improve the wet suit based on Bradner's design, making it more fitted, lightweight, and flexible. In 1953, they debuted their version, the Dive N' Surf Thermocline,[14] and began selling it in their store. Their suit would become one of the top-selling wet suits in the world. In 1958, Morgan sold his portion of Dive N' Surf to the Meistrells, who renamed it Body Glove, after their wet-suit slogan "fits like a glove."

Meanwhile, up north in San Francisco, surfer Jack O'Neill was trying to find a way to stay warm in frigid Bay Area waters that rarely exceeded 50 degrees Fahrenheit. At that temperature, O'Neill's surf time was limited to twenty-minute segments, before needing to warm up next to a beach fire. He began experimenting with wool sweaters soaked in oil, and later, vests made of polyvinyl chloride (PVC) foam and plastic to insulate the chest. In 1952, he opened his first surf shop in a garage along the Great Highway in San Francisco. One of O'Neill's surfing buddies, pharmacist Harry Hind, suggested that O'Neill try neoprene because of its insulating properties. By 1956, O'Neill had fully developed his neoprene wet suit and showcased it at a sporting-goods trade show in San Francisco. However, at that time there were very few surfers willing to endure the cold water. Charlie Grimm, another local surfer, discouraged O'Neill going forward with the design saying, "You're going to sell to five guys on the beach and you're out."[15] With this in mind, O'Neill moved his operation to Santa Cruz in 1959, where the water was warmer, but still required a wet suit. He shifted his business from surfboards to focus on wet suits. Over the following decades, O'Neill would continue to improve wet-suit technology and release new styles until 1985, when he retired from his role as CEO—announcing his son Pat as his successor—to pursue environmental projects and surfing. O'Neill and his competitor Body Glove have become wet-suit empires: in 2005 the *Los Angeles Times* noted that the two brands accounted for half a billion dollars in annual sales.[16]

Hugh Bradner, Bev Morgan, and Jack O'Neill have all been credited with inventing the wet suit—and each man has, in his turn, claimed to be its originator. In truth, it is difficult to determine the original creator. Did multiple people simultaneously create the same item in isolation, or were they influenced by each other? It is not uncommon for this kind of situation to arise, as different individuals identify the same niche, and then set out to find a way to fill it. In fashion, there is a similar history regarding the emergence of the miniskirt. Mary Quant, John Bates, and André Courrèges have all been credited with its invention—and have claimed credit—yet all that fashion historians can conclusively say is that the miniskirt, like the neoprene wet suit, was the right idea at the right time.

### Improving Wet-Suit Construction

Early neoprene wet suits were rigid and unlined, making it difficult to get in and out of them. Talcum powder was applied to the body before putting on the wet suit, to prevent the rubber from sticking to the body. Over time, the suit would tear from the wear of pulling and tugging it on and off. Surfers would often complain of horrible rashes around their arms caused by the friction of paddling (this was not as much of a problem for divers, since most of their motion came from kicking). Suits were later lined with nylon to reduce friction and chafing against the body. Some wet suits are designed with a layer of nylon, which increases the life of the neoprene. Wet suits without the nylon layer are called smooth-skin wet suits, which refers to the sleek appearance of neoprene.

Traditional sewing machines were used to construct the early wet suits; however, the needle created holes, of course, which allowed large amounts of water to enter the suit. These holes became larger when worn, and would result in the seams tearing. During the 1970s, seam tape made of nylon cloth and waterproof rubber backing was used to resolve this issue. It was applied using a chemical solvent or heat rollers that melted the tape. Later in the decade, the blind stitch revolutionized the wet suit, eliminating holes by passing through only part of the fabric. In the early 1970s, Jack

O'Neill and his sons Pat and Mike tested the latest seam technology by inflating their wet suits to a degree that resembled the Michelin Man (fig. 131). A long zipper plays an important role in allowing the wearer to get in and out of the suit with ease. To prevent the zipper from becoming undone, a flap, referred to as a batwing, is secured with a Velcro closure.

The air bubbles trapped within the neoprene fabric created a buoyant suit that allowed surfers to float. This was a vast safety improvement from the heavy wool sweaters that weighed them down. However, buoyancy posed a problem for divers. Even though the bubbles compressed the deeper a diver went, making the suit denser, additional weight was needed to allow the diver to fully submerge. The weight of the scuba equipment helped, but a weighted belt and buoyancy compensator were needed. The buoyancy compensator permits the diver to increase or decrease the volume of air, so he or she can go deeper; it also aids in returning to the surface.

Another important factor to take into account is the rate at which the body temperature reduces over time. Wet suits

131
Jack O'Neill with his sons, Pat and Mike, testing the latest wet-suit seam technology for their company, O'Neill, in the early 1970s

are manufactured in different thicknesses, ranging from two to eight millimeters, which allows some flexibility when calculating insulation against water temperature. This is especially critical for divers, who are generally exposed to colder waters than surfers: the deeper a diver goes, the colder the water, and the faster a wet suit loses it thermal qualities.

## Scuba Diving as a Popular Sport

The emergence of scuba and wet-suit technology during the 1950s marked a dramatic shift for both professional and amateur divers. Professional divers began to employ streamlined equipment, and amateur divers were now able to explore the depths of the oceans for themselves up to 130 feet (40 meters) below sea level. Interest in underwater exploration grew throughout the decade and was covered in popular magazines such as *Time, Vogue,* and *Harper's Bazaar.* In July 1959, *Harper's Bazaar* featured a supplement, "The Fifties," that highlighted important events of the previous ten years. The supplement juxtaposed a mention of couturier Cristóbal Balenciaga introducing the color white into his collections, with a story about the popularity of skin diving. Headlined "Skin-Divers Abound," the short feature discussed the influence of the books by Rachel Carson and Jacques Cousteau, stating: "Snorkels, fins, spears, seaproof cameras and other skin-diving paraphernalia have become almost as familiar under-sea, offshore phenomena as the indigenous fish and crustaceans. Spurred on by Rachel Carson's *The Sea Around Us* and Jacques Cousteau's *The Silent World*, everyone from small boys to women old enough to know better has felt inclined to take the plunge."[17]

Rachel Carson, a marine biologist and accomplished author, published her 1951 book, *The Sea Around Us*, as part of a trilogy. The book drew from Carson's eight years of research, exploring the formation of hidden mountains and canyons in the deep sea, as well as how plants and animals came to occupy these spaces. *The Sea Around* Us piqued public curiosity about the oceans. The book was on the *New York Times* best-seller list for eighty-six weeks and

was also translated into twenty-eight languages. Carson licensed the rights to a documentary based on her book, but was unsatisfied with the version of the final script because it incorrectly depicted her book and the scientific facts.[18] Despite its inaccuracies, the 1953 film won the Academy Award for the Best Documentary Feature. After this negative experience, Carson refused to license the rights to her books for future projects.

Written in 1953, *The Silent World* was Cousteau's first book. The Aqua-Lung appears in print for the first time on page three. Over the next two years, Cousteau and his team of twelve divers used Aqua-Lungs and underwater cameras to film ocean life at 165 feet (50 meters) below sea level. In 1956, Cousteau released his documentary, also named *The Silent World*, which won the Academy Award for the Best Documentary Feature. One of the first underwater films in color, it marked an important milestone. It provided actual footage of the deep sea—filmed by Cousteau's team—a world that previously had been only imagined in illustrations for works of fiction, such as Jules Verne's *Twenty Thousand Leagues under the Sea*. Cousteau's film was more successful and accurate than Carson's because he had complete creative control over the production. For its March 28, 1960, issue, *Time* honored Cousteau with his own cover and nine- page feature story. The article highlighted the free-diving (scuba diving without a wet suit) phenomenon stating, "This week some 1,000,000 dedicated U.S. skin-divers are getting ready for their biggest year. They are pro halfbacks, harried housewives, gawky teenagers."[19]

## Female Divers and Surfers in Vogue

Although atmospheric and standard diving suits are used by professional divers to explore the deepest parts of the ocean, the wet suit is the garment that is most familiar to the average person. Beginning in the 1960s, society's fascination with deep-sea exploration inspired fashion magazines to feature female deep-sea divers and their likenesses in editorials. A two-page spread in *Vogue*'s September 1967

**132**
Diver Valerie Taylor featured in *Vogue*, September 15,
1967, photograph by Arnaud de Rosnay

—

SUSAN COCHRAN

**133**
*Vogue,* May 1, 1971,
photograph by Irving Penn

—

## THE GOOD SPORTS
# WATER-BABIES

**Down, down, down, she goes,** left, shining all the way in a two-piece black wet-suit: deep-sea photographer Susan Cochran, totally covered—literally and figuratively—for a shot in the dark. Her own flippers and gloves, plus goggles, weight, belt, and a Nikonos II underwater camera from Richards Aqualung Center. Parkway/Recreonics wet-suit; Neoprene rubber bonded with Du Pont nylon. $65. To order, at Abercrombie & Fitch.

**Between perfect waves,** right, intrepid surfers like Minnie Cushing keep warm out there —and visible—in seal-slick wet-suits such as this: One-piece, black, of Neoprene rubber lined with nylon. From Richards Aqualung Center; about $35. The surf board, from Post Ski & Sport Shops. **MINNIE CUSHING**

PENN

134
*Vogue*, May 1, 1971,
photograph by Irving Penn

—

**135**
"Fashion Below Sea Level," *Harper's Bazaar*, May 1963,
photograph by James Moore

**136**
*Vogue*, December 1, 1965,
photograph by Irving Penn

—

issue highlighted a glamorous photograph taken by Arnaud de Rosnay (an avid surfer and adventurer) of Valerie Taylor, a blonde Australian diver elegantly floating next to an eight-foot-long whaler shark (fig. 132). The caption reads, "A small, feminine diver who wears eye makeup behind her mask, Miss Taylor wears a blue riband [ribbon] in her blonde hair, fake eyelashes, and an orange wet suit."[20] *Vogue* also highlighted the contributions of other female divers, such as Judy Joye. They described her as "the best-looking oceanographic specialist we've ever met, and she owns a consulting service."[21] Joye would lead diving expeditions for pharmaceutical companies looking for ways to create new drugs from marine organisms. Joye said, "I love deep-sea diving so much, I asked myself one day if I couldn't make a profession out of it? The answer was yes."[22]

Irving Penn first photographed a professional deep-sea diver in a standard diving suit in 1951 (fig. 128); two decades later, he brought diving back to the pages of *Vogue* in a 1971 spread featuring a female deep-sea photographer and a surfer in full gear (figs 133, 134). Diving and surfing are often featured together because both utilize wet suits. Smiling women, dressed in fitted wet suits rather than bulky, standard diving suits, are obviously more relatable to a fashion audience. The article described the wet suit as if it were the latest fashion trend, providing detailed information about the material and where the wet suit could be purchased. "Down, down, down, she goes," says the article, "shining all the way in the two-piece black wet-suit, deep-sea photographer Susan Cochran, totally covered—literally and figuratively—for a shot in the dark … neoprene rubber bonded with DuPont nylon. $65. To order, at Abercrombie & Fitch."[23]

## Models in Wet Suits

The skintight fit of the wet suit made it irresistible to the fashion world. The popularity of diving and surfing, coupled with Diana Vreeland's pioneering predilection for photography done outside the studio in exotic locales, brought adventurous editorials featuring models in wet suits to the pages of *Vogue* and *Harper's Bazaar*. A 1963 story in *Harper's*

*Bazaar* titled "Fashion Below Sea Level" showcased a model taking on the role of an explorer, wearing a camouflage wet suit, and stretching across a rocky tide pool overlooking the ocean (fig. 135). The moss on the rocks created a pattern that is reflected in the wet suit. *Harper's Bazaar* commented on this pattern, "The streaks, particularly attractive beneath the foam, guaranteed to make a fish feel you're simply part of life's rich pattern (and, thereby, not take alarm.)"[24] Prior to this, aesthetics were not considered when developing the wet suit—they were typically made from plain black neoprene. The introduction of color and pattern in this wet suit better positions its inclusion in a fashion magazine.

For a 1965 *Vogue* editorial, Irving Penn captured the movement of water running down the sleek surface of a neoprene wet suit, making it seem that the model had just walked out of the ocean and onto Penn's set (fig. 136). The smooth surface of this suit prevents a surfer from sticking to the board, while in this image, the structure of the neoprene conforms to the curved pose of the model's body. Her sharp, geometric ponytail, manicured nails, and prominent eyelashes add a fashionable aspect to the photograph. The caption credits the wet suit to Aqua-Lung, the manufacturer of scuba gear. The inclusion of a sporting-goods brand was a notable departure from the fashion brands typically featured.

Photographer David Bailey caught the energetic splashes of his two favorite models—Jean Shrimpton and Penelope Tree—jumping into the water sporting full wet suits for a 1970 "*Vogue*'s Eye View" feature (fig. 137). Although their bodies are completely covered, the figures underneath are more exposed than normal because the wet suits are made from nylon instead of neoprene. (Bailey's idea to focus on the beauty of the models' faces is evocative of Richard Avedon's 1965 photograph of Jean Shrimpton in a NASA space helmet, mentioned in Elizabeth Way's essay.) "The playful nature of Bailey's photograph is highlighted in the commentary, "Here are our friends Jean and Penelope, the Shrimp and the Tree, just grooving with it—scuba-ing, duba-ing, dancing on sea spray—two hale, happy water babies simply enjoying themselves in their own way. "[25]

APRIL 1, 1970

# VOGUE'S EYE VIEW

## o joy!

**O bliss!
O frabjous
day!—**

the sun is high, the water like looking glass, and here are our friends Jean and Penelope, the Shrimp and the Tree, just grooving with it—scuba-ing, duba-ing, dancing on sea spray—two hale, happy water babies simply enjoying themselves in their own way. Having their own kind of fun. And fun, chums, has got to be part of life or there's no life—no real life—at all....Let's face it, as a disc jockey recently observed, "you can't dance to the news." But there are a lot of other things you can dance to, and never forget it—if you don't like the music, make up your own—kick up your heels! Enjoy yourself...it's earlier than you think.... Black stretch nylon wet suits, $60 each. By Parkway Fabricators. At Altman's.

DAVID BAILEY

137
*Vogue*, April 1, 1970,
photograph by David Bailey

Fashion Thunderball, diving into the underwater world in full snorkel. Bikini top and skirt of yellow vinyl, glowing bright enough to make a fish blink. By Robert Sloan. Top, about $12; skirt, about $23. (Photographic license; they're not meant to be worn underwater.) Ensemble at Miss Bergdorf of Bergdorf Goodman; Neiman-Marcus; I. Magnin. Emme hat. Sheffield watch. These pages: all skin diving equipment from Abercrombie and Fitch.

In 1985, fashion designer Robin Piccone approached the wet-suit brand Body Glove about designing a line for the company. Within a year, Piccone had created a fifty-piece collection of fluorescent designs that incorporated a lightweight version of neoprene. She presented her collection to the editors of *Vogue*, *Harper's Bazaar*, and *Elle*, recalling, "All the assistants wanted to keep the pieces. In the end, I had to hide my stuff from them, because I was running out."[26] Spreads featuring Body Glove began appearing in major fashion magazines. Thus, Piccone had successfully transformed the wet-suit company into a fashion brand.

A November 1986 editorial in *Vogue* featured model Robbi Chong basking in the sun—a less active pose than

seen in previous pictorials—wearing a fluorescent yellow Body Glove wet-suit jacket, paired with a sexy blue thong and sunglasses to match. Titled "Shock Waves," the editorial highlights the surfing jacket with a caption that further describes fashion tapping into the surfing industry: "Just when it seemed everything that could be done to a bathing suit, had been done . . . . Here, straight from the water sports world, Body Glove's wet-suit 'jacket' over a thong from Diva."[27] The Body Glove jacket transitioned from being sold in sporting-goods stores to the trendy New York fashion boutique, Patricia Field. Another 1986 editorial featuring Body Glove takes a cold-weather approach to the wet suit by layering a fur coat over a full-length Body Glove wet suit.

138
*Harper's Bazaar*, May 1966,
photograph by Bob Richardson

—
**176**

The trend for Body Glove continued into 1988, as evidenced in a *Vogue* article that states, "Another trend: neoprene and 'rubber' surfing gear worn in—and out of—the water by Robin Piccone for Body Glove."[28]

## Accessorizing the Shoot

Styling plays an important role in creating the fantasy of a fashionable woman dabbling in the sport of scuba diving. By removing certain elements—such as the scuba tank—necessary to survive underwater, we begin to move away from realistic representations. Fashion garments—not visually related to diving—were accessorized with certain forms of diving gear, like fins, to draw a connection to diving. Editors pick and choose which type of equipment to include in a feature, for example, one might use a mask and fins, while another uses a mask and scuba tank, but no regulator for the tank.

Fashion photographer Hiro photographed models suspended from aerobics rings for the January 1963 *Harper's Bazaar* feature, "Sea Sirens '63." An overlaid image gives the illusion that the models are underwater. Rather than a wet suit, one model wears a red swimsuit by Rudi Gernreich made of what the magazine describes as "simulated patent leather." The material, most likely vinyl, provided a glistening wet look, similar to a wet suit. However, it would not hold up well if it were actually underwater. The photo shoot is accessorized with a mask and flippers that recall the idea of underwater aerobics. The caption described the swimsuit on the opposite page as "deep-sea black," which refers to the pitch-black darkness at depths of more than half a mile below sea level.

The 1965 James Bond film *Thunderball* includes an epic nine-minute underwater fight that ignited the public's fascination with scuba diving. The film became a pop culture phenomenon and spurred a trend for underwater editorials in fashion magazines. *Harper's Bazaar*, for example, shot an underwater story in Acapulco titled "On The Land, In The Sea, It's Fluorescence," in which a model casually floats in a

**139**
Two-piece "beavertail" wet suit with zipper and twistlock fasteners featured in Parkway Fabricators 1969 catalogue

177

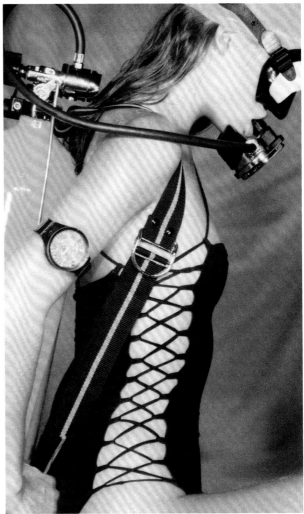

curved position with her hands waving to the camera. Her fashionable bandeau bikini-top and skirt are juxtaposed with a mask and a scuba (fig. 138). The double-hose breathing apparatus, referred to as a rebreather, is the same style used by the villainous divers in the *Thunderball* fight scene; it allowed for oxygen to be recycled in a closed circuit instead of being expelled into the water, which creates bubbles that could give away a diver's location. This apparatus was useful for the photo shoot because it prevented bubbles from blocking the model's face. The magazine describes the scene: "Fashion Thunderball, dives into the underwater world in full snorkel. Bikini top and skirt of yellow vinyl, glowing bright enough to make a fish blink."[29] The caption mentions that the top and skirt should not be worn underwater, pointing out the creative license taken by the stylist. A similar example to the wet suit worn by Sean Connery in

140, 141
"The Bond Girls," *L'Officiel*, no. 683,
1982, photographs by Claus Wickrath

**142**
Grace Coddington modeling a Courrèges
scuba-diving ensemble from spring/summer 1970,
photograph by Clive Arrowsmith

—

**179**

the film is a two-piece, beavertail-style wet suit modeled by a glamorous blonde for a 1969 Parkway Fabricators catalogue (fig. 139). The influence of *Thunderball* was not limited to the 1960s—the 1982 editorial "The James Bond Girls," featured in the French fashion magazine *L'Officiel*, depicts athletic women in swimsuits and diving gear. One model was dressed in a diving jacket holding fins; another had a scuba tank on her back (figs 140, 141).

André Courrèges is best known for his space-age fashion designs. However, for his spring 1970 collection he briefly explored scuba diving, creating his version of a wet suit, nicknamed "Scuba-Duba" by the press (fig. 142). The black vinyl ensemble included a hooded short-sleeve shirt, shorts, and flippers to match. White trim and buttons defined the plackets and tab details. *Vogue* UK featured his creation, accessorizing it with a faux scuba tank, mask, and snorkel. Grace Coddington—who would become the legendary fashion editor for American *Vogue*—stepped in when the model was late to the shoot. She playfully fluttered her flippers while casually smiling at the camera as she adjusted her mask. It is worth noting that if the accessories and blade from the flippers were removed, the ensemble would look like a typical Courrèges design.

*L'Officiel* staged an underwater fight between two elegant models in Paris's Hotel Nikko swimming pool for a June 1978 article about scuba-diving equipment (fig. 143).

143

*L'Officiel*, no. 643, 1978, photographs by
(left) T. P. Trosset and (right) Michel Picard

A photograph captures the moment that a model equipped with a mask, diving knife, and fins gracefully chokes another model, who is wearing a sheer swimsuit with triangular inserts. The fight is meant as a metaphorical reminder that proper survival equipment is essential in order to survive the rough conditions of the sea. *L'Officiel* warns, "Like the mountain, the sea is lively and temperamental. She does not like to be treated lightly."[30] The drama of the image is intensified by the models' mouths, open underwater without a scuba tank. The exaggerated image was juxtaposed with an organized layout of essential scuba-diving gear. The article reviews the benefits and different styles of diving equipment, while also encouraging the recreational diver to join a diving club for safety's sake. The void of scuba gear on the models is similar to the fantasized image of Miranda Kerr mentioned in the letter to *Vogue* at the introduction to this essay.

## The Curved Body as a Styling Tool

To enhance the deep-sea theme in editorials, photographers often placed models in elongated, curved positions in order to give the illusion that they were floating underwater or diving to the depths of the ocean. The May 1961 issue of *Harper's Bazaar* showcased a number of such shoots. A full-page photograph by Hiro featured a model gracefully suspended within a rocky cavern—as if she were weightlessly floating underwater—wearing a hooded tunic resembling the fitted headpiece used by scuba divers. The model's extended legs and arms curve to form an inverted "L" that mimics the shape of the cavern. *Harper's Bazaar* described her as "hooded, warm, wonderful-looking—and shaped with a kind of interplanetary zing."[31]

An elegantly curved Kristen McMenamy stretches across two pages of *Vogue* in the May 1995 feature "Good Sports." The arch of her body suggests a diver entering the water. Body Glove booties, a scuba tank, and a regulator are used to accessorize her silver bikini. Throughout the eight-page editorial, diving gear is used to style the metallic swimsuits,

which picked up on the athletic trend in fashion during the 1990s, and the term "tank" is used in a variety of ways, including scuba tank, tank-style swimsuit, and think tank.

In a June 2011 travel feature, *Vogue* highlighted swimsuits that closely resemble wet suits. Diving accessories are almost nonexistent in the feature, leaving the viewer reliant on other visual cues to make the deep-sea connection. Raquel Zimmermann models a long-sleeve top and shorts by Marni that are color-blocked in a manner similar to a wet suit, with white-stripe details that highlight the seams (fig. 144). Although the fabric hugs the body like knitted nylon, it was actually made of cotton and leather. A safety pin, bottle opener, and whistle dangle from a chain mail Paco Rabanne bag that resembles the net a scuba diver might use to collect scientific data. Finally, the swinging motion of body, bag, and laces create the illusion of Zimmermann gracefully floating underwater. Caption headers such as "Deep Blue" and "Scuba Do" further ground the abstract visual references to the diving world.

## Wet Suits Spark a Fashion Trend

"Ten years ago, sports gear consisted of tennis whites, grey sweats, and a pair of Keds. But the fitness movement changed all that: exercise gear—along with exercise—suddenly became fashion conscious," said *Vogue* in September 1988.[32] Previously, magazines had simply referenced scuba diving using accessories, photographic illusions, and the occasional wet suit. But now that was changing. Between 1989 and 1991, top designers began using surfing and wet suits as inspiration for their fashion collections. This was seen in a variety of ways, ranging from sparkling garments directly based on wet suits, to more abstract interpretations using fitted fabrics that resembled neoprene and nylon.

Japanese fashion designer Junko Koshino took an avantgarde approach when designing neoprene coats circa 1989. Fashion curator Harold Koda wrote, "Koshino challenges almost every preconception about fashion, from the materials available for clothing to the way in which clothing serves

the commonwealth and the individual."[33] Koshino was one of the first designers to use neoprene as a fashion fabric; other designers often referenced the fit and sculptural quality of neoprene while using more traditional fabrics. Her coats ranged from oversized, full-length garments to tailored, cutaway tailcoats. The nylon lining provided comfort to the wearer, while the trim added fashionable detail. A turnlock closure referenced the fastener used in the 1960s beaver-tail-style wet suits. In some of the coats, thick industrial zippers were incorporated to create a securely sealed pocket.

Bob Mackie, a "designer to the stars" known for his glitzy evening pieces, was inspired by the surfers at Malibu beach. He said to *Vogue* in 1989, "Sports are a way of life. So it comes naturally to take that athletic influence to clothes, then add a little dazzle."[34] He designed a short, evening jumpsuit that glistened with bugle beads in blocks of color that ran down the side of the body and on the shoulders. The front zipper referenced the closure on a surfer's wet suit. Herb Ritts illustrated the athletic aspect of the jumpsuit by photographing it on Naomi Campbell while she ran along the beach. An editorial, titled "Close Fit," discussed the fashionable trend of exercising that was influenced by the Summer 1988 Olympics in Seoul. The tight fit of wet suits was perfectly in sync with the body-conscious style of the time.

Christian Francis Roth took a more playful approach to his scuba reference in 1990. Black trompe l'oeil straps were stitched around the waist and over the shoulders to connect with a metallic tank appliqué on the back of a navy, cotton sateen jacket (fig. 145). The tank was inscribed "CFR 1990," an abbreviation of the designer's name combined with the year of the collection. The piece was available for special order at exclusive boutiques for $1,900.

The spring 1991 collections by Chanel (Karl Lagerfeld), Donna Karan, and Geoffrey Beene were inspired by surfing wet suits. Karl Lagerfeld transformed the wet suit into a chic, two-piece suit and referred to the look as "the city surfer, because it's perfect for diving into the nightlife from Paris to Rome to London to New York."[35] The long boxy jacket, available in four colorways—blue, yellow, red, and

white—was covered in sequins, trimmed with the classic black Chanel braid, and finished off with a full-length zipper (fig. 146). The sequins glistened in a way identical to the sleek surface of neoprene, and the braid highlighted the lines similar to the seams of a wet suit. Lagerfeld explained, "I simply took the sporty style of the surfer and stamped it out in sequins the color of the California waves."[36] Lagerfeld replaced the typical Chanel skirt with a pair of black Lycra pedal pushers to give the suit a sportier look. Supermodel Linda Evangelista, walking down the runway wearing the blue-sequined jacket and carrying a matching surfboard

144
(facing) *Vogue*, June 2011, photograph by Craig McDean, model Raquel Zimmermann

145
Christian Francis Roth scuba jacket, 1990, model Pamela Telford

1991" to Chanel, Donna Karan, and Geoffrey Beene, who took "inspiration from the zip-up-the-front wet suits surfers wear."[37] The red "Scuba watch" header again uses the term incorrectly. This confusion continues to occur throughout other fashion magazines and it is understandable, because both sports utilize wet suits. To further complicate matters, the Dive N' Surf shop has, since its incarnation, sold wet suits for both scuba diving and surfing, as have other similar retailers.

Karan's spring 1991 collection was inspired by the simplicity and sculptural quality of the neoprene wet suit. Picking up on the shifting silhouette she said, "The narrow jacket is the cut of the new age for me. Sloppy, long, and overscale looks wrong suddenly. The key is double-faced wool. That allows for a modern, molded silhouette."[38] The thickness of double-faced wool allows the fabric to hold its shape, similar to neoprene, and was often used by couturiers such as André Courrèges during the 1960s to create structural, futuristic-looking fashions. Karan's elongated white jacket was paired with a short shirt that extended an inch below the jacket, closely resembling the length of a surfer's wet suit. Further mirroring the look of the wet suit were the jacket's long sleeves and high neckline. The long center zipper allowed for ease getting in and out of the jacket, similar to a wet suit, while the bias-side zippers were more aesthetic and followed the curve of the hips. Karan said, "For me, the zip-front narrow jacket is the natural evolution from soft and fluid to sharp and graphic."[39] The $1,390 jacket proved to be the cornerstone of her collection, and was reordered continuously until she was completely sold out. In one interview, Karan's spokesperson referred to it as a scuba jacket.

Geoffrey Beene often used sports references in his collections. The most famous examples were part of his spring 1967 collection, which included a sequined evening dress inspired by a football jersey. For spring 1991, he designed form-fitting black jackets paired with short-sleeve and strapless dresses that were contrasted with long, white, industrial zippers. In André Leon Talley's cover story for January 1991 Vogue, "Fashion 1991," Beene explains, "This

was, according to the press, the highlight of the show. Lagerfeld's jackets graced the cover of Vogue in January 1991, modeled by Niki Taylor, Stephanie Roberts, and Audrey Benoit, each wearing a different colorway. These were incorrectly described as "scuba jackets" by the magazine.

Fashion often misuses the term "scuba" by treating it as if it were a general term to describe surfing, when it is actually the acronym for the *self-*contained *underwater breathing apparatus* used for deep-sea diving. Inside the aforementioned January 1991 issue of Vogue, editor André Leon Talley dedicated four pages of the eighteen-page editorial "Fashion

**146**
CHANEL, spring/summer 1991 ready-to-wear collection,
*Vogue*, January 1991, photograph by Guy Marineau,
model Linda Evangelista

spring, the white zipper replaces the white piqué collar of the past seasons. It is an accent that brings a sense of clarity and neatness. The surfer's wet suit is an inspiration … because it affords natural elegance and comfort in movement".[40] Similar to Karan, Beene used the characteristics of the fabric—in this case stretch material—to create a second skin.

Two months later, the style section of the *Los Angeles Times* published a major article on the wet-suit trend, titled, "'I'd Like to Be Under the Sea' Is Back in Fashion, in a Slick Wet Suit Look."[41] This article discussed the major success of the Chanel collection and how it spurred a trend for other designers to create less expensive versions of the "wet suit" ensemble. Some of these could be purchased for $250, as compared to $4,110 for the Chanel version. "Like catsuits and leggings, the scuba suit owes its popularity to stretchy Lycra-blend fabrics," said the article, "the jackets themselves hug the torso and look best paired with biker shorts, leggings or a short, slim skirt."[42]

Three years after *Vogue*'s cover story "Fashion 1991," the magazine featured a two-page editorial, entitled "Talking Fashion: Fit and Fashionable," that highlighted the sports-influence trend at its peak. Within the editorial, the spring 1991 collections by Chanel and Geoffrey Beene were shown alongside Donna Karan's fall 1994 collection for DKNY. The caption reads, "Making Waves: The last thing a surfer wants is to find himself at scuba depths, but when Karl Lagerfeld for Chanel and Geoffrey Beene dipped into these influences, they were inspired. Now Donna Karan hopes DKNY's neoprene styles will swim off her racks for spring."[43] Neoprene fabric coated with nylon created incredible volume in a fuchsia dress from her fall 1994 DKNY collection (fig. 147). The curved seams shaped the bodice of the dress—similar to the way a corset is constructed—and connected to a box-pleated skirt that created a voluminous, feminine effect. In contrast to Junko Koshino's more avant-garde neoprene tailcoat, Karan designed a practical dress that could easily be worn off the runway. One would assume she meant to reference deep-sea diving or surfing based on the use of

neoprene and nylon for her dresses, but Karan styled the looks with swimming goggles on the runway, further blurring her sports references.

Beginning in the early 2000s, a second wave of designers, including Yohji Yamamoto, Balenciaga (by Nicolas Ghesquière), Alexander McQueen, Burberry, and Raf Simons were inspired by neoprene and wet suits. One of the most intriguing was Junya Watanabe's spring 2000 collection, "Function and Practicality." Models wearing evening dresses passed under a section of water that rained down on them, while audience members were stunned that the

**147**
DKNY, dress, neoprene, nylon, fall/winter 1994,
New York, The Museum at FIT

148
Junya Watanabe, spring/summer
2000 runway

fabrics were unaffected by the water. This performance revealed Watanabe's masterfully engineered waterproof fabrics, and these garments were juxtaposed with permeable fabrics, such as wool and silk, covered with a protective layer of plastic. Four looks were inspired by scuba-diving wet suits, including two sculptural suits that Watanabe tailored out of thick, silver, synthetic fabric to create a sleek appearance. The suits featured sheer circular cutouts and piping details that mirrored the seam tape in wet suits (fig. 148). A dress style appeared to be constructed from the flat pattern pieces of a wet-suit jacket. Vogue.com described the collection as "a seamless display of refinement, architectural construction, and clarity of vision that relied on technologically advanced fabric and techniques coupled with Watanabe's impeccably pure sense of style."[44]

French shoe designers Pierre Hardy and Christian Louboutin have also been fascinated with scuba diving. In 2008, Hardy introduced a collection of deep-sea- and scuba-inspired stilettos. His fashionable, lace-up booties reference those worn by scuba divers, which completely cover the foot (fig. 149). The tongue of the shoe is flipped over to secure the laces, similar to the extra flap on the zipper of a wet suit. Evocative of the bright colors and seams used in wet suits, Hardy outlines the color-blocked sections of neoprene using thin black piping. That season, Vogue featured another pair of his scuba-inspired stilettos, saying, "Though we would never recommend you go deep-sea diving in these extreme neoprene stilettos, designer Pierre Hardy had that exact ocean sport in mind."[45] The shoe combined wet-suit materials, seen in the three, bright-blue nylon bands and the black neoprene base (fig. 150). The magazine said the shoe's back-zipper detail was taken from surfing wet suits (although Hardy was actually referencing a diving wet suit) and that the unique shape of the heel was inspired by waves. Hardy joked that when "turned upside down it [the heel] transforms into a shark fin." In this feature, the lines between scuba diving and surfing were once again blurred.

On its June/July 2010 cover, L'Officiel featured model Ali Stephens in a Chloé swimsuit and scuba gear. Inside

the magazine, a two-page story highlighted images from the spring 2010 runway collections—inspired by deep sea and surfing—interspersed with photographs of Jacques Cousteau's deep-sea expeditions. The title of the story, "The Fashion of Silence," played on the title of Cousteau's book and documentary film, *The Silent World.* The write-up of the spring 2010 collections announced, "It is the call of the open sea that guides the fashion planet this summer . . . this season, the icon, the one, the only, Commander Cousteau."[46] The feature discussed a number of collections, such as that by Frida Giannini for Gucci, which included a ribbed leather jacket and swimsuit, both fastened with thick industrial zippers that resembled those on a diving jacket. The designers at Proenza Schouler looked to their childhood surfing memories when designing blue-green iridescent dresses and skirts that recalled the colors of the ocean. Peter Dundas's collection for Pucci was inspired by his scuba-diving explorations. His vision was translated into a variety of aquatic-blue printed dresses and neoprene suits.

Alexander McQueen's spring 2010 collection, "Plato's Atlantis"—the last presented by McQueen himself—is described as one of the most innovative and breathtaking collections in recent fashion history. McQueen was an avid scuba diver, and his collection was inspired by a 2009 scuba-diving trip to the Maldives. Journalist Sarah Mower described his collection as "casting an apocalyptic forecast of the future ecological meltdown of the world: mankind is made up of creatures that evolved from the sea, and we may be heading back to an underwater future as the ice caps dissolve."[47] Within the collection, McQueen designed intricate computerized prints of fish, giant squid, and fictional deep-sea creatures. Each print was uniquely engineered to complement the shape of the dress. Voluminous circular tops and dresses made out of iridescent fabrics evoked bioluminescent creatures in the deepest reaches of the ocean (fig. 152). McQueen also referenced the standard diving suit in a green, shot-silk jumpsuit adorned with a multicolored jeweled collar that extended up the length of the neck (fig. 151).

More recently, Thom Browne experimented with the use of neoprene and the idea of surfing wet suits in his men's spring 2017 collection. The seventeen-minute presentation took place in three stages, beginning with models shuffling down the runway in full-length, oversized surfing wet suits

**149**
Pierre Hardy, neoprene, 2008

**150**
Pierre Hardy, 2008,
photograph by Richard Pierce

embossed to resemble Browne's signature gray suit (fig. 153). They then removed the gray wet suits to showcase variations of colorful, three-piece neoprene suits that were finely tailored to fit the body—typical of Browne's style (fig. 154). Next, these suits were unzipped in the back, revealing that the three-piece suits had been an illusion—in actuality they were single wet suits. The final garment revealed was a vintage-style, unitard bathing suit. Journalist Alexander Fury enthused, "kudos to Browne, because when all the layers were peeled off these were wonderfully inventive,

technically stunning clothes."[48] Browne's innovative, tailored neoprene suits challenged the characteristics of the fabric as well as fashion's perception of the wet suit.

### The Future of our Oceans and Fashion

Dr. Sylvia Earle began exploring the oceans in 1953. She has spent a total of seven thousand hours underwater. In 1970, she led the Tektite II mission, a team of female aquanauts who lived underwater for two weeks. Through her seven

151<br>Alexander McQueen, spring/summer 2010 runway<br>ensemble inspired by standard diving suit,<br>photograph by Marcio Madeira

152<br>Alexander McQueen, spring/summer 2010 runway<br>ensemble inspired by bioluminescent deep-sea<br>creatures, photograph by Marcio Madeira

**153, 154**
Thom Browne, spring/summer 2017, menswear presentation,
photographs by Dan and Corina Lecca

decades of exploring, she has seen the discovery of new ocean species and has also witnessed the destruction of many of the same species by overfishing. Environmentalist Al Gore described her as "the face of marine biology. She has taken a lifetime to make herself an expert in a topic that is central to the future of human civilization."[49] In her 2014 documentary *Mission Blue,* she explains the significance of our oceans as the main supplier of the oxygen we consume, poignantly stating, "No ocean, no life, no ocean, no us." She has made it her mission to educate the public and to protect endangered parts of the oceans. She recently partnered with Google Earth to begin mapping life under the sea. This technology has enabled the public to explore the oceans from a diver's perspective without stepping into the water. While Earle is focused on restoring the oceans' ecosystems, other explorers are discovering new regions.

Jacques Cousteau once said, "Impossible missions are the only successful ones." As technology continues to advance, explorers are able to unearth new life-forms. In the latter part of the twentieth century, two new ecosystems were discovered, revealing that life could exist in the extreme conditions of the deep sea. Creatures were discovered, such as mussels and tube worms, that do not need sunlight to survive; they receive their energy from methane and sulfides rising from the earth's core. Despite these findings, most of the ocean floor is still largely unknown, with only about 10 percent currently explored.[50] Today, explorers are pushing the boundaries and depths of the ocean. In 2012, the filmmaker James Cameron—of *Titanic* and *Avatar* fame—became the third person to reach the deepest known point on earth: the Mariana Trench, located in the western Pacific Ocean. In 1960, Don Walsh and Jacques Piccard made the first descent into the Trench, 6.8 miles down, in four hours and forty-eight minutes; however, they were unable to take any photographs because of the dust cloud they created when they landed. Improvements in technology allowed Cameron to reach the bottom in about half that time. The *Deepsea Challenger* submersible (2.5 stories high) was equipped with a variety of customized instruments designed to collect scientific data and specimens. Cameron's 3-D cameras filmed his expedition for his 2014 documentary, *Deepsea Challenge 3D.* His findings continue to inspire further exploration and to expand the range of possibilities regarding new habitats and life-forms under the sea.

Back on dry land, groundbreaking fashion designer Iris van Herpen pushes the limits of her materials and silhouettes, and especially through her unique collaborations. For her fall 2012 collection, she collaborated with architect Philip Beesley to create biomorphic-shaped garments previously unseen in fashion. The press release said that van Herpen's "inspiration is yet another scientific experiment; this time her inspiration is drawn from a project led by Philip Beesley called *Hylozoic Ground.* His almost living sculptures and environments suggest that a future city could operate as a living being."[51] Layered strips of coated metallic gather to form curved extensions of the arm, and the result is a look that closely resembles structures seen in deep sea (fig. 155). Van Herpen's unique creations offer an avant-garde vision of fashion for the future, while deep-sea explorers continue to ponder all the possibilities of life underwater.

**155**
Iris van Herpen, fall/winter 2012

# NOTES

## Expedition: Fashion from the Extreme

1   Cousteau's phrase about Verne's *Twenty Thousand Leagues under the Sea* is frequently cited, most often by one of Verne's leading English-language translators, Frederick Paul Walter.

2   Cited James E. Gunn, *Inside Science Fiction* (Lanham, MD: Scarecrow Press, 2006), 210.

3   "French Cheer Frank Borman," *Daytona Beach Morning Journal*, February 6, 1969, 37.

4   Edward R. Tufte, *Visual Explanations: Images and Quantities, Evidence and Narrative* (Cheshire, CT: Graphics Press, 1997), 95.

5   Cited Gunn, *Inside Science Fiction*, 210.

## Dress, Image, and Cultural Encounter in the Heroic Age of Polar Exploration

1   Barbara Schweger, "Documentation and Analysis of the Clothing Worn by Non-native Men in the Canadian Arctic Prior to 1920, with an Emphasis on Footwear" (master's thesis, University of Alberta, Faculty of Home Economics, 1983).

2   It was also a logistical headache, requiring the ability to marshal and organize huge amounts of people, money, and supplies. See Felix Driver, *Geography Militant: Cultures of Exploration and Empire* (Oxford: Blackwell, 2001), 9.

3   Nicholas Thomas, "Appropriation/Appreciation: Settler Modernism in Australia and New Zealand," in *The Empire of Things: Regimes of Value and Material Culture*, ed. Fred R. Myers (Santa Fe: School of American Research Press, 2001), 139.

4   Ruth Phillips, *Trading Identities: The Souvenir in Native North American Art from the Northeast, 1700–1900* (Seattle: University of Washington Press, 1998), xiii.

5   Some scholars have suggested that the phenomenon of explorers modeling garments on clothing of the North American Inuit specifically is the result of historical accidents. Early European explorers searching westward for the legendary Northwest Passage encountered Greenlandic and eastern Canadian Inuit peoples before, almost inevitably, their ships became locked in winter ice and they were unable to move further west. Thus, the material culture of these areas, including local dress as well

as dogsleds and snow igloos, largely became the Western image of all Arctic peoples by the nineteenth century. See Hugh Brody, *Living Arctic: Hunters of the Canadian North* (Seattle: University of Washington Press, 1987), 17–19.

6   There are undoubtedly specific factors that influence each human's ability to survive in an extremely cold, dry, windy climate for long periods of time: nutrition, preexisting medical conditions, etc. As this paper is less concerned with the science of the human body in polar regions and more with the cultural and symbolic dimensions of clothing, the response of the body to cold will be assumed to be the same from person to person. However, there is now an extensive body of scientific work on the response of the human body to polar environments, including the variable of clothing. For just a few examples, see Ken Parsons, *Human Thermal Environments: The Effects of Hot, Moderate, and Cold Environments on Human Health, Comfort, and Performance* (Boca Raton: CRC/Taylor & Francis, 2002), M. K. Bakkevig and R. Nielsen, "Optimal Combination of Garments in Work Clothing for Cold and Wet Environments," *Arctic Medical Research* 53 (1994), 311–13, and A. F. Rogers, "Antarctic Climate, Clothing and Acclimatization," in *Polar Human Biology*, ed. O. G. Edholm and E. K. E. Gunderson (London: Heinemann, 1973), 265–89. This last article discusses research conducted on clothing in the field during the 1955–1958 Commonwealth Trans-Antarctic Expedition.

7   Schweger, "Clothing Worn by Non-native Men," 1983.

8   Marionne Cronin, "Dog Sleds, Parkas, and Airplanes: Material Histories of Polar Exploration," in *Moving Worlds* vol. 15, no. 2, "The Postcolonial Arctic" (2015), 76–78.

9   Nicholas Thomas, *Entangled Objects: Exchange, Material Culture, and Colonialism in the Pacific* (Cambridge, MA: Harvard University Press, 1991), 4.

10  A note on terminology: The term "Eskimo" has been used historically to describe all peoples of the Arctic region who spoke languages of the Eskaleutian family (and culturally, were often conflated by outsiders with each other),

and is still in use today in Alaska. However, the term has fallen out of favor in Canada and Greenland, where it is considered pejorative. Today, most of the peoples formerly referred to as Eskimos prefer to use self-names from their own respective languages: Inuit (Canadian Arctic and Greenland), Yuit (northeastern Siberia and St. Lawrence Island, Alaska), Yupik (southwestern Alaska) and Iñupiat (northern Alaska). In 1977, in order to present a unified nomenclature, the Inuit Circumpolar Conference deemed that all present-day persons formerly described as Eskimos should be called Inuit. See Betty Issenman and Catherine Rankin, *Ivalu: Traditions of Inuit Clothing* (Montreal: McCord Museum of Canadian History, 1988), 18–19, and Shari M. Huhndorf, *Going Native: Indians in the American Cultural Imagination* (Ithaca: Cornell University Press, 2001), 79.

11  For a more extensive discussion of regional differences in the North American Arctic, across time and place, see J. C. H. King, Birgit Pauksztat, and Robert Storrie, eds., *Arctic Clothing* (London: The British Museum Press, 2005). As Julia Emberley has noted, it is important to understand these fashionable components of Inuit dress: "The symbolic dimensions of Inuit fashion must be foregrounded because too often the assumption is that such clothing functions solely in a utilitarian manner and indeed lacks the signifying capacities already associated with 'Western dress.'" See Emberley, *The Cultural Politics of Fur* (Ithaca: Cornell University Press, 1997), 178.

12  For a more comprehensive survey of traditional fur clothing in the North American Arctic, see Betty Issenman, "Inuit Skin Clothing: Construction and Motifs," in *Études/Inuit/Studies* vol. 9, no. 2 (1985), 101–119, *Sinews of Survival: The Living Legacy of Inuit Clothing* (Vancouver: University of British Columbia Press, 2000), and Birgit Pauksztat, "The Arctic," in *Berg Encyclopedia of World Dress and Fashion: The United States and Canada*, ed. Phyllis G. Tortora (Oxford: Bloomsbury, 2010), 366–75. For more on gut parkas, see Erin Freedman, "Sheer Boundaries: Gutskin in Indigenous Arctic Material Culture" (master's thesis, Bard Graduate

Center, Decorative Arts, Design History, Material Culture, 2015). Like all forms of dress, Inuit fashion has changed over time, and after contact with whalers, traders, and missionaries it began to incorporate imported materials, including woven and knitted textiles, and modern synthetic fabrics. For a cheeky and stereotype-busting look at contemporary Inuit dressing, see Joseph Flowers's blog *Folks Dressed Up Like Eskimos* (folksdresseduplikeeskimos.tumblr.com).

13  J. C. H. King, "Introduction," in *Arctic Clothing*, ed. J. C. H. King, et al. (London: The British Museum Press, 2005), 12.

14  Issenman, *Sinews of Survival*, 38–39, 176.

15  V. Kapsali, "Biomimetics and the Design of Outdoor Clothing," in *Textiles for Cold Weather Apparel*, ed. J. T. Williams (Cambridge: Woodhead Publishing, 2009), 120. While they are made of high-tech synthetic fabrics instead of fur, even modern military clothes for cold weather are made according to traditional Inuit design principles. See C. Thwaites, "Cold-weather Clothing," in Eugene Wilusz, ed. *Military Textiles* (Cambridge: Woodhead Publishing, 2008), 156–79.

16  King, "Introduction," 12.

17  For an introduction to the chronology of Arctic and Antarctic expeditions, see William J. Mills, *Exploring Polar Frontiers: A Historical Encyclopedia, Volumes 1 and 2* (Santa Barbara, CA: ABC-CLIO, 2003).

18  Ibid. See also Barbara Schweger, "Clothing and Textiles as Symbol on Nineteenth Century Arctic Expeditions," in *Ethnicity and Culture (Boreal Institute for Northern Studies Contribution Series)*, ed. Reginald Auger et al. (Calgary: Archaeological Association, University of Calgary, 1987), 288–89.

19  Charles Officer and Jake Page, *A Fabulous Kingdom: The Exploration of the Arctic* (Oxford: Oxford University Press, 2012), 64.

20  Simon Carter, *Rise and Shine: Sunlight, Technology and Health* (Oxford: Berg, 2007), 15–18, and E. T. Renbourn, "The Spine Pad: A Discarded Item of Tropical Clothing," *Journal of the Royal Army Medical Corps*, 102, no. 3 (July 31, 1956), 217–33.

21  Thomas S. Abler, *Hinterland Warriors and Military Dress: European Empires and Exotic Uniforms* (Oxford: Berg, 1999), 111–29.

22  Donald Clay Johnson, "Clothes Make the Empire: British Dress in India," *The Berg Fashion Library*, 2007.

23  Schweger, "Clothing Worn by Non-native Men," 76–134.

24  One notable example of this information sharing comes from the British explorer Francis Leopold McClintock (1819–1907) who wrote up a report entitled "Description of Travelling Equipments" after returning from his Arctic expedition of 1857–1859, which included recommendations for clothing. Later, he passed the manuscript to several members of the British Arctic Expedition (1875–1876) with the request that after their return they would add their comments on the suggested equipment and give the edited

manuscript to the Admiralty, to continue this circulation of knowledge. See Hall to McClintock, October 11, 1877, and "Arctic Committee: Description of Travelling Equipments," both National Maritime Museum archives MCL/38. As Schweger notes, though, many British explorers still made their crews wear European-style "Sunday best" clothes for occasions like weekly prayer services, and British explorers were seldom depicted in native dress in paintings or engravings, no matter what they wore in the field. See Schweger, "Clothing and Textiles," 288. Schweger has noted that even in the mid-nineteenth century, middle men were beginning to emerge who could arrange the manufacture of fur clothing in bulk quantities for large expeditions. See Barbara Schweger, "Clothing in Early Expeditions: An Essential Contribution by the Native Seamstress," University of Alberta Boreal Institute for Northern Studies Contribution Series no. 190 (1980), 46–47.

25  Ann Fienup-Riordan, *Freeze Frame: Alaska Eskimos in the Movies* (Seattle: University of Washington Press, 2003), 13.

26  Ibid., 11–12. See also Huhndorf, *Going Native*, 100–104, and Francis Spufford, *I May Be Some Time* (London: Faber and Faber, 1996), 188–90, 231.

27  Russell Potter, *Arctic Spectacles: The Frozen North in Visual Culture, 1818–1875* (Seattle: University of Washington Press, 2007), 3. See also Brody, *Living Arctic*, 19–21.

28  Stuart A. Weaver, *Exploration: A Very Short Introduction* (Oxford: Oxford University Press, 2015), 4. All three of the explorers profiled in this essay named landmarks they encountered after supporters, including the King Haakon VII Plateau, Mount Don Pedro Christophersen, and the Axel Heiberg Glacier in Antarctica (Amundsen); King Edward VII Land, Mount Longstaff, and Mount Harmsworth, also in Antarctica (Scott); and Cape Thomas Hubbard, Cape Morris Jesup, and Crocker Land in Nunavut and Greenland (Peary).

29  Flaherty's film was sponsored in part by the fur company Revillon Frères. For more on "Northerns" see *Return to the Land of the Head Hunters: Edward S. Curtis, the Kwakwaka'wakw, and the Making of Modern Cinema*, eds. Brad Evans and Aaron Glass (Seattle: University of Washington Press, 2013), 11, 201, and Russell Potter, "Before Nanook: Fact and Fiction in Early Arctic Films" (presentation, Third Annual Explorers Club Polar Film Festival, New York, November 21–22, 2014). In addition to live displays and films, stereotypical images of Inuit were popular in advertising, and continued to be so into the 1960s. For more on the "smiling Eskimo" in advertising, see Amanda Brownridge, "Images that Injure: Stereotypical Representations of the 'Eskimo' in Advertising," in *Aboriginate: Aboriginal Art Research Group [Concordia University]* vol. 1 (2014–2015), 6–21.

30  Beau Riffenburgh, *The Myth of the Explorer: The*

*Press, Sensationalism and Geographic Discovery* (Oxford: Oxford University Press, 1994), 165–90. The most famous example of the intersection of newspapers and explorers, also discussed by Riffenburgh in the same book, was the 1871 meeting between missionary and explorer David Livingstone and explorer and reporter Henry Morton Stanley, which was essentially a publicity stunt orchestrated by James Gordon Bennett Jr., publisher of the *New York Herald*. Bennett went on to sponsor the disastrous *Jeannette* expedition to the Arctic. See ibid., and Hampton Sides, *In the Kingdom of Ice: The Grand and Terrible Polar Voyage of the USS* Jeannette (New York: Doubleday, 2014).

31  This phenomenon in Victorian and Edwardian America has been well documented in work such as Gail Bederman, *Manliness and Civilization: A Cultural History of Gender and Race in the United States, 1880–1917* (Chicago: University of Chicago Press, 1995), and Michael Kimmel, *Manhood in America: A Cultural History* (New York: Oxford University Press, 2011).

32  Lisa Bloom, *Gender on Ice: American Ideologies of Polar Expeditions* (Minneapolis: University of Minnesota Press, 1993), 6.

33  Huhndorf, *Going Native*, 72.

34  Michael F. Robinson, *The Coldest Crucible: Arctic Exploration and American Culture* (Chicago: University of Chicago Press, 2006), 2, 124.

35  Theodore Roosevelt, *Presidential Addresses and State Papers: April 14, 1906, to January 14, 1907* (New York: Review of Reviews, 1910), 1001. For Peary, the admiration was mutual; he named the ship that carried him to the Arctic on his last two voyages the *Roosevelt*.

36  Mills, *Exploring Polar Frontiers, Volume 1*, 510.

37  Quoted in Riffenburgh, *Myth of the Explorer*, 165, emphasis Peary's.

38  For more on Peary's celebrity and connections with elite American benefactors, see Lyle Dick, "'The men of prominence are "among those present" for him': How and Why America's Elites Made Robert Peary a National Icon," in *North by Degree: New Perspectives on Arctic Exploration*, ed. Susan A. Kaplan and Robert McCracken Peck (Philadelphia: American Philosophical Society, 2013), 3–48.

39  Ernest Ingersoll, *The Conquest of the North* (New York: C. S. Hammon & Co., 1909), 21. For more examples of Peary's nationalistic rhetoric, see Robert Peary, "The Value of Arctic Exploration," *National Geographic* vol. 14, no. 12 (1903), 429–36.

40  Riffenburgh, *Myth of the Explorer*, 166.

41  Quoted in Robinson, *The Coldest Crucible*, 120.

42  Robert Peary, *Secrets of Polar Travel* (New York: Century, 1917), 160–61. This entire chapter provides a fascinating look at Peary's typical polar ensembles.

43  Quoted in Riffenburgh, *Myth of the Explorer*, 166.

44  Robinson, *The Coldest Crucible*, 120.

45  Bruce Henderson, *True North: Peary, Cook and the Pole* (New York: W. W. Norton, 2005), 81.

46  James Hanson, "Laced Coats and Leather Jackets: The Great Plains Intercultural Clothing

Exchange," in *Plains Indian Studies: Collection in Honor of John Ewers and Waldo Wedel*, eds. Douglas Ubelaker and Herman Viola (Washington, DC: Smithsonian, 1982), 105–117. This kind of cross-dressing was not limited to flashy entertainers or explorers. At the same time, anthropologists were also known to pose in indigenous clothing for photographs, to use as models for later museum dioramas and book illustrations, to serve as salvage of certain cultural practices, or to prove their fieldwork credentials. Pioneering anthropologist Franz Boas posed in a Baffin Island fur ensemble for images that were later reproduced in his work *The Central Eskimo*. An interesting future research project might be to compare "native cross-dressing" for entertainment vs. scholarly purposes. For a genealogy of the Boas images, see Jenna Grant, "Screening Room: Collecting in the Collection," Fieldsights—Visual and New Media Review, *Cultural Anthropology Online*, January 14, 2015, www.culanth.org/fieldsights/628-screening-room-collecting-in-the-collection.

47 Hanson, "Laced Coats and Leather Jackets." Historian Michael F. Robinson has argued that in addition to fears about over-civilization, in American cities there was often additional anxiety about the robustness of nativist white culture in the face of "hordes" of recently arrived immigrants. He writes that American polar explorers like Peary "gave voice to hopes and fears that seem, at first glance, far removed from the Arctic regions: about the status of the United States as a civilized nation, about threats to its manly character and racial purity . . . about the dangers of progress. The Arctic, in other words, presented a faraway stage on which explorers played out dramas that were unfolding very close to home." Peary's white-man-turned-native act might then have played particularly well in the cities of the northeast, especially New York, that were his fundraising bases. See Robinson, *The Coldest Crucible*, 3. Schweger has noted a connection between American polar explorers of the nineteenth century and American romanticism and a spirit of frontier self-reliance, but fails to note a contradiction between this professed self-reliance and actual reliance on the Inuit. See Schweger, "Clothing and Textiles as Symbol," 289–91.

48 Robert Peary, *The North Pole: Its Discovery in 1909 Under the Auspices of the Peary Arctic Club* (New York: Frederick A. Stokes, 1910), 272.

49 Ibid., 43.

50 Kenn Harper, *Give Me My Father's Body* (New York: Pocket Books, 2000). Harper's book also gives an overview of Peary's 1909 museum exhibit featuring models of native "helpers," and an account of the six Inughuit individuals he brought to New York as living specimens, in conjunction with the American Museum of Natural History—an institution headed by Morris K. Jesup, a founding member of the Peary Arctic Club—and anthropologist Franz Boas.

51 Spufford, *I May Be Some Time*, 213, 232. Peary's performance of white masculinity has often been discussed in the context of his relationships with Inuit men and women *and* with Henson, who was African-American. See Bloom, *Gender on Ice*, 96–109, and Emma Bonanomi, "To be Black and American: Matthew Henson and His Post-Pole Lecture Tour, 1909–1910," in *North by Degree*, 185–210.

52 Riffenburgh, *Myth of the Explorer*, 168–69.

53 See Roland Huntford, *The Last Place on Earth: Scott and Amundsen's Race to the South Pole* (New York: Random House Modern Library, 1999) and Stephen R. Bown, *The Last Viking: The Life of Roald Amundsen* (Philadelphia: Da Capo Press, 2012).

54 See Huntford, *Last Place on Earth*, and Spufford, *I May Be Some Time*.

55 See Ranulph Fiennes, *Race to the Pole: Tragedy, Heroism and Scott's Antarctic Quest* (New York: Hyperion, 2004) and Susan Solomon, *The Coldest March: Scott's Fatal Antarctic Expedition* (New Haven: Yale University Press, 2002). While Scott did bring some sled dogs, as well as Manchurian ponies and three early motorized sleds to Antarctica, he used them only for the initial work of setting up supply depots and to support the core South Pole team for the beginning of their journey. The men who made the final trek to the South Pole manhauled their supplies.

56 Though Peary was enlisted in the US Navy for twenty-nine years, he was only on active duty for about twelve, with the rest of the time spent on extended leave for exploring and fundraising. See Harper, *Give Me My Father's Body*, 205. Scott, who had joined the British Royal Navy as a thirteen-year-old cadet, was released on half pay to plan and execute his second Antarctic expedition. See Max Jones, "Introduction," in *Journals: Captain Scott's Last Expedition*, by Robert F. Scott, ed. Max Jones (Oxford: Oxford University Press, 2005), lvi.

57 Quoted in Huntford, *Last Place on Earth*, 57–58. Though Cook gave Amundsen his first direct experience with fur garments, Amundsen had likely first heard of the benefits of Inuit clothing in 1893 as a twenty-year-old student in Christiania (now Oslo), when he attended a lecture given by the explorer Eivind Astrup, who had accompanied Peary to Greenland in 1891–1892. See Huntford, *Last Place on Earth*, 29.

58 For this expedition, Amundsen received a grant of 10,000 kroner from King Oscar II (king of a combined Sweden-Norway) in 1901). Yet he had no other major sponsors, and relied largely on the support of family members and his own accumulation of debt. Amundsen famously cast off the *Gjøa* from its dock in Christiania in the middle of the night as he feared his creditors would have his boat impounded for his unpaid bills. See Bown, *The Last Viking*, 54, and Tor Bomann-Larsen, *Roald Amundsen*, trans. Ingrid Chistophersen (Stroud, Gloucestershire: Sutton Publishing, 2006), 34.

59 By the turn of the twentieth century, Nansen (1861–1930) was considered an elder statesman of polar exploration, and was consulted by numerous individuals traveling to the far north or Antarctica. Like Amundsen, he favored bringing both Inuit-style fur clothing and clothes of Scandinavian-style densely woven wool to cope with changing temperatures, precipitation, and types of physical activity. See Hjalmar Johansen, *With Nansen in the North: A Record of the* Fram *Expedition in 1893–1896*, trans. H. L. Brækstad (London: Ward, Lock, 1899), 44, 156.

60 Roald Amundsen, "To the North Magnetic Pole and through the Northwest Passage (presentation, Royal Geographical Society, London, February 11, 1907), text reprinted in Geir Kløver, ed., *Cold Recall: Reflections of a Polar Explorer* (Oslo: The Fram Museum, 2009), 23, 30. Amundsen especially sought out Netsilingmiut clothes made from the dense fur of caribou calves killed in autumn, when the animals grow their winter coats. Caribou fur is especially insulating because the hair follicles are hollow, and these trap warm air against the skin. See J. C. H. King, *First Peoples, First Contacts: Native Peoples of North America* (Cambridge, MA: Harvard University Press, 1999), 189. For more of Amundsen's thoughts about clothing on this expedition, see Roald Amundsen, *The North West Passage* (New York: E. P. Dutton & Co., 1908), vol. 1, 149–50.

61 Riffenburgh, *Myth of the Explorer*, 114.

62 Amundsen, "To the North Magnetic Pole," 30.

63 Huntford, *Last Place on Earth*, 92. Amundsen saw his Inuit "allies" according to Darwinian terms, once remarking that, among the Netsilingmiut, "the adaptation [to the environment] is perfect." See Bown, *The Last Viking*, 79. Although Amundsen's primary goal in Uqsuqtuuq was not anthropological study, he did collect many Netsilingmiut objects, which survive in the collection of the Museum of Cultural Heritage at the University of Oslo. Discussion of the clothing items in this collection can be found in Torunn Klokkernes and Nalini Sharma, "The Impact of a Skin Preparation Method on Preservation," in *Arctic Clothing*, ed. J. C. H. King, et al., 91–94.

64 Roald Amundsen, *My Life as an Explorer* (Garden City, NY: Doubleday, Page, 1927), 48.

65 Ibid., 49. Amundsen goes on to say that while the white man may even be brutal toward the "savage" and retain the savage's respect, such respect would dissipate if the white man took liberties with the savage's women, and so Amundsen had urged his men "not to yield to this kind of temptation." Perhaps the strangest chapter in Amundsen's relationship with native polar peoples occurred on the later *Maud* expedition to the Arctic, when he unofficially adopted two native Siberian girls, named Kakonita and Camilla, and brought them home with him to Norway in 1922. They were cared for by Amundsen's brother Leon and his wife for two years before Roald sent them back to live with Camilla's father, a fur trader. Relatively little information survives on Amundsen's

relationship with the girls, whose adoption he later described as an "experiment." See Bown, *The Last Viking*, 220–221, and Bomann-Larsen, *Roald Amundsen*, 195–96, 200, 246, 316–17.

66 Roald Amundsen, *The North West Passage*, 259–60. Despite incidents like this, Dorothy Eber's records of oral histories from the modern community at Gjoa Haven show that Amundsen ("Amusi") and his crew are largely recalled fondly by the Netsilingmiut who knew them, as well as by their descendants. See Dorothy Harley Eber, *Encounters on the Passage: Inuit Meet the Explorers* (Toronto: University of Toronto Press, 2008), 116–30. A more recent biography of Amundsen likewise cites interviews with modern residents of Gjoa Haven who expressed pride that the skills, including making fur clothing, that their ancestors taught Amundsen helped him successfully sail the Northwest Passage and reach the South Pole. See Lynne Cox, *South with the Sun: Roald Amundsen, His Polar Explorations, and the Quest for Discovery* (New York: Knopf, 2011), 148.

67 For more on the Peary-Cook controversy, see Riffenburgh, *Myth of the Explorer*, Henderson, *True North*, Wally Herbert, *The Noose of Laurels: Robert E. Peary and the Race for the North Pole* (New York: Anchor Books, 1990), and Robert M. Bryce, *Cook & Peary: The Polar Controversy, Resolved* (Mechanicsburg, PA: Stackpole Books, 1997).

68 Quoted in Huntford, *Last Place on Earth*, 293.

69 Roald Amundsen, *The South Pole: An Account of the Norwegian Expedition in the* Fram, *1910–1912* (London and New York: J. Murray and L. Keedick, 1913), 78. The prepared reindeer skins were obtained from groups of Sami, the indigenous reindeer-herding peoples of northern Scandinavia, through Amundsen's friend Fritz Zapffe, a Tromsø pharmacist who had connections to local Sami communities.

70 Ibid. Though further research is needed to confirm this, he likely gave the tailor clothing he had obtained and worn at Gjoa Haven as a model.

71 Quoted in Huntford, *Last Place on Earth*, 208. It is Amundsen's letter to Daugaard-Jensen requesting the clothes, dated September 9, 1909, which also provides the earliest evidence of Amundsen's secret change in plans to attempt a voyage to the South Pole.

72 Amundsen, *The South Pole*, 81. This, Amundsen's published account of the voyage, has an extensive discussion of his selection process for all of his gear, including clothing. Amundsen's team switched from wearing the fur outer garments to the gabardine ones after reaching the plateau surrounding the South Pole, when the temperature had warmed to a more moderate –6°F (–21°C) and strenuous skiing and dog-sledding was in order, although the men cut off the hoods from their fur parkas and attached them to the gabardine ones for extra protection for their faces. See Roland Huntford, *Race for the South Pole: The Expedition Diaries of Scott and*

*Amundsen* (New York and London: Continuum, 2010), 160. While the rest of the assemblage had been purchased, Amundsen wrote, "Of our inner garments, we are fondest of the woollen [*sic*] vests Betty [Gustavson, Amundsen's beloved housekeeper] knitted for us." Ibid., 368.

73 Perhaps more than any other textile and clothing company, Burberry has a long history of outfitting polar expeditions, including those led by Scott, Amundsen, Ernst Shackleton, Fridtjof Nansen, Frederick Jackson, Douglas Mawson, and Hubert Wilkins, among others. Anne Melgård of the National Library of Norway has investigated a group of extant fragments of one of Amundsen's tent coverings, which may be the same Burberry fabric as that used to manufacture the men's ski suits. I am very grateful to her for sharing her ongoing research with me.

74 Amanda Lynnes, "Clothing," in *Encyclopedia of the Antarctic, Volume 1*, ed. Beau Riffenburgh (New York: Routledge/Taylor & Francis, 2007), 264.

75 Huntford, *Last Place on Earth*, 364.

76 Not that the Norwegians had no problems at all with their clothes. Anxious that Scott's team would start for the Pole as early as possible, Amundsen ordered his men out of their base camp on September 8, 1911, but within a few days the temperature had dropped to –72°F (–58°C). Amundsen wrote in the middle of a howling blizzard that "when all is said and done, the greatest danger of these low T. [temperatures] is the damage to one's clothes. If we only had a chance to dry out [in calm weather], things would be completely different." See Huntford, *Race for the South Pole*, 43. The team eventually turned back to wait for warmer temperatures and for several of the men to recover from frostbite. Smoothing over this last detail, Amundsen later remarked that, "We human beings might have kept going for some time in this temperature, well clothed as we were, but our dogs could not stand it very long." See Roald Amundsen, "The Norwegian South Polar Expedition" (presentation, Royal Geographical Society, London, November 15, 1912), text reprinted in Kløver, *Cold Recall*, 130.

77 Amundsen's hardest lesson in this area came after the successful end of the *Gjøa* expedition in 1906. Then, problems cabling his message to London's *Times* newspaper, which Amundsen had promised to provide with an exclusive scoop, caused the story to leak and the *Times* subsequently refused to pay. See Bown, *Last Viking*, 86–89.

78 Gerald Christy to Leon Amundsen, June 8, 1911, reprinted in Kløver, *Cold Recall*, 209. Leon secured a lecture tour in Britain through Gerald Christy's The Lecture Agency, Ltd. ("Sole Agents for Sir Ernest Shackleton and Commander Peary").

79 Lee Keedick to Leon Amundsen, May 27, 1912, ibid., 228.

80 Ross D. E. MacPhee, *Race to the End: Amundsen,*

*Scott, and the Attainment of the South Pole* (New York and London: Sterling Innovation, 2010), 7. The 1899 session in the Christiania studio of Daniel Georg Nyblin, with Amundsen dressed in a full Inuit-style fur ensemble, with skis and snowshoes, against a faux background of snow and ice, produced two photos.

81 After detailing all of his preparations for the South Pole expedition, including the selection of clothing, Amundsen summed up his approach to exploration thus: "It is not money alone that makes for the success of such an expedition . . . the greatest factor—the way in which the expedition is equipped—the way in which every difficulty is foreseen, and precautions taken for meeting or avoiding it. Victory awaits him who has everything in order—luck, people call it. Defeat is certain for him who has neglected to take the necessary precautions in time; this is called bad luck." Amundsen, *The South Pole*, 370. This excerpt reads like a subtle dig at Scott's defenders who blamed his defeat and death on bad luck, especially bad weather.

82 "Robert Falcon Scott and H. R. Bowers, Stores Lists, 1910–1913: List B. Main Party Relief Stores. Clothing, Coal, Oil, etc." Scott Polar Research Institute archives, MS 1453/30/D and British Antarctic Expedition, 1910–1913 Volume 2: Part 2 of E. L. Atkinson's report. Ship, Equipment, Hut, etc. Scott Polar Research Institute archives, MS 280/28/2; ER. This report from Atkinson, expedition surgeon, contains perhaps the most extensive discussion of the team's clothing, as well as notes on manhauling technique.

83 Ibid. Writing his report of the expedition in 1913, Atkinson attributed the need for this special preparation to the fact that the feet of Scott's British men were larger than those of Sami men.

84 Scott famously wrote, "In my mind, no journey ever made with dogs can approach the height of that fine conception which is realized when a party of men go forth to face hardships, dangers, difficulties with their own unaided efforts. . . . Surely in this case the conquest is more nobly and splendidly won." See R. F. Scott, *The Voyage of the Discovery, Volume 1* (London: Smith, Elder, 190), 343. As MacPhee has noted, by this time dogsledding had long been embraced by Western men working as agents for the Hudson's Bay Company in the Arctic, "who had no need to prove their manhood by self-haulage." See MacPhee, *Race to the End*, 76.

85 Lynnes, *Encyclopedia of the Antarctic*, s.v. "Clothing."

86 The expedition diaries kept by Scott and others on both the *Discovery* and *Terra Nova* expeditions are riddled with anecdotes about the difficulties of drying out clothing, trying to keep it from freezing, and having to wear it even when it became stuck in strange shapes. The men on the march to the South Pole slept with their sleeping bags closed around their heads, and condensation from their breath froze inside the sleeping bags too. For a brief summary of these incidents, see Solomon, *The Coldest March*, 23–24.

87  For more on the medical aspects of Scott's return journey, including their relationship to clothing, see Lewis George Halsey and Mike Adrian Stroud, "Could Scott Have Survived With Today's Physiological Knowledge?," *Current Biology* vol. 21, no. 12 (June 2011), R457–R461.

88  Atmospheric chemist Susan Solomon has used the meteorological data collected as part of Scott's expedition, as well as modern climate modeling, to argue that the winter of 1912 on Antarctica's Ross Ice Shelf where Scott's team perished was colder than usual. See Solomon, *Coldest March*.

89  For a thorough examination of the historiography of Scott, see Stephanie Barczewski, *Antarctic Destinies: Scott, Shackleton and the Changing Face of Heroism* (London and New York: Hambledon Continuum, 2007).

90  Stephanie Barczewski, "The Historiography of Antarctic Exploration," in *Reinterpreting Exploration: The West in the World*, ed. Dane Kennedy (Oxford: Oxford University Press, 2014), 217–18. One newspaper article on the *Terra Nova* expedition summed up the popular sentiment thus: "Through the energy and daring of Commander Peary the hope that the Union Jack would fly first at the North Pole has been taken from us forever. . . . The people of this country have not been accustomed to take second place in any field of human endeavour." "For the Honour of the Flag," *Daily Mail*, September 13, 1909, in "Album of Press Cuttings," Scott Polar Research Institute archives MS 1453/38; BPC.

91  Historian Max Jones also cites the embarrassments of the Boer War, the looming threat of German industrial and military expansion, Irish nationalism, and labor unrest at home as factors that stoked British popular support for a great national endeavor such as Scott's expedition. See Jones, "Introduction," xxxii.

92  "20,000 GBP for Capt. Scott," *Daily Chronicle*, January 7, 1910, in "Album of Press Cuttings," Scott Polar Research Institute archives MS 1453/38; BPC.

93  Robert F. Scott, "Plans of the British Antarctic Expedition, 1910," *Geographical Journal* 36 (1910), 11–12.

94  MacPhee, *Race to the End*, 18. Scott sent certificates to members of the public who purchased subscriptions, with the note, "With our most sincere gratitude for your patriotic support." "Acknowledgements (3) of receipt of subscriptions, 1909–1910," Scott Polar Research Institute archives MS 1319/14/1-3; D. Scott also received the approval of the Royal Geographical Society but only a paltry £500 financial contribution from them, even though they had previously lavished support on polar expeditions. Leonard Darwin to Robert F. Scott, November 9, 1909, Royal Geographical Society (with IBG) archives RGS/RFS/4a.

95  R. F. Scott, letter to Joseph Kinsey, 22 January, 1910, quoted in Diana Preston, *A First Rate Tragedy* (London: Constable, 1997), 117. Amundsen too received offers from corporate sponsors while he was planning his expedition to the (at the time, stated North) Pole. He wrote to a friend and business associate, "Offers for goods are pouring in: toothpaste, shoe polish, and the most extraordinary articles in a motley mess. Not to forget mouth organs and remedies against hair loss." Quoted in Bomann-Larsen, *Roald Amundsen*, 70.

96  Preston, *First Rate Tragedy*, 39.

97  "1–5 Catalogue, Posters, Invitations, etc. *Discovery* Antarctic Expedition, London, 1904," Scott Polar Research Institute archives, MS 366/14; ER. Jeff Blumenfeld, author of a funding guide for aspiring modern explorers, uses the example of modern explorer Robert Swan, who was able to procure sponsorship from Burberry for an Antarctic trek in the 1980s by citing the company's earlier sponsorship of Scott. See Blumenfeld, *Get Sponsored: A Funding Guide for Would-Be Explorers, Adventurers and Travelers* (New York: Skyhorse Publishing, 2014), 34.

98  Scott to Möller, no date [possibly January 1901], Royal Geographical Society [with IBG] archives RGS/AA/7/1/7 and RGS/AA/7/1/8). Koettlitz, who had earlier served on the Jackson-Harmsworth Expedition to Franz Josef Land in the Arctic between 1894 and 1897, wrote to several Arctic veterans, including Nansen, to inquire about where to purchase fur clothing and boots (Koettlitz to Scott, November 9, 1900, Royal Geographical Society [with IBG] archives RGS/AA/7/1/2), and he investigated prices for Scott (Koettlitz to Scott, November 15, 1900, Royal Geographical Society (with IBG) archives RGS/AA/7/1/3). Scott also relied on Albert Arrmitage, a career sailor and the expedition's navigator, who had also been on the Jackson-Harmsworth Expedition. Scott enlisted him to correspond with a British expat living in Oslo about purchasing furs for Scott through Möller (Somerville to Armitage, March 31, 1901, Royal Geographical Society [with IBG] archives RGS/AA/7/1/9). In a letter to Sir Clements Markham, Armitage made recommendations for a combination of fur and textile clothing: sheepskin coats to be worn onboard the ship; reindeer boots for cold weather and walrus hide for warmer temperatures; rubber boots for wet conditions; tweed breeches; Jaeger wool blouses, singlets, and long drawers; both Jaeger and "Norwegian dog skin" mittens; and "gabardine to cover everything [around the head] when sledging." Armitage also suggested having the British Foreign Office bring a few indigenous Samoyed families from Siberia to London or Norway and "with the skins being supplied to them they could make all necessary fur-garments under supervision." Armitage to Markham, June 5, 1900, Royal Geographical Society (with IBG) archives RGS/AA/7/1/1.

99  Scott, *Voyage of the Discovery*, 319. In this chapter Scott gives a more thorough description of the clothing worn during manhauling, including his praise of the finneskoes. The idea to use reindeer suits to sleep in may have come from Koettlitz, who suggested in his correspondence with Scott (see note 101) to use something akin to a *malitza*, a sack-like fur tunic worn by the indigenous peoples of the Siberian Arctic.

100 Ibid.

101 Scott and others Britons made tantalizing suggestions, here and there, that they suspected the furs they were able to obtain were of poor quality and did not perform as they were supposed to, or that they lacked the ability to judge good quality furs from bad ones and so were taken advantage of by their suppliers. See sources mentioned in n. 98, above; Royal Geographical Society, *The Antarctic Manual, for the Use of the Expedition of 1901*, ed. George Murray (London: Royal Geographical Society, 1901), 258, and E. L. Atkinson's report, MS 280/28/2; ER (Atkinson writes, "He [the explorer choosing furs] must have experience with requirements if he is not himself skilled in the choice of furs. Good finneskoe on snow surfaces will last for a year with good treatment, bad ones will last only a month or less even with good treatment."). David E. Yelverton has written that Scott was forced by his budget to buy lower quality furs from Möller, but I have examined the same correspondence in the Royal Geographical Society archives and not reached the same conclusion. See David E. Yelverton, *Antarctica Unveiled: Scott's First Expedition and the Quest for the Unknown Continent* (Boulder: University Press of Colorado, 2000), 59, 157–58. More research needs to be done to follow up on these threads.

102 E. R. G. R. Evans, "Outfit and Preparation," in R. F. Scott, *Scott's Last Expedition in Two Volumes, Second Volume*, arranged by Leonard Huxley (New York: Dodd, Mead, 1913), 340. Wolsey used the photo of the *Terra Nova* team (fig. 31) as an advertisement in programs for Evans's 1913 lectures on "Captain Scott's Expedition," see Max Jones, *The Last Great Quest: Scott's Antarctic Sacrifice* (Oxford: Oxford University Press, 2003), xi and plate 9.

103 G. H. Boroughs, "Tailoring at the South Pole," *The American Tailor & Cutter*, vol. 34, no. 12 (June 1913), 336–37.

104 Fiennes, *Race to the Pole*, 10. Fiennes continues that ". . . Eskimos, he [Markham] pointed out, had no need to extend their geographical knowledge," using Markham's reasoning that Inuit could never be true explorers, in part to explain why Scott should not be criticized for not adopting more native technologies in his exploratory voyages. While the Inuit may not have had the same goals as Western explorers, it is misguided to suggest that the Inuit would *never* need new geographical information for any reason. For more on Markham's attitudes towards the Inuit, see Heather Davis-Fisch, *Loss and Cultural Remains in Performance: The Ghosts of the Franklin Expedition* (New York: Palgrave Macmillan, 2012), 70–72, and Spufford, *I May Be Some Time*, 234–35.

105 MacPhee has noted that in championing Scott's Antarctic expeditions, Markham never seemed bothered by Scott's lack of Arctic experience: "Scott, the product of a Navy education, had in Markham's estimation all the theoretical background needed to plunge into his new job and succeed brilliantly." See MacPhee, *Race to the End*, 30. For more on Markham's attitudes and Scott's lack of experience, see Spufford, *I May Be Some Time*, 339–415. At the time, Amundsen also noticed this attitude among British explorers. On July 11, 1912, he recorded in his diary an extensive critique of the British explorer Ernest Shackleton, with whom Scott shared many of his methods and gear items: "Then comes S's reference to fur clothes [in his book *The Heart of the Antarctic*]. Furs are not necessary, he opines [because they were not used] on [British Antarctic expeditions on the ships] *Discovery* or *Nimrod*. That is enough to prove that furs are unnecessary. Very possibly so. But [why then] does S. complain so often about the cold on his long Southern journey? . . . One thing, I think I can . . . say, if Shackleton had been equipped in a practical manner, dogs, fur clothes . . . and naturally understood their use . . . well then, the South Pole would have been a closed chapter. . . . The English have loudly and openly told the world that skis and dogs are unusable in these regions and that fur clothes are rubbish. We will see, we will see." Quoted in Huntford, *Last Place on Earth*, 375.

106 Dane Kennedy, "Introduction," in *Reinterpreting Exploration: The West in the World*, ed. Dane Kennedy (Oxford: Oxford University Press, 2014), 2. Kennedy's assertion is echoed somewhat in the comments of J. C. H. King, discussing Inuit clothing's spiritual meanings for its makers, by connecting hunters and makers to fur-bearing animals: "In contemporary Western thought technical achievements have symbolic value, but lack a spiritual unity with the source material. Indeed, for Westerners it could be said that the more efficient a technology, the less it may be endowed with spiritual value." See King, "Introduction," 13.

107 Some historians, including Max Jones, have cited Scott's need to include a scientific program as part of his expedition as a reason for his failure to attain the South Pole first, as it split his planning energy and resources across multiple goals. See Jones, "Introduction," xl. Scott's ideas of modernity and science may have contributed to his rejection of dogsleds, an Inuit mode of transportation, as well as Inuit clothing. Scott experimented with other modern Western technologies, including a hot air balloon on the *Discovery* expedition and the first telephone in Antarctica at his base camp. See Preston *First Rate Tragedy*, 218. For further discussion of modern technology and transportation in polar exploration, see Cronin, "Dog Sleds, Parkas, and Airplanes," 70–80.

108 Amundsen, *The South Pole*, 44.

109 Henry Robertson Bowers, "Conclusion of Lecture on Polar Clothing," Scott Polar Research Institute archives MS 1505 3/3/2/18; BJ.

110 Scott, *Journals: Captain Scott's Last Expedition*, 283.

111 Ibid., 260.

112 Ibid.

113 Cherry-Garrard went on to write a memoir of his time in Antarctica, entitled *The Worst Journey in the World*, a title that referred to the Cape Crozier excursion, not the march to the South Pole. See Apsley Cherry-Garrard, *The Worst Journey in the World: With Scott in Antarctica, 1910–1913* (Mineola, New York: Dover, 2010 [1922]). Scott continued to reassure himself that the textile clothing was adequate, if not ideal. For example, while on the trek to the South Pole, he wrote on Sunday, December 24, 1911, that hauling in "wind blouses" stiff with frozen perspiration was difficult: "With our present clothes it is a fairly heavy plod, but we get over the ground." Scott, *Journals: Captain Scott's Last Expedition*, 358.

114 Huntford, *Race for the South Pole*, 39.

115 Scott wrote a letter to his secretary Francis Drake in October of 1911, while at McMurdo Sound, explaining that "I have written a number of advertisement letters and given Ponting a list of the advertisement photos to be taken." Letter to Francis Drake, October 1911, Scott Polar Research Institute archives MS 1493; D. In contrast, Amundsen put comparatively little effort into photography in Antarctica. He had no dedicated photographer like Ponting. His crew brought a moving-film camera and still cameras south, but Amundsen himself had no photography training to speak of, and the camera he took to the South Pole broke on the return journey. All surviving photos from the trek itself were taken by crew member Olav Bjaaland, with a Kodak pocket camera he brought as part of his twenty-pound allotment of personal gear. Norwegian photographer Anders Beer Wilse, who prepared the surviving photographs as lantern slides for Amundsen's lecture tours, concluded that the explorer had lost "many thousands of kroners' income" in reproduction rights by his lack of attention to good photography. See MacPhee, *Race to the End*, 171.

116 Scott, *Journals: Captain Scott's Last Expedition*, 377. Interestingly, when Scott's diaries were later published the words in bold were removed, likely a choice by the editorial committee—including Scott's widow and a few surviving crew members—to make Scott seem uninterested in publicity and fame, and thus more heroic in his quest. Ibid., 470.

117 R. F. Scott, *Scott's Last Expedition in Two Volumes, First Volume*, arranged by Leonard Huxley (New York: Dodd, Mead and Company, 1913), 416. Several months later, the article in the *American Tailor & Cutter* written by Mandelberg's G. H. Boroughs claimed that "Whatever may have been the cause or causes of the tragic termination of the venture . . . it seems certain that the special clothing which had been produced in accordance with Captain Scott's own carefully planned instructions was in no way responsible for the disaster." See Boroughs, "Tailoring at the South Pole," 336. Scott's eloquent final journal entry, on March 29, 1912, also betrays how exploration had become a profession. He wrote, "For God's sake, look after our people," imploring the British public to financially support his family and the families of his dead crew members, who would be left without their breadwinners and the expected income from publications and lecturing. See Janice Cavell, "Manliness in the Life and Posthumous Reputation of Robert Falcon Scott," *Canadian Journal of History* no. 45 (winter 2010), 546–47.

118 Preston, *First Rate Tragedy*, 120.

119 Measured in clo value, a measurement of the thermal insulation of clothing. One clo unit represents clothing that will allow a person at rest to maintain thermal equilibrium at 70°F (21° C). George Havenith, "Benchmarking Functionality of Historical Cold Weather Clothing: Robert F. Scott, Roald Amundsen, George Mallory," *Journal of Fiber Bioengineering and Informatics* vol. 3 (2010), 121–29. Havenith's research also compared the replica ensembles to a modern ensemble for polar wear made from synthetic fabrics. For a brief introduction to modern polar dressing, see Lynnes, "Clothing," 264–65, and Natalie Cadenhead, "Antarctic Explorer Wear," in *Berg Encyclopedia of World Dress and Fashion: Australia, New Zealand, and the Pacific Islands*, ed. Margaret Maynard (Oxford: Bloomsbury: 2010), 326–331, dx.doi.org/10.2752/BEWDF/EDch7050.

120 Havenith, "Benchmarking Functionality."

121 Thomas, "Appropriation/Appreciation," in *The Empire of Things*, 160.

122 Weaver, *Exploration*, 91.

123 As anthropologist Gísli Pálsson has explained, in the case of the Arctic even the boundaries of the region itself are ambiguous. Some definitions hinge on a certain latitude, others on the tree line, and others on temperature or the length of winter darkness and summer sun. See Gísli Pálsson, "Hot Bodies in Cold Zones: Arctic Exploration," *Scholar & Feminist Online* vol. 7, no. 1 (fall 2008), sfonline.barnard.edu/ice/palsson_01.htm.

124 Thomas, *Entangled Objects*, 26.

125 It is interesting to note the remarks of Captain Robert Bartlett (1875–1946), a Canadian-American sailor who took part in several of Peary's Arctic expeditions. Like Amundsen, he recorded what he saw as the particularly British features of polar exploration. He was invited to see the preparations on board Scott's *Terra Nova* before it departed, and he wrote in his memoir, "Two things especially struck me about what I saw . . . the attitude of the country and the kind of equipment. England really felt this was her own expedition. [Secondly] the basis of all Peary's work was application of Eskimo methods to the white man's problem. The Eskimo for many centuries has learned to clothe himself properly. . . . In contrast to this, the British

worked out their own theories. The old English explorers proved on paper that it wasn't worth while to use dogs . . . Scott's men pulled their sledges to the South Pole. They suffered terribly from frozen feet and wet garments. Despite the windproof fabric of their outer shirts the cold sapped their energy until, in a pinch, they perished. I thought of these things as I looked at the fine woolen clothing, the specially designed (in England) sledges, and the other gear. None of it looked like the Eskimo stuff that we were used to. It wasn't many months afterwards that the suffering and death of the men who used them confirmed my thoughts." Robert Bartlett, *The Log of Bob Bartlett: The True Story of Forty Years of Seafaring and Exploration* (New York: G. P. Putnam & Sons, 1928), 224–25.

126  In the words of MacPhee, "For Amundsen, significance always came from the difficulty of attaining the goal, or more precisely, succeeding where others had failed." See MacPhee, *Race to the End*, 214. However, in one case Amundsen's actions unintentionally caused a small diplomatic crisis in Europe. His mentor Nansen became the Norwegian ambassador to Britain in 1906, and Britain was potentially a powerful ally for a fledgling country. Nansen felt compelled to defend Amundsen's actions in switching his expedition to the South Pole from the British press, public, and government. He did not want it to appear that Amundsen had acted in a malicious or "ungentlemanly" way by not giving Scott some kind of priority to reach the South Pole first. See Huntford, *Last Place on Earth*, 304–308.

127  Peter Beck, *The International Politics of Antarctica* (Abingdon and New York: Routledge, 2014), 95–182. The treaty entered into force on June 23, 1961. The original text of the treaty can be retrieved from the National Science Foundation, www.nsf.gov/geo/plr/antarct/anttrty.jsp.

128  Jenny Johnson, "Who Owns the North Pole? Debate Heats Up as Climate Change Transforms Arctic," Bloomberg News Agency, April 4, 2011, www.bloomberg.com/news/2014-04-04/who-owns-the-north-pole-debate-heats-up-as-climate-change-transforms-arctic.html.

129  Ben Saunders, "Why Britain Should Have an Ambassador for the Arctic," *The Guardian*, March 3, 2015, www.theguardian.com/commentisfree/2015/mar/03/why-britain-ambassador-arctic.

130  King, "Introduction," 15.

**Fashion from the Extreme:**
**The Poles, Highest Peaks, and Beyond**

1  Sarah Pickman, "Of Khaki and Hair Pins: Early Women's Safari Clothing" (unpublished paper, Bard Graduate Center, New York, fall 2014).

2  Alice La Varre, "Vanity in the Jungle," *Vogue*, November 1935, 125.

3  Lantern slides dating to the early twentieth century taken on Peary's journeys, and now in the archives of the Explorers Club in New York, depict numerous men, women, and children in similar types of clothing.

4  Ann Marguerite Tartsinis, *An American Style: Global Sources for New York Textile and Fashion Design, 1915–1928*, New York: Bard Graduate Center, 2013.

5  Ibid., 81.

6  The Ainu are a unique indigenous people living in the northern Japanese island of Hokkaido and far eastern Russia.

7  Randy Kennedy, "Getty Museum Acquires Penn Photographs" *New York Times*, February 7, 2008, E1, E9.

8  "Beautiful Barbarians," *Harper's Bazaar*, October 1962, 139–147.

9  Ibid., 139.

10  Victoria and Albert Museum, London, online collection database, retrieved September 24, 2016.

11  Jill Kennington quoted by Philippe Garner, "Photos: Antonioni's *Blow-Up* and Swinging 1960s London," *Vanity Fair*, April 2011, online interview.

12  Laird Borrelli-Persson, "How to Look Chic in the Antarctic, the *Vogue* Way," Vogue.com, February 14, 2016.

13  "Arctic White and Pale Blue Photographed Above the Arctic Circle," *Vogue*, November 1964, 137, 210-12.

14  Ibid., 210.

15  Ibid.

16  Janet Maslin, "A Madcap Maestro of Haute Couture: Ode to Isaac Mizrahi," *New York Times*, August 4, 1995, C1, C16.

17  Hamish Bowles, "Yohji Yamamoto," Vogue.com, February 26, 2000, online review.

18  Ibid.

19  Sarah Mowers, "Chanel," Vogue.com, March 8, 2010, online review.

20  Tim Blanks, "Moncler Gamme Rouge," Vogue.com, March 5, 2013, online review.

21  Ibid.

22  Robert Spector, "Eddie Bauer: The Man Behind the Name," *Pacific NW Magazine*, May 1983.

23  Victoria and Albert Museum, London, online collection database, retrieved October 1, 2016.

24  Ann Coleman, *The Genius of Charles James* (Brooklyn, New York: The Brooklyn Museum, distributed by Holt, Rinehart and Winston, New York, 1982), 23.

25  *Harper's Bazaar*, October 1938, 67.

26  Coleman, *The Genius of Charles James*, 23.

27  "Everest" Color Supplement, *The Times*, September 1953. No page numbers were included but this information appeared on page 4 of the supplement.

28  The horrific Scott expedition is documented in the essays by Lacey Flint and Sarah Pickman. One of the reasons Scott and his team died was their sole reliance on British-made clothing. Eschewing Inuit designs in favor of Western menswear, in combination with other strategically flawed decisions, resulted in clothing that was ill-suited to the environment.

29  Mike Parsons and Mary B. Rose, in their 2003 publication, *Invisible on Everest: Innovation and the Gear Makers*, discuss a number of innovations and detail the clothing worn by climbers. Aside from outerwear, they also discuss down sleeping bags and other equipment.

30  Stephen Regenold, "Everest Climbing Gear: Hillary to Hilaree," *National Geographic* magazine online, March 15, 2012.

31  Ibid.

32  Victoria and Albert Museum, London, online collection database, retrieved October 1, 2016.

33  *Vogue*, July 1978, 132.

34  *Vogue*, September 1978, 491.

35  Hamish Bowles, "Altuzarra fall 2011," Vogue.com, February 13, 2011, online review.

36  Author's phone interview with Joseph Altuzarra, September 19, 2016.

37  Ibid.

38  Balenciaga popularized the *sacque* back jacket and coat. Its fullness began at the shoulder blades and culminated at the hipline. Gvasalia inverted the volume by placing the fullness at the top and gradually narrowing around the hips.

39  Imran Amed, "Demna Gvasalia Reveals Vetements' Plan to Disrupt the Fashion System," *Business of Fashion*, February 5, 2016, online.

40  William J. Broad, "Scientist at Work: Graham Hawkes; Racing to the Bottom of the Deep, Black Sea," *New York Times*, August 3, 1993.

**Fur: The Final Frontier**

1  C. S. Lewis, *The Lion, the Witch and the Wardrobe* (London: Harper Collins, 1999), 12.

2  "The 'Force' of Fur," American *Vogue*, November 1970, 308–15.

3  Philippe Perrot, *Fashioning the Bourgeoisie: A History of Clothing in the Nineteenth Century* (Princeton: Princeton University Press, 1994), 7.

4  Christopher Breward. *Fashioning London: Clothing and the Modern Metropolis* (Oxford: Berg, 1999), 11.

5  Immanuel Kant, "Book II Analytic of the Sublime," *The Critique of Judgement* (Oxford: Oxford University Press, 1952), 107.

6  Ibid.

7  Gen. 3:21 and Matt. 3:4 (King James Version).

8  "Law of 1294," Peter McNeil & Giorgio Riello, eds., *Luxury: A Rich History* (Oxford: Oxford University Press, 2016), 53.

9  Gaston Bachelard, *Poetics of Space* (Boston: Beacon Press, 1992), 217.

10  James Laver, *Taste and Fashion* (London: George Harrap, 1948), 169–70.

11  Samuel Pepys, *The Diary of Samuel Pepys*, "Monday 17th August 1663," www.pepysdiary.com/diary/1663/08/17/.

12  Lewis, *The Lion, the Witch and the Wardrobe*, 12–13.

**Looking Back at the Future:**
**Space Suits and Space Age Fashion**

1  David Michaelis, "The Now of Avedon," *Vanity Fair*, December 2009, 184.

2  Ibid., 184.

3   "Table of Contents," *Harper's Bazaar*, April 1965, 2.

4   "Moon Magnetics," *Harper's Bazaar*, April 1965, 158–59.

5   Michaelis, "The Now of Avedon," 184.

6   Georges Le Faure and Henry de Graffigny, *Aventures extraordinaires d'un savant russe, vol. 1. La lune* (Paris: Edinger, 1888), www.gutenberg.org/ebooks/19738. Author's translation.

7   Le Faure and de Graffigny, *Aventures extraordinaires d'un savant russe, vol. 2. Le soleil et les petites planètes* (Paris: Edinger, 1889), www.gutenberg.org/ebooks/24962. Author's translation.

8   Emily S. Rosenberg, "Far Out: The Space Age in American Culture," *Remembering the Space Age*, ed. Steven J. Dick (Washington, DC: National Aeronautics and Space Administration, 2008), 173.

9   Lloyd Mallan, *Suiting Up For Space: The Evolution of the Space Suit* (New York: John Day Company, 1971), 1; Lillian D. Kozloski, *U.S. Space Gear: Outfitting the Astronaut* (Washington, DC: Smithsonian Institution Press, 1994), 9.

10  Mallan, *Suiting Up For Space*, 10–20; Kozloski, *U.S. Space Gear*, 10–11.

11  Mallan, *Suiting Up For Space*, 21–37; Kozloski, *U.S. Space Gear*, 11–14; Amanda Young, *Spacesuits: The Smithsonian National Air and Space Museum Collection* (Brooklyn: powerHouse Books, 2009), 12.

12  Nicholas de Monchaux, *Spacesuit: Fashioning Apollo* (Cambridge, MA: MIT Press, 2011), 56–59, 65.

13  Kozloski, *U.S. Space Gear*, 11–14, 30; Mallan, *Suiting Up For Space*, 54; Young, *Spacesuits*, 22; de Monchaux, *Fashioning Apollo*, 89.

14  Mallan, *Suiting Up For Space*, 100, 107; Lillian D. Kozloski, *U.S. Space Gear*, 26–27; Young, *Spacesuits*, 19.

15  Mallan, *Suiting Up For Space*, 100.

16  De Monchaux, *Fashioning Apollo*, 82, 92, 117.

17  Ibid., 92.

18  Ibid., 95.

19  Ibid., 92–95, Mallan, *Suiting Up For Space*, 156–57; Kozloski, *U.S. Space Gear*, 33–34.

20  De Monchaux, *Fashioning Apollo*, 95; Kozloski, *U.S. Space Gear*, 38–39.

21  Mallan, *Suiting Up For Space*, 188.

22  De Monchaux, *Fashioning Apollo*, 11.

23  Mallan, *Suiting Up For Space*, 212.

24  Ibid., 188.

25  De Monchaux, *Fashioning Apollo*, 99.

26  Ibid., 104; Kozloski, *U.S. Space Gear*, 66.

27  De Monchaux, *Fashioning Apollo*, 104.

28  Mallan, *Suiting Up For Space*, 128. Partial-pressure suits were also developed starting in the 1930s to combat the gravitational forces on the body during high speeds of air travel. Pilots could endure larger g-forces if their lower extremities were tightly bound to prevent blood pooling in legs.

29  Kozloski, *U.S. Space Gear*, 34.

30  Mallan, *Suiting Up For Space*, 103.

31  Ibid., 212; de Monchaux, *Fashioning Apollo*, 219; Young, *Spacesuits*, 26; Kozloski, *U.S. Space Gear*, 47.

32  De Monchaux, *Fashioning Apollo*, 209.

33  Ibid., 209–11, 193, 219; Kozloski, *U.S. Space Gear*, 80.

34  De Monchaux, *Fashioning Apollo*, 228, 264.

35  Rosenberg, "Far Out: The Space Age in American Culture," 179.

36  "André Courrèges: Space Age Couturier," *Women's Wear Daily*, January 10, 2016, wwd.com/fashion-news/designer-luxury/andre-courreges-space-age-couturier-10307711/; Suzanne Baldaia, "Space Age Fashion," *Twentieth-Century American Fashion*, eds. Linda Welters and Patricia A. Cunningham (New York: Bloomsbury, 2005), e-book.

37  Norman Norell, et al., "Is Fashion Art?" *The Metropolitan Museum of Art Bulletin*, vol. 26, no. 3 (November 1967), 139.

38  "André Courrèges, Fashion Designer—Obituary," *The Telegraph*, January 10, 2016, www.telegraph.co.uk/news/obituaries/12091078/Andre-Courreges-fashion-designer-obituary.html.

39  Norell, et al., "Is Fashion Art?," 138.

40  Diana Vreeland, "Paris Report," *Vogue*, September 1, 1963, 243.

41  Valérie Guillaume, *Courrèges* (New York: Assouline, 2004), 15.

42  "Paris 1964: Vogue's First Report on the Spring Collections," *Vogue*, March 1, 1964, 128a.

43  Lisa Eisner and Roman Alonso, "The White House: After Turning Fashion On Its (White-Boot) Heel In The 60s, Courrèges Is Back In . . ." *New York Times*, August 19, 2001, SM149.

44  "André Courrèges: Space Age Couturier."

45  J. Krige and A. Russo, *A History of the European Space Agency 1958–1987: Volume I. The Story of ESRO and ELDO, 1958–1973*, European Space Agency, April 2000, 10. e-book. www.esa.int/esapub/sp/sp1235/sp1235v1web.pdf.

46  John Krige, "Building Space Capability Through European Regional Collaboration," *Remembering the Space Age*, 46; J. Krige, and A. Russo, *A History of the European Space Agency 1958–1987*, 13, 55–56.

47  Françoise Giraud, "After Courrèges, What Future for Haute Couture?" *New York Times*, September 12, 1965, SM50.

48  Ibid.

49  Ibid.

50  Ibid.

51  Kathryn Ann Dwyer, "Courrèges: The Last Couturier?" (master's thesis, Fashion Institute of Technology, 1988) 18–20.

52  "André Courrèges: Space Age Couturier."

53  Thelma Sweetinburgh, "Cardin—L'Industriel," *Women's Wear Daily*, May 12, 1967, 1.

54  Guillaume, *Courrèges*, 4.

55  Valerie Mendes, *Pierre Cardin Past Present Future* (London: Dirk Nishen Publishing, 1990), 10.

56  Jean-Pascal Hesse and Benaïm Laurence, *Pierre Cardin: 60 Years of Innovation* (New York: Assouline, 2010), 12–13.

57  Ibid., 16.

58  Mendes, *Pierre Cardin Past Present Future*, 10.

59  "The Moulded Dress of Cardin," *Vogue*, October 1, 1968, 128; Lydia Kamitsis, *Paco Rabanne: A Feeling for Research* (Neuilly-sur-Seine: Michel Lafon, 1996), 65.

60  Suzy Menkes, "Pierre Cardin: One Step Ahead of Tomorrow," *New York Times*, March 22, 2010, www.nytimes.com/2010/03/23/fashion/23iht-fcardin.html.

61  Sweetinburgh, "Cardin—L'Industriel," 18.

62  "Paris," *Vogue*, March 15, 1968, 54.

63  "Beauty Words: Paris," *Harper's Bazaar*, June 1968, 113.

64  "Silver Streak: The Speed Boutique," *Harper's Bazaar*, December 1969, 18.

65  Sweetinburgh, "Cardin—L'Industriel," 18.

66  Marylin Bender, "Maxi? To Cardin, C'est Bon," *New York Times*, October 14, 1969, 42.

67  Benjamin Loyauté, *Pierre Cardin Evolution: Furniture and Design* (New York: Rizzoli, 2006), 26.

68  Kamitsis, *Paco Rabanne: A Feeling for Research*, 65.

69  Ibid., 50.

70  Ibid., 42.

71  Claude de Leusse, "The Accessories: They're 'Dingues,'" *Women's Wear Daily*, October 15, 1965, 14.

72  Sean Topham, *Where's My Space Age? The Rise and Fall of Futuristic Design* (New York: Prestel, 2003), 91–92, 99.

73  Kamitsis, *Paco Rabanne*, 10–25, 28.

74  De Leusse, "The Accessories," 14.

75  "Vogue's Eye View: The Girl in the Chips," *Vogue*, April 1, 1966, 117.

76  "See Legs In Bright White Hip Pants and Shorts," *Vogue*, May 1, 1966, 185; "Skirts From the Portuguese," *Vogue*, May 1, 1966, 156–57.

77  "Vogue's Eye View: Fashion Forecast," *Vogue*, July 1, 1966, 40–41.

78  Kamitsis, *Paco Rabanne*, 38.

79  "Paris: Explosion Plastique—Paco Rabanne's Discs Are It," *Vogue*, April 1, 1966, 115; T. T., "The Plastic World of Paco Rabanne," *Women's Wear Daily*, March 29, 1966, 8.

80  Kamitsis, *Paco Rabanne*, 38–39.

81  Peter Braunstein, "Visiting Planet Paco," *Women's Wear Daily*, February 21, 2001, 10.

82  Kamitsis, *Paco Rabanne*, 42.

83  "A Month of Sun-Days." *Harper's Bazaar*, June 1966, 68–69.

84  Kamitsis, *Paco Rabanne*, 82, 88–90; Topham, *Where's My Space Age?*, 60.

85  Kamitsis, *Paco Rabanne*, 134, 138–40, 144–46, 161.

86  Ibid., 68.

87  Ibid., 158.

88  Roman Alonso and Lisa Eisner, "Man of Steel," *New York Times*, March 10, 2002, F49.

89  Ibid.

90  Ibid.

91  Kamitsis, *Paco Rabanne*, 66.

92  Ibid., 54.

93  "Courrèges: Lord of the Space Ladies," *Life*, May 21, 1965, 47.

94  Jason Roberts, "The NASA Z-2 Suit," *NASA Johnson Space Center Features* blog, April 30, 2014, jscfeatures.jsc.nasa.gov/z2.

95 Chris Heath, "The Martian," *Gentleman's Quarterly*, December 2015, 136.

96 Ibid., 136.

97 Ryan Brinso, "Jose Fernandez: The Man Sculpting and Shaping the Most Iconic Characters in Film," *Bleep Magazine*, February 18, 2016, bleepmag.com/2016/02/18/jose-fernandez-the-man-sculpting-and-shaping-the-most-iconic-characters-in-film.

98 "Virgin Galactic And Y-3 Announce Exclusive Space-Apparel Partnership," *Virgin Galactic* press release, January 14, 2016, www.virgingalactic.com/virgin-galactic-and-y-3-announce-exclusive-space-apparel-partnership.

**Ocean Exploration: Fashions from the Deep**

1 "Turning the Tide," *Vogue*, July 2010, 146–47.

2 "Talking Back: Letters from Readers," *Vogue*, October 2010, 110.

3 Problems of atmospheric pressure and mobility were not exclusive to the deep-sea diving suit. In fact, the creation of the spacesuit—outlined in Elizabeth Way's essay in this book, "Looking Back at the Future: Spacesuits and Space Age Fashion," was informed by designs for deep-sea suits by the British manufacturer Siebe Gorman, founded in 1788.

4 Tony Loftas, "JIM: Homo Aquatic-Metallicum," *New Scientist*, 58, no. 849 (1973), 621.

5 Ibid. A little over three decades after the Tritonia suit went into storage, Joseph Salim Peress (the original inventor) assisted Mike Humphrey and Mike Borrow, partners in the English firm Underwater Marine Equipment Ltd (UMEL), in developing an improved atmospheric diving suit based on the design of the Tritonia. The updated suit was unveiled in November 1971, and named JIM after Peress's chief diver Jim Jarrett. Humphrey and Borrow used the same cast-magnesium and oil-cushion technology employed in the Tritonia suit. Improved versions of the JIM suit were created up until the late 1980s, when the Canadian engineer Phil Nuytten began introducing his atmospheric diving suits. The latest version of the Newtsuit, Exosuit 2000, is the most current innovation in these suits.

6 Loftas, "JIM: Homo Aquatic-Metallicum," 623.

7 Willard Bascom, a research engineer at Scripps Institution of Oceanography, recommended Bradner use neoprene, from a company called Rubatex. At this time neoprene was only available in strips, used as a sealant for gaskets in cars and planes. Neoprene was invented in 1931 by DuPont. By 1937 they changed the name from Duprene to neoprene to show it was an ingredient and not a finished product. During World War II, neoprene was taken off the commercial market and used only by the military after their natural-rubber supply was cut off by the Japanese. By January 1, 1949, the Louisville, Kentucky, neoprene plant was back under the sole ownership of DuPont, and neoprene was back on the commercial market.

8 Carolyn Rainey, "Wet Suit Pursuit: Hugh Bradner's Development of the First Wet Suit" (November 1998), 3; scilib.ucsd.edu/sio/hist/rainey_wet_suit_pursuit.pdf.

9 Ibid., 5.

10 Ibid., 4.

11 In the early 2000s, when asked for the original wet suit to display at the Smithsonian Institution in Washington, DC, Bradner said, "They were all gone by then." David Eisenstadt, "Surfing Whodunit," *Los Angeles Times*, October 11, 2005, articles.latimes.com/2005/oct/11/news/os-neoprene11.

12 In 1961, Hugh Bradner would join the faculty at Scripps College and continue to teach until he retired in 1980.

13 Eisenstadt, "Surfing Whodunit."

14 The name "Thermocline" refers to the temperature of water changing quickly.

15 Eric Gustafson, "How Wet-Suit Pioneer Jack O'Neill Shaped Surfing Culture," *Huron Herald Tribune*, August 7, 2015, www.michigansthumb.com/travel/article/How-wet-suit-pioneer-Jack-O-Neill-shaped-6431340.php#photo-8380929.

16 Eisenstadt, "Surfing Whodunit."

17 "Special Supplement: The Fifties," *Harper's Bazaar*, July 1959, 7.

18 Linda Lear, *Rachel Carson: Witness for Nature* (New York: Henry Holt, 1997), 239–40.

19 "Sport: Poet of the Depths," *Time*, March 28, 1960, content.time.com/time/subscriber/article/0,33009,826158-1,00.html

20 "Australia: Country of Champs," *Vogue*, September 15, 1967, 162.

21 "Beauty Checkout: The Beautiful Activists," *Vogue*, January 1974, 32.

22 Ibid.

23 Sanche de Gramont, "Can a Man Lose to a Woman in a Love Game? Yes, But . . . . /The Good Sports: Golf/Bicycling/SCUBA/Surfing," *Vogue*, May 1, 1971, 136–37.

24 "Fashion You Need Now: Fashion Below Sea Level," *Harper's Bazaar*, May 1963, 88.

25 "Vogue's Eye View: O Joy!," *Vogue*, April 1, 1970, 127.

26 Caroline Ryder, "Robin Piccone and Body Glove: When the Beach Arrived," *Los Angeles Times*, articles.latimes.com/2009/may/24/image/ig-bodyglove24.

27 "Shock Waves," *Vogue*, November 1986, 392.

28 "Vogue Beauty: What's Hot", *Vogue*, September 1988, 292.

29 "On The Land, In The Sea, It's Florescence," *Harper's Bazaar*, May 1966, 168.

30 "Les Grands Fonds," *L'Officiel*, no. 643, 1978, 156–157, patrimoine.editionsjalou.com/lofficiel-de-la-mode-numero_643-1978-detail-13-637.html.

31 "Young Perfectionist: By the Beautiful Sea," *Harper's Bazaar*, May 1961, 158.

32 "Vogue Beauty: What's Hot," *Vogue*, September 1988, 292.

33 Harold Koda, "Junko Koshino," *Encyclopedia of Fashion*, www.fashionencyclopedia.com/Ki-Le/Koshino-Junko.html.

34 "Close Fit," *Vogue*, April 1980, 410.

35 "Fashion 1991," *Vogue*, January 1991, 135.

36 Ibid.

37 Ibid., 134.

38 Ibid., 132.

39 Ibid.

40 Ibid.

41 Kathryn Bold, "'I'd Like to Be Under the Sea' Is Back in Fashion, in a Slick Wet Suit Look," *Los Angeles Times*, March 29, 1991, articles.latimes.com/1991-03-29/news/vw-1089_1_scuba-suit.

42 Ibid.

43 "Talking Fashion: Fit and Fashionable," *Vogue*, January 1, 1994, 164–95.

44 "Junya Watanabe, Spring 2000 Runway Review," Vogue.com, www.vogue.com/fashion-shows/spring-2000-ready-to-wear/junya-watanabe.

45 "Last Look: Pierre Hardy Neoprene Stilettos," *Vogue*, April 2008, 368.

46 Omaima Salem, "La Mode Du Silence," *L'Officiel*, no. 946, June/July 2010, 42–43.

47 Sara Mower, "Alexander McQueen, Spring 2010, Vogue Runway Review," www.vogue.com/fashion-shows/spring-2010-ready-to-wear/alexander-mcqueen.

48 Alexander Fury, "Thom Browne, Spring 2017, Vogue Runway Review," http://www.vogue.com/fashion-shows/spring-2017-menswear/thom-browne.

49 "The Explorer: Sylvia Earle," *Glamour*, November 5, 2014, www.glamour.com/story/sylvia-earle.

50 Chris Dixon, "Do Humans Have a Future in Deep Sea Exploration," *New York Times*, September 14, 2015.

51 Iris Van Herpen press release, Iris van Herpen website, www.irisvanherpen.com/DOCS/IVH-hybrid_holism.pdf.

# ACKNOWLEDGMENTS

This publication could not have been done without the incredible input and efforts of many.

I am especially grateful to my fellow essayists and expeditioneers. Despite the countless demands on their time, they generously donated their compelling insights and brilliant analyses. The book is a viable scholarly resource thanks in large part to the participation of doctoral candidate, Sarah Pickman, and Dr. Jonathan Faiers. I am also indebted to Lacey Flint, curator of The Explorers Club, not only for the essay she contributed, but for her assistance with the many research requests and the numerous contacts she provided.

Special thanks go to two members of the MFIT curatorial staff: assistant curators Elizabeth "Liz" Way and Ariele Elia. Not only did Liz do the legwork to secure most of the images, she did a great deal of independent research on a crucially important aspect of expedition and fashion—outer space. And thanks to Ariele for her research and essay on deep-sea exploration. This book would simply not exist without them and their contributions.

Content for this book could only have come about due to the generosity of the designers and photographers whose gorgeous objects and images are the stars of *Expedition: Fashion from the Extreme*. We are most grateful to Carolyn Cowan of the John Cowan Archive; Karl Lagerfeld and Cécile Goddet-Dirlès of Chanel; Joseph Altuzarra, Michelle No, and Jodie Chan of Joseph Altuzarra; Clara Berg of the Museum of History and Industry; Conrad Froehlich, director of the Martin and Osa Johnson Safari Museum; Judith Levinson, Dr. Laurel Kendall, Dr. Peter Whiteley, Dr. Adam Watson, David Harvey, Joel Sweimler, Katherine Skaggs, and Colin Woodward at the American Museum of Natural History Library; Federica Gamba at Moncler; Hong Jang Hyun and Lee Kyung-Kim; Colin Berg of the Eddie Bauer Archives; Paul Caranicas for Antonio Lopez; Terrence Abbott of the David Winton Bell Gallery, Brown University; Luke Mayes of OWENSCORP / Valerio Mezzanotti; Meghan Grossman Hansen of the Museum at the Fashion Institute of Design & Merchandising; Rose Chiango of the Philadelphia Museum of Art; Guro Tangvald of the National Library of Norway; the family of Leonard Matero; Peter Knapp and Mimi Knapp; Clive Arrowsmith; Richard Pierce; Pierre Hardy; the Irving Penn Foundation; the Richard Avedon Foundation; the Arnaud de Rosnay Estate; Kieran Horn of O'Neill; James Moore; Christian Francis Roth; Guy Marineau; Thom Browne, Miki Higasa, and Mari Fujiuchi of Thom Browne; Dan and Corina Lecca; Special Collections & Archives, UC San Diego; Daphne Seybold of Comme des Garçons; William Ayrey of ILC Dover; Jackie Nickerson; Peter Wories; Pierre Cardin, Yoshi Takata, and Mélanie Bouexiere of DR.

Sarah Pickman wishes to thank Aaron Glass, Peter Miller, Gregory Raml, Lacey Flint, Naomi Boneham, Anne Melgård, Kate Wodehouse, Sara Martinetti, Robyn Fleming, Sarah Airriess, Max Shron, the archival staff of the Royal Geographical Society (with IBG), the National Maritime Museum, and the Scott Polar Research Institute for their assistance and support. Her essay is based on her master's thesis, "'Not a Trouser Button Must Be Missing': Dress, Image, and Cultural Encounter in the Heroic Age of Polar Exploration" (unpublished, Bard Graduate Center: Decorative Arts, Design History, Material Culture, 2015).

All of us are grateful to FIT President, Dr. Joyce F. Brown, and MFIT director, Dr. Valerie Steele, for their continual support on this project.

My editors at Thames & Hudson, Jamie Camplin, Will Balliett, Elizabeth Keene, copyeditor Sharon Lucas, proofreader Neil Mann, and especially designer Paul Sloman, deserve gratitude for their input and diligence on *Expedition: Fashion from the Extreme*. This is the first project on which we collaborated, and I thank them for their professionalism and critical insight, as well as their kindness, patience, and encouragement.

My thanks to the incredibly talented team at MFIT: conservators Ann Coppinger and Nicole Bloomfield for their enthusiasm and insight; curator Colleen Hill for her editorial guidance; curator Fred Dennis; photographer Eileen Costa; registrar Sonia Dingilian; and Nateer Cirino for performing countless duties necessary to make this book.

Last but certainly not least, I thank the unsung heroes of this project, our longtime editor and partner-in-prose, Julian Clark, and the book's project lead, Beth Tondreau. Julian deserves special and heartfelt thanks for his scrupulous work on all the essays, as well as his keen insights and attention to detail. We are all grateful to Beth for managing this mighty project, and for aligning so many diverse components into a cohesive and compelling whole. And I especially appreciate the humor that both of them brought to this demanding task.

# BIBLIOGRAPHY

## The Explorers Club: A Brief History

Amundsen, Roald. *The South Pole*. New York: Trow Press, 1913.

Cook, James. *A Voyage Towards the South Pole, and Round the World. Performed in His Majesty's Ships the Resolution and Adventure, in the Years 1772, 1773, 1774, and 1775*. Vol. 1. London, 1777.

Dick, Steven J. "The Importance of Exploration." November 22, 2007. Accessed: www.nasa.gov/missions/solarsystem/Why_We_01pt1.html.

Earhart, Amelia. *The Fun of It: Random Records of My Own Flying and of Women in Aviation*. Chicago, IL: Academy Press, 1977.

Greely, Adolphus, Lt. *Three Years of Arctic Service: An Account of the Lady Franklin Bay Expedition of 1881–1884*. New York: Charles Scribner's Sons, 1886.

Hayes, J. Gordon. *Antarctica: A Treatise on the Southern Continent*. London: Richards Press Limited, 1928.

Henderson, Bruce. *True North: Peary, Cook, and the Race to the Pole*. New York: W. W. Norton & Company, 2005.

Henson, Matthew Alexander. *Matthew A. Henson's Historic Arctic Journey: The Classic Account of One of the World's Greatest Black Explorers*. Guilford, CT: Lyons Press, 2009.

Herbert, Kari. *Polar Wives: The Remarkable Women Behind the World's Most Daring Explorers*. Vancouver: Greystone Books, 2012.

Hillary, Edmund. *High Adventure*. New York: E. P. Dutton & Company, 1955.

Holzel, Tom, and Audrey Salkeld. *First on Everest: The Mystery of Mallory and Irvine*. New York: H. Holt, 1986.

Piccard, Jacques, and Robert S. Dietz. *Seven Miles Down: The Story of the Bathyscaph Trieste*. New York: Putnam, 1961.

Plimpton, George. *As Told at The Explorers Club: More than Fifty Gripping Tales of Adventure*. Guilford, CT: Lyons Press, 2003.

Shackleton, Ernest Henry. *South: The Last Antarctic Expedition of Shackleton and the Endurance*. New York, NY: Lyons Press, 1998.

"The Sixth International Geographical Congress." *The Geographical Journal*, vol. 5, no. 4, April 1, 1895: 369–73. Accessed: www.jstor.org/stable/10.2307/1774104.

Sullivan, Robert, Robert Andreas, and Will Steger. *The Greatest Adventures of All Time: The Explorers Club 100th Anniversary Edition*. Des Moines, IA: LIFE Books/Time, 2002.

Thomas, Lowell, and Lowell Thomas, Jr. *Famous First Flights That Changed History: Sixteen Dramatic Adventures*. New York: MJF Books, 2004.

## Dress, Image, and Cultural Encounter in the Heroic Age of Polar Exploration

"20,000 GBP for Capt. Scott." *Daily Chronicle*, January 7, 1910. "Album of Press Cuttings." Scott Polar Research Institute archives MS 1453/38; BPC.

Abler, Thomas S. *Hinterland Warriors and Military Dress: European Empires and Exotic Uniforms*. Oxford: Berg, 1999.

Amundsen, Roald. *My Life as an Explorer*. Garden City, NY: Doubleday, Page & Company, 1927.

———. *The North West Passage*. New York: E. P. Dutton & Company, 1908.

———. "The Norwegian South Polar Expedition." Lecture to the Royal Geographical Society, London, November 15, 1912. Reprinted in Kløver, Geir, ed. *Cold Recall: Reflections of a Polar Explorer*. Oslo: The Fram Museum, 2009.

———. *The South Pole: An Account of the Norwegian Expedition in the Fram, 1910–1912*. London and New York: J. Murray and L. Keedick, 1913.

———. "To the North Magnetic Pole and through the Northwest Passage." Lecture to the Royal Geographical Society, London, February 11, 1907.

Reprinted in Kløver, Geir, ed. *Cold Recall: Reflections of a Polar Explorer*. Oslo: The Fram Museum, 2009.

Armitage to Markham, June 5, 1900, Royal Geographical Society (with IBG) archives RGS/AA/7/1/1.

Atkinson, E. L. British Antarctic Expedition, 1910–1913 Volume 2: Part 2 of E. L. Atkinson's report. Ship, Equipment, Hut, etc. Scott Polar Research Institute archives, MS 280/28/2; ER.

Bakkevig, M. K. and R. Nielsen. "Optimal Combination of Garments in Work Clothing for Cold and Wet Environments." *Arctic Medical Research* vol. 53 (1994), 311–13.

Barczewski, Stephanie. *Antarctic Destinies: Scott, Shackleton and the Changing Face of Heroism*. London and New York: Hambledon Continuum, 2007.

———. "The Historiography of Antarctic Exploration." In *Reinterpreting Exploration: The West in the World*, edited by Dane Kennedy, 214–30. Oxford: Oxford University Press, 2014.

Bartlett, Robert. *The Log of Bob Bartlett: The True Story of Forty Years of Seafaring and Exploration*. New York: G. P. Putnam & Sons, 1928.

Bederman, Gail. *Manliness and Civilization: A Cultural History of Gender and Race in the United States, 1880–1917*. Chicago: University of Chicago Press, 1995.

Beck, Peter. *The International Politics of Antarctica*. Abingdon, Oxfordshire, and New York: Routledge, 2014.

Bloom, Lisa. *Gender on Ice: American Ideologies of Polar Expeditions*. Minneapolis: University of Minnesota Press, 1993.

Blumenfeld, Jeff. *Get Sponsored: A Funding Guide for Would-Be Explorers, Adventurers and Travelers*. New York: Skyhorse Publishing, 2014.

Bomann-Larsen, Tor. *Roald Amundsen*. Translated by Ingrid Chistophersen. Stroud, Gloucestershire: Sutton Publishing, 2006.

Bonanomi, Emma. "To be Black and American: Matthew Henson and His Post-Pole Lecture Tour, 1909–1910." In *North by Degree: New Perspectives on Arctic Exploration*, edited by Susan A. Kaplan and Robert McCracken Peck, 185–210. Philadelphia: American Philosophical Society, 2013.

Boroughs, G. H. "Tailoring at the South Pole." *The American Tailor & Cutter*, vol. 34, no. 12, June 1913: 336–38.

Bowers, Henry Robertson. "Conclusion of Lecture on Polar Clothing." Scott Polar Research Institute archives MS 1505 3/3/2/18; BJ.

Bown, Stephen R. *The Last Viking: The Life of Roald Amundsen*. Philadelphia: Da Capo Press, 2012.

British Antarctic Expedition, 1910–1913 Volume 2: Part 2 of E. L. Atkinson's Report. Ship, Equipment, Hut, etc. Scott Polar Research Institute archives, MS 280/28/2; ER.

Brody, Hugh. *Living Arctic: Hunters of the Canadian North*. Seattle: University of Washington Press, 1987.

Brownridge, Amanda. "Images that Injure: Stereotypical Representations of the 'Eskimo' in Advertising." *Aboriginate: Aboriginal Art Research Group [Concordia University]* vol. 1 (2014–2015), 6–21.

Bryce, Robert M. *Cook & Peary: The Polar Controversy, Resolved*. Mechanicsburg, PA: Stackpole Books, 1997.

Burton, Pierre. *The Arctic Grail: The Quest for the North West Passage and the North Pole, 1818–1909*. Toronto: Anchor Canada, 2001.

Cadenhead, Natalie. "Antarctic Explorer Wear." In *Berg Encyclopedia of World Dress and Fashion: Australia, New Zealand, and the Pacific Islands*, edited by Margaret Maynard, 326–31. Oxford: Bloomsbury, 2010. Accessed: dx.doi.org/10.2752/BEWDF/EDch7050.

Carter, Simon. *Rise and Shine: Sunlight, Technology and Health*. Oxford: Berg, 2007.

Cavell, Janice. "Manliness in the Life and Posthumous Reputation of Robert Falcon Scott." *Canadian Journal of History* no. 45, winter 2010, 537–64.

Cherry-Garrard, Apsley. *The Worst Journey in the World: With Scott in Antarctica, 1910–1913*. Mineola, NY: Dover, 2010 [1922].

Christy to Amundsen, June 8, 1911. Reprinted in Kløver, Geir, ed. *Cold Recall: Reflections of a Polar Explorer*. Oslo: The Fram Museum, 2009.

Cox, Lynne. *South with the Sun: Roald Amundsen, His Polar Explorations, and the Quest for Discovery*. New York: Knopf, 2011.

Cronin, Marionne. "Dog Sleds, Parkas, and Airplanes: Material Histories of Polar Exploration." *Moving Worlds* vol. 15, no. 2, "The Postcolonial Arctic," (2015), 70–80.

Darwin to Scott, November 9, 1909. Royal Geographical Society (with IBG) archives RGS/RFS/4a.

Davis-Fisch, Heather. *Loss and Cultural Remains in Performance: The Ghosts of the Franklin Expedition*. New York: Palgrave Macmillan, 2012.

Dick, Lyle. "'The men of prominence are "among those present" for him': How and Why America's Elites Made Robert Peary a National Icon." In *North by Degree: New Perspectives on Arctic Exploration*, edited by Susan A. Kaplan and Robert McCracken Peck, 3–48. Philadelphia: American Philosophical Society, 2013.

Driver, Felix. *Geography Militant: Cultures of Exploration and Empire*. Oxford: Blackwell, 2001.

Eber, Dorothy Harley. *Encounters on the Passage: Inuit Meet the Explorers*. Toronto: University of Toronto Press, 2008.

Emberley, Julia. *The Cultural Politics of Fur*. Ithaca: Cornell University Press, 1997.

Evans, Brad and Aaron Glass, eds. *Return to the Land of the Head Hunters: Edward S. Curtis, the Kwakwaka'wakw, and the Making of Modern Cinema*. Seattle: University of Washington Press, 2013.

Evans, E. R. G. R., "Outfit and Preparation." In Scott, Robert Falcon, Leonard Huxley, and Edward Adrian Wilson. *Scott's Last Expedition in Two Volumes*. Arranged by Leonard Huxley, 338–44. New York: Dodd, Mead and Company, 1913.

Fiennes, Ranulph. *Race to the Pole: Tragedy, Heroism and Scott's Antarctic Quest*. New York: Hyperion, 2004.

Fienup-Riordan, Ann. *Freeze Frame: Alaska Eskimos in the Movies*. Seattle: University of Washington Press, 2003.

"For the Honour of the Flag." *Daily Mail*, September 13, 1909. "Album of Press Cuttings," Scott Polar Research Institute archives MS 1453/38; BPC.

Freedman, Erin. "Sheer Boundaries: Gutskin in Indigenous Arctic Material Culture." Master's thesis, Bard Graduate Center: Decorative Arts, Design History, Material Culture, 2015.

Grant, Jenna. "Screening Room: Collecting in the Collection." Fieldsights—Visual and New Media Review, *Cultural Anthropology Online*. January 14, 2015. Accessed: www.culanth.org/fieldsights/628-screening-room-collecting-in-the-collection.

Hall to McClintock, October 11, 1877, National Maritime Museum archives MCL/38.

Halsey, Lewis George and Mike Adrian Stroud. "Could Scott have survived with today's physiological knowledge?" *Current Biology* vol. 21, no. 12, June 2011: R457–R461.

Hanson, James. "Laced Coats and Leather Jackets: The Great Plains Intercultural Clothing Exchange." In *Plains Indian Studies: Collection in Honor of John Ewers and Waldo Wedel*, edited by Douglas Ubelaker and Herman Viola, 105–17. Washington, DC: Smithsonian, 1982.

Harper, Kenn. *Give Me My Father's Body*. New York: Pocket Books, 2000.

Havenith, George. "Benchmarking Functionality of Historical Cold Weather Clothing: Robert F. Scott, Roald Amundsen, George Mallory." *Journal of Fiber Bioengineering and Informatics*, vol. 3, no. 3, 2010: 121–29.

Henderson, Bruce. *True North: Peary, Cook and the Pole*. New York: W. W. Norton, 2005.

Herbert, Wally. *The Noose of Laurels: Robert E. Peary and the Race for the North Pole*. New York: Anchor Books, 1990.

Huhndorf, Shari M. *Going Native: Indians in the American Cultural Imagination*. Ithaca: Cornell University Press, 2001.

Huntford, Roland. *Race for the South Pole: The Expedition Diaries of Scott and Amundsen*. New York and London: Continuum, 2010.

———. *The Last Place on Earth: Scott and Amundsen's Race to the South Pole*. New York: Random House Modern Library, 1999.

Ingersoll, Ernest. *The Conquest of the North*. New York: C. S. Hammon & Co., 1909.

Betty Issenman. "Inuit Skin Clothing: Construction and Motifs." *Études/Inuit/Studies* vol. 9, no. 2, 1985: 101–19.

———. *Sinews of Survival: The Living Legacy of Inuit Clothing*. Vancouver: University of British Columbia Press, 2000.

Issenman, Betty and Catherine Rankin. *Ivalu: Traditions of Inuit Clothing*. Montreal: McCord Museum of Canadian History, 1988.

Johansen, Hjalmar. *With Nansen in the North: A Record of the Fram Expedition in 1893–1896*. Translated by H. L. Brækstad. London: Ward, Lock and Co., 1899.

Johnson, Donald Clay. "Clothes Make the Empire: British Dress in India." In *The Berg Fashion Library*, 2007.

Johnson, Jenny. "Who Owns the North Pole? Debate Heats Up as Climate Change Transforms Arctic." Bloomberg News Agency, April 4, 2011. Accessed: www.bloomberg.com/news/2014-04-04/who-owns-the-north-pole-debate-heats-up-as-climate-change-transforms-arctic.html.

Jones, Max. "Introduction." In *Journals: Captain Scott's Last Expedition*, by Robert F. Scott, edited by

Max Jones, xvii–xli. Oxford: Oxford University Press, 2005.

Kapsali, V. "Biomimetics and the Design of Outdoor Clothing. In *Textiles for Cold Weather Apparel*, edited by J. T. Williams, 113–30. Cambridge: Woodhead Publishing, 2009.

Keedick to Amundsen, May 27, 1912. Reprinted in Kløver, Geir, ed. *Cold Recall: Reflections of a Polar Explorer*. Oslo: The Fram Museum, 2009.

Kennedy, Dane. "Introduction." In *Reinterpreting Exploration: The West in the World*, edited by Dane Kennedy, 1–18. Oxford: Oxford University Press, 2014.

Kimmel, Michael. *Manhood in America: A Cultural History*. New York: Oxford University Press, 2011.

King, J. C. H. *First Peoples, First Contacts: Native Peoples of North America.* Cambridge, MA: Harvard University Press, 1999.

King, J. C. H., Birgit Pauksztat, and Robert Storrie, eds. *Arctic Clothing*. London: The British Museum Press, 2005.

King, J. C. H., "Introduction." In *Arctic Clothing*, edited by J. C. H. King, Birgit Pauksztat and Robert Storrie, 12–22. London: The British Museum Press, 2005.

Klokkernes, Torunn and Nalini Sharma. "The Impact of a Skin Preparation Method on Preservation." In *Arctic Clothing*, edited by J. C. H. King, Birgit Pauksztat and Robert Storrie, 91–94. London: The British Museum Press, 2005.

Kløver, Geir, ed. *Cold Recall: Reflections of a Polar Explorer*. Oslo: The Fram Museum, 2009.

Koettlitz to Scott, November 9, 1900, Royal Geographical Society (with IBG) archives RGS/AA/7/1/2.

———, November 15, 1900, Royal Geographical Society (with IBG) archives RGS/AA/7/1/3.

Lynnes, Amanda. "Clothing." In *Encyclopedia of the Antarctic, Volume 1*, edited by Beau Riffenburgh, 264. New York: Routledge/Taylor & Francis Group, 2007.

MacPhee, Ross D. E. *Race to the End: Amundsen, Scott, and the Attainment of the South Pole.* New York and London: Sterling Innovation, 2010.

McClintock, Francis Leopold. "Arctic Committee: Description of Travelling Equipments." National Maritime Museum archives MCL/38.

McGhee, Robert. *The Last Imaginary Place: A Human History of the Arctic World.* Chicago: University of Chicago Press, 2007.

Mills, William J. *Exploring Polar Frontiers: A Historical Encyclopedia, Volumes 1 and 2*. Santa Barbara, CA: ABC-CLIO, Inc., 2003.

Officer, Charles, and Jake Page. *A Fabulous Kingdom: The Exploration of the Arctic*. Oxford: Oxford University Press, 2012.

Pálsson, Gísli. "Hot Bodies in Cold Zones: Arctic Exploration." *Scholar & Feminist Online* vol. 7, no. 1, fall 2008. Accessed: sfonline.barnard.edu/ice/palsson_01.htm.

Parsons, Ken. *Human Thermal Environments: The Effects of Hot, Moderate, and Cold Environments on Human Health, Comfort, and Performance*. Boca Raton: CRC/Taylor & Francis, 2002.

Pauksztat, Birgit. "The Arctic." In *Berg Encyclopedia of World Dress and Fashion: The United States and Canada*, edited by Phyllis G. Tortora, 366–75. Oxford: Bloomsbury, 2010.

Peary, Robert. *Secrets of Polar Travel*. New York: The Century Co., 1917.

———. *The North Pole: Its Discovery in 1909 Under the Auspices of the Peary Arctic Club*. New York: Frederick A. Stokes Company, 1910.

———. "The Value of Arctic Exploration," *National Geographic* vol. 14, no. 12, 1903: 429–36.

Phillips, Ruth. *Trading Identities: The Souvenir in Native North American Art from the Northeast, 1700–1900*. Seattle: University of Washington Press, 1999.

Potter, Russell. *Arctic Spectacles: The Frozen North in Visual Culture, 1818–1875*. Seattle: University of Washington Press, 2007.

———. "Before Nanook: Fact and Fiction in Early Arctic Films." Paper presented at the Third Annual Explorers Club Polar Film Festival, New York, November 21–22, 2014.

Preston, Diana. *A First Rate Tragedy*. London: Constable, 1997.

Program of *Discovery* exhibit. "1–5 Catalogue, posters, invitations, etc. *Discovery* Antarctic Expedition, London, 1904." Scott Polar Research Institute archives, MS 366/14; ER.

Renbourn, E. T. "The Spine Pad: A Discarded Item of Tropical Clothing." *Journal of the Royal Army Medical Corps*, vol. 102, no. 3, July 31, 1956: 217–33.

Riffenburgh, Beau. *The Myth of the Explorer: The Press, Sensationalism and Geographic Discovery*. Oxford: Oxford University Press, 1994.

———. ed. *Encyclopedia of the Antarctic, Volume 1*. New York: Routledge/Taylor & Francis Group, 2007.

Robinson, Michael F. *The Coldest Crucible: Arctic Exploration and American Culture*. Chicago: University of Chicago Press, 2006.

Rogers, A. F. "Antarctic climate, clothing and acclimatization." In *Polar Human Biology*, edited by O. G. Edholm and E. K. E. Gunderson, 265–89. London: Heinemann, 1973.

Roosevelt, Theodore. *Presidential Addresses and State Papers: April 14, 1906, to January 14, 1907*. New York: The Review of Reviews Company, 1910.

Royal Geographical Society. *The Antarctic Manual, for the Use of the Expedition of 1901*. Edited by George Murray. London: Royal Geographical Society, 1901.

Saunders, Ben. "Why Britain Should Have an Ambassador for the Arctic." *Guardian*, March 3, 2015. Accessed: www.theguardian.com/commentisfree/2015/mar/03/why-britain-ambassador-arctic.

Schweger, Barbara. "Clothing and Textiles as Symbol on Nineteenth Century Arctic Expeditions." In *Ethnicity and Culture (Boreal Institute for Northern Studies Contribution Series)*, edited by Reginald Auger et al., 287–91. Calgary: Archaeological Association, University of Calgary, 1987.

———. "Clothing in Early Expeditions: An Essential Contribution by the Native Seamstress." In University of Alberta Boreal Institute for Northern Studies Contribution Series no. 190, 1980: 42–55.

———. "Documentation and Analysis of the Clothing Worn by Non-native Men in the Canadian Arctic Prior to 1920, with an Emphasis on Footwear." Master's thesis, University of Alberta, Faculty of Home Economics, 1983.

Scott, Robert Falcon. "Acknowledgements (3) of receipt of subscriptions, 1909–1910," Scott Polar Research Institute archives MS 1319/14/1-3; D.

———. *Journals: Captain Scott's Last Expedition*. Edited by Max Jones. Oxford: Oxford University Press, 2005.

———. "Plans of the British Antarctic Expedition, 1910." *Geographical Journal* 36, 1910, 11–12.

———. *The Voyage of the* Discovery, *Volume 1*. London: Smith, Elder & Co., 1907.

Scott, Robert Falcon and Henry R. Bowers. "Robert Falcon Scott and H. R. Bowers, Stores Lists, 1910–1913: List B. Main Party Relief Stores. Clothing, Coal, Oil, etc." Scott Polar Research Institute archives, MS 1453/30/D.

Scott to Drake, October 1911. Scott Polar Research Institute archives MS 1493; D.

Scott, Robert Falcon, Leonard Huxley, and Edward Adrian Wilson. *Scott's Last Expedition in Two Volumes*. Arranged by Leonard Huxley. New York: Dodd, Mead and Company, 1913.

Scott to Möller, no date [possibly January 1901], Royal Geographical Society (with IBG) archives RGS/AA/7/1/7.

Scott to Möller, no date [possibly January 1901], Royal Geographical Society (with IBG) archives RGS/AA/7/1/8.

Sides, Hampton. *In the Kingdom of Ice: The Grand and Terrible Polar Voyage of the USS* Jeannette. New York: Doubleday, 2014.

Solomon, Susan. *The Coldest March: Scott's Fatal Antarctic Expedition*. New Haven: Yale University Press, 2002.

Somerville to Armitage, March 31, 1901, Royal Geographical Society (with IBG) archives RGS/AA/7/1/9.

Spufford, Francis. *I May Be Some Time*. London: Faber and Faber, 1996.

Thomas, Nicholas. "Appropriation/Appreciation: Settler Modernism in Australia and New Zealand." In *The Empire of Things: Regimes of Value and Material Culture*, edited by Fred R. Myers, 139–63. Santa Fe: School of American Research Press, 2001.

———. *Entangled Objects: Exchange, Material Culture and Colonialism in the Pacific*. Cambridge, MA: Harvard University Press, 1991.

Thwaites, C. "Cold-Weather Clothing." In *Military Textiles*, edited by E. Wilusz, 158-82. Cambridge: Woodhead Publishing, 2008.

Weaver, Stuart A. *Exploration: A Very Short Introduction*. Oxford: Oxford University Press, 2015.

Yelverton, David E. *Antarctica Unveiled: Scott's First Expedition and the Quest for the Unknown Continent*. Boulder: University Press of Colorado, 2000.

## Fashion from the Extreme: The Poles, Highest Peaks, and Beyond

### Books and Articles

Cherry-Garrard, Apsley. *The Worst Journey in the World: Antarctica 1910–1913*. New York: Skyhorse Publishing, 2013. (Originally published 1922.)

Coleman, Ann. *The Genius of Charles James*. Brooklyn: The Brooklyn Museum, distributed by Holt, Rinehart and Winston, New York, 1982.

Darwin, Charles. *On the Origin of Species: By Means of Natural Selection or the Preservation of Favoured Races in the Struggle for Life*. New York: The Heritage Press, 1963. (Originally published 1859.)

"Everest," *The Times* (London), September, 1953.

Garner, Philippe. "Photos: Antonioni's Blow-Up and Swinging 1960s London," *Vanity Fair*, April 2011, online.

Herzog, Maurice, translated by Nea Morin and Janet Adam Smith. *Annapurna: The First Conquest of an 8,000-Meter Peak*. Guilford, CT: Globe Pequot Press, 2010.

Huguier, Françoise. *En route pour Behring: Notes de voyage en Sibérie*. Paris: Maeght, 1993.

Kavanagh, Julie. *Secret Muses: The Life of Frederick Ashton*. New York: Pantheon Books, 1996.

King, Alan C. J., Birgit Pauksztat, and Robert Storrie. *Arctic Clothing of North America*. Canada: McGill-Queen's University Press, 1995.

Koda, Harold, and Jan Glier Reeder. *Charles James: Beyond Fashion*. New York: Metropolitan Museum of Art, distributed by Yale University Press, 2014.

Loti, Pierre. *An Iceland Fisherman*. Translated by M. Jules Cambon. Reprinted, New York: P. F. Collier & Son, 1902.

Mears, Patricia. *American Beauty: Aesthetics and Innovation in Fashion*. New Haven and London: Yale University Press, 2010.

Nadeau, Chantal. *Fur Nation: From the Beaver to Brigitte Bardot*. London: Routledge, 2005.

Nansen, Fridtjof. *Farthest North: An Epic Adventure of a Visionary Explorer*. New York: Skyhorse Publishing, 2008. (Originally published 1897.)

Oakes, Jill, and Rick Riewe. *Our Boots: And Inuit Women's Art*. London: Thames & Hudson, 1996.

Onozato, Minoru. *My Rugged 211: Unfashionable Fashion*. Tokyo: East Communications, 2010.

Pearlman, Chee. *Isaac Mizrahi: An Unruly History*. New York: The Jewish Museum, distributed by Yale University Press, 2016.

Quinn, Stephen Christopher. *Windows on Nature: The Great Habitat Dioramas of the American Museum of Natural History*. New York: Abrams, 2006.

Regenold, Stephen. "Everest Climbing Gear: Hillary to Hilaree." *National Geographic* magazine online. March 15, 2012.

Spector, Robert. "Eddie Bauer: The Man Behind the Name," *Pacific NW Magazine*, May 1983.

———. *The Legend of Eddie Bauer*. Lyme, Connecticut: Greenwich Publishing Group, 1994.

Strauss, Mark. "Ten Inventions Inspired by Science Fiction." Smithsonianmag.com, March 15, 2012.

Tartsinis, Ann Marguerite. *An American Style: Global Sources for New York Textile and Fashion Design, 1915–1928*. New York: Bard Graduate Center, 2013.

Verne, Jules. *From the Earth to the Moon (De la terre à la lune)*, 1865. Translated by Edward Roth, 1874. Reprinted 1976, Mattituck, New York: Aeonian Press.

———. *Twenty Thousand Leagues under the Sea*. New York: Scribner's and Sons, 1956.

### Fashion Periodicals and Websites

*Harper's Bazaar*, 1937–2016

*Vogue*, 1916–2016

Vogue.com

### Films

Keeve, Douglas. *Unzipped*. Distributed by Miramax, 1995.

Flaherty, Robert J. *Nanook of the North*. Distributed by Pathé Exchange, 1922.

### Archives

Max Meyer sketches, 1915–1922. Special Collections, Library at the Fashion Institute of Technology.

## Fur: The Final Frontier

### Books and Articles

Bachelard, Gaston. *Poetics of Space*. Boston: Beacon Press, 1992. (Originally published 1958.)

Blum, Dilys, E. *Shocking! The Art and Fashion of Elsa Schiaparelli*. Philadelphia: Philadelphia Museum of Art, 2004.

Böhme, Hartmut. *Fetishism and Culture*. Berlin: De Gruyter, 2014.

Breward, Christopher. *Fashioning London: Clothing and the Modern Metropolis*. Oxford: Berg, 1999.

Davey, Richard. *Furs and Fur Garments*. London: The Roxburghe Press, 1895.

Faiers, Jonathan. *Dressing Dangerously: Dysfunctional Fashion in Film*. New Haven and London: Yale University Press, 2013.

Hunt, Alan. *Governance of the Consuming Passions: A History of Sumptuary Law*. New York: Palgrave Macmillan. 1996.

Johnston, Lucy. *Nineteenth Century Fashion in Detail*. London: V&A Publications, 2005.

Kant, Immanuel. "Book II Analytic of the Sublime" in *The Critique of Judgement*. Oxford: Oxford University Press, 1952. (Originally published 1790.)

Laver, James. *Taste and Fashion*. London: George Harrap & Co. Ltd., 1948.

Lewis, C. S. *The Lion, the Witch and the Wardrobe*. London: Harper Collins, 1999. (Originally published 1950.)

Links, J. G. *The Book of Fur*. London: James Barrie, 1956.

McNeil, Peter & Giorgio Riello, eds. *Luxury: A Rich History*. Oxford: Oxford University Press, 2016.

Perrot, Philippe. *Fashioning the Bourgeoisie: A History of Clothing in the Nineteenth Century*. Princeton: Princeton University Press, 1994.

Walker, Myra. *Balenciaga and His Legacy: Haute Couture from the Texas Fashion Collection*. New Haven and London: Yale University Press, 2006.

**Fashion Periodicals and Websites**

"The 'Force' of Fur." American *Vogue*, November 1970.

"Fur Coats and Cadillacs." American *Vogue*, November 1957.

The Diary of Samuel Pepys. www.pepysdiary.com/diary/1663/08/17/.

**Looking Back at the Future: Space Suits and Space Age Fashion**

Alonso, Roman and Lisa Eisner. "Man of Steel," *New York Times*, March 10, 2002, F49.

"A Month of Sun-Days," *Harper's Bazaar*, June 1966, 68–69.

"André Courrèges, Fashion Designer—Obituary," *The Telegraph*, January 10, 2016. Accessed: www.telegraph.co.uk/news/obituaries/12091078/Andre-Courreges-fashion-designer-obituary.html.

"André Courrèges: Space Age Couturier," *Women's Wear Daily*, January 10, 2016. Accessed: wwd.com/fashion-news/designer-luxury/andre-courreges-space-age-couturier-10307711/.

Baldaia, Suzanne. "Space Age Fashion" in *Twentieth-Century American Fashion*, edited by Linda Welters and Patricia A. Cunningham. New York: Bloomsbury, 2005 (e-book). "Beauty Words: Paris," *Harper's Bazaar*, June 1968, 112–13.

Bender, Marylin. "Maxi? To Cardin, C'est Bon," *New York Times*, Oct 14, 1969, 42.

Braunstein, Peter. "Visiting Planet Paco," *Women's Wear Daily*, February 21, 2001, 10–11.

Brinso, Ryan. "Jose Fernandez: The Man Sculpting and Shaping the Most Iconic Characters in Film,"

*Bleep Magazine*, February 18, 2016. Accessed: bleepmag.com/2016/02/18/jose-fernandez-the-man-sculpting-and-shaping-the-most-iconic-characters-in-film/.

Chu, Jennifer. "Shrink-Wrapping Spacesuits," *MIT News*, September 18, 2014. Accessed: news.mit.edu/2014/second-skin-spacesuits-0918.

"Courrèges: Lord of the Space Ladies," *Life*, May 21, 1965, 47–65.

De Leusse, Claude. "The Accessories: They're 'Dingues,'" *Women's Wear Daily*, October 15, 1965.

De Monchaux, Nicholas. *Spacesuit: Fashioning Apollo*. Cambridge: The MIT Press 2011.

Dwyer, Kathryn Ann. "Courrèges: The Last Couturier?" Master's thesis, Fashion Institute of Technology, August 16, 1988.

Eisner, Lisa, and Roman Alonso. "The White House: After Turning Fashion On Its (White-Boot) Heel In The 60s, Courrèges Is Back In . . . ," *New York Times*, August 19, 2001, SM149.

Giraud, Francoise. "After Courrèges, What Future for Haute Couture?," *New York Times*, September, 12, 1965, SM50.

Guillaume, Valérie. *Courrèges*. New York: Assouline, 2004.

Hansen, James R., and NASA Langley Research Center Office of Public Affairs. *The Rendezvous That Was Almost Missed: Lunar Orbit Rendezvous and the Apollo Program*, Nasa Facts series, NF175, December 1992. Accessed: www.nasa.gov/centers/langley/news/factsheets/Rendezvous.html.

Heath, Chris. "The Martian," *Gentleman's Quarterly*, December 2015, 130–36.

Hesse, Jean-Pascal and Benaïm Laurence. *Pierre Cardin: 60 Years of Innovation*. New York: Assouline, 2010.

Kamitsis, Lydia. *Paco Rabanne: A Feeling for Research*. Neuilly-sur-Seine: Michel Lafon, 1996.

Kozloski, Lillian D. *U.S. Space Gear: Outfitting the Astronaut*. Washington, DC: Smithsonian Institution Press, 1994.

Krige, John. "Building Space Capability Through European Regional Collaboration." In *Remembering the Space Age*, edited by Steven J. Dick. Washington, DC: National Aeronautics and Space Administration, 2008.

Krige, J., and A. Russo. *A History of the European Space Agency 1958–1987: Volume I The Story of ESRO and ELDO, 1958–1973*. European Space Agency, April 2000. PDF e-book. Accessed: www.esa.int/esapub/sp/sp1235/sp1235v1web.pdf.

Le Faure, Georges, and Henry de Graffigny. *Aventures extraordinaires d'un savant russe, vol. 1. La lune* (Paris: Edinger, 1888). Accessed: www.gutenberg.org/ebooks/19738.

———. *Aventures extraordinaires d'un savant russe, vol. 2. Le soleil et les petites planètes* (Paris: Edinger, 1889). Accessed: www.gutenberg.org/ebooks/24962.

Loyauté, Benjamin. *Pierre Cardin Evolution: Furniture and Design*. New York: Rizzoli, 2006.

Mallan, Lloyd. *Suiting Up For Space: The Evolution of the Space Suit*, New York: John Day Company, 1971.

Mendes, Valerie. *Pierre Cardin Past Present Future*. London: Dirk Nishen Publishing, 1990.

Menkes, Suzy. "Pierre Cardin: One Step Ahead of Tomorrow," *New York Times*. March 22, 2010. Accessed: www.nytimes.com/2010/03/23/fashion/23iht-fcardin.html.

Michaelis, David. "The Now of Avedon," *Vanity Fair*, December 2009, 184.

"Moon Magnetics," *Harper's Bazaar*, April 1965, 158–59.

Norell, Norman, Louise Nevelson, Irene Sharaff, Alwin Nikolais, Andre Courrèges, and Priscilla Tucker. "Is Fashion Art?" *The Metropolitan Museum of Art Bulletin* vol. 26, no. 3 (November 1967), 129–40.

"Paris," *Vogue*, March 15, 1968, 54–55.

"Paris: Explosion Plastique—Paco Rabanne's Discs Are It," *Vogue*, April 1, 1966, 115.

"Paris 1964: Vogue's First Report on the Spring Collections," *Vogue*, March 1, 1964, 128–37.

Roberts, Jason. "The NASA Z-2 Suit," *NASA Johnson Space Center Features* blog, April 30, 2014. Accessed: jscfeatures.jsc.nasa.gov/z2/.

Rosenberg, Emily S. "Far Out: The Space Age in American Culture." In *Remembering the Space Age* edited by Steven J. Dick. Washington, DC: National Aeronautics and Space Administration, 2008.

"See Legs In Bright White Hip Pants and Shorts," *Vogue*, May 1, 1966, 184–191.

"Silver Streak: The Speed Boutique," *Harper's Bazaar*, December 1969, 184–91.

"Skirts From the Portuguese," *Vogue*, May 1, 1966, 156–57.

Sweetinburgh, Thelma. "Cardin—L'Industriel," *Women's Wear Daily*, May 12, 1967, 1, 18.

Sweetinburgh, Thelma. "First Paris Report," *Women's Wear Daily*, December 9, 1966, 1, 22.

"Table of Contents" *Harper's Bazaar*, April 1965, 2.

"The Moulded Dress of Cardin," *Vogue*, October 1, 1968, 128.

Topham, Sean. *Where's My Space Age? The Rise and Fall of Futuristic Design*. New York: Prestel, 2003.

T. T., "The Plastic World of Paco Rabanne," *Women's Wear Daily*, March 29, 1966, 8.

"Virgin Galactic and Y-3 Announce Exclusive Space-Apparel Partnership," *Virgin Galactic press release*, January 14, 2016. Accessed: www.virgingalactic.com/virgin-galactic-and-y-3-announce-exclusive-space-apparel-partnership/.

"Vogue's Eye View: Fashion Forecast," *Vogue*, July 1, 1966, 37–59.

"Vogue's Eye View," *Vogue*, October 15, 1964, 117–21.

"Vogue's Eye View: The Girl in the Chips," *Vogue*, April 1, 1966, 117.

Vreeland, Diana. "Paris Report," *Vogue*, September 1, 1963, 169, 243–45.

Young, Amanda. *Spacesuits: The Smithsonian National Air and Space Museum Collection*. Brooklyn: powerHouse Books, 2009.

**Ocean Exploration: Fashions from the Deep**

"Australia: Country of Champs," *Vogue*, September 15, 1967, 162.

"Beauty Checkout: The Beautiful Activists," *Vogue*, January 1974, 32.

Bold, Kathryn. "I'd Like to Be Under the Sea Is Back in Fashion, in a Slick Wet Suit Look," *Los Angeles Times*, March 29, 1991. Accessed: http://articles.latimes.com/1991-03-29/news/vw-1089_1_scuba-suit.

Carson, Rachel. *The Sea Around Us*. Oxford: Oxford University Press, 1951.

Chabenès, Bernard. "Les Grands Fonds," *L'Officiel*, no. 643, June 1978, 152–55. Accessed: patrimoine.editionsjalou.com/lofficiel- de-la-mode-numero 643-1978-detail- 13-637.html

"Close Fit," *Vogue*, April 1980, 410.

Cousteau, Jacques-Yves, and Frédéric Dumas. *The Silent World*. New York: Harper & Brothers Publishers, 1953.

De Gramont, Sanche. "Can a Man Lose to a Woman in a Love Game? Yes, But . . . /The Good Sports: Golf/Bicycling/SCUBA/Surfing," *Vogue*, May 1, 1971, 136–37.

Dixon, Chris. "Do Humans Have a Future in Deep Sea Exploration?" *New York Times*, September 14, 2015.

Eisenstadt, David. "Surfing Whodunit" *Los Angeles Times*, October 11, 2005. Accessed: articles.latimes.com/2005/oct/11/news/os-neoprene11.

"Fashion 1991," *Vogue*, January 1991, 135.

"Fashion You Need Now: Fashion Below Sea Level," *Harper's Bazaar*, May 1963, 88.

Gustafson, Eric. "How Wet-Suit Pioneer Jack O'Neill Shaped Surfing Culture," *Huron Herald Tribune*, August 7, 2015. Accessed: www.michigansthumb.com/travel/article/How-wet-suit-pioneer-Jack-O-Neill-shaped-6431340.php#photo-8380929.

Iris Van Herpen press release, Iris van Herpen website. Accessed: www.irisvanherpen.com/DOCS/IVH-hybrid_holism.pdf.

"Junya Watanabe Spring 2000 Runway Review," Vogue.com. http://www.vogue.com/fashion-shows/spring-2000-ready-to-wear/junya-watanabe.

Koda, Harold, Junko Koshino. *Encyclopedia of Fashion*. Accessed: www.fashionencyclopedia.com/Ki-Le/Koshino-Junko.html.

"Last Look: Pierre Hardy Neoprene Stilettos," *Vogue*, April 1, 2008, 368.

Lear, Linda. *Rachel Carson: Witness for Nature*. New York: Henry Holt, 1997.

Loftas, Tony. "JIM: homo aquatic-metallicum," *New Scientist*, 58, no. 849 (1973): 621.

Mower, Sara. "Vogue Runway Review, Spring 2010 Alexander McQueen." Accessed: www.vogue.com/fashion-shows/spring-2010-ready-to-wear/alexander-mcqueen.

Omaima, Salem. "La Mode Du Silence," *L'Officiel*, no. 946, June/July 2010, 42–43.

"On The Land, In The Sea, It's Fluorescence," *Harper's Bazaar*, May 1966, 168.

Rainey, Carolyn. "Wet Suit Pursuit: Hugh Bradner's Development of the First Wet Suit" (November 1998), 3. Accessed: scilib.ucsd.edu/sio/hist/rainey_wet_suit_pursuit.pdf.

Ryder, Caroline. "Robin Piccone and Body Glove: When the Beach Arrived," *Los Angeles Times*. Accessed: articles.latimes.com/2009/may/24/image/ig-bodyglove24.

"Shock Waves," *Vogue*, November 1986, 392.

"Special Supplement: The Fifties," *Harper's Bazaar*, July 1959.

"Sport: Poet of the Depths," *Time*, March 28, 1960. Accessed: content.time.com/time/subscriber/article/0,33009,826158-1,00.html.

"Talking Back: Letters from Readers," *Vogue*, October 2010, 110.

"Talking Fashion: Fit and Fashionable," *Vogue*, January 1994, 164–95.

"The Explorer: Sylvia Earle," *Glamour*, November 5, 2014. Accessed: www.glamour.com/story/sylvia-earle.

"Thom Browne Runway Review," VogueRunway.com. Accessed: http://www.vogue.com/fashion-shows/spring-2017-menswear/thom-browne.

"Turning the Tide," *Vogue*, July 2010, 146–47.

Verne, Jules. *Twenty Thousand Leagues under the Sea*, New York: Scribner's and Sons, 1956.

"Vogue Beauty: What's Hot", *Vogue*, September 1988, 292.

"Vogue's Eye View: O Joy!," *Vogue*, April 1, 1970, 127.

"Young Perfectionist: By the Beautiful Sea," *Harper's Bazaar*, May 1961, 158.

**Films**

Allen, Irwin. *The Sea Around Us*, distributed by RKO Pictures, 1953.

Cousteau, Jacques-Yves, and Louis Malle. *The Silent World*, distributed by Columbia Pictures, 1956.

Cousteau, Jacques-Yves. *World Without Sun*, distributed by Columbia Pictures, 1964.

Young, Terence. *Thunderball*, distributed by United Artists, 1965.

# PICTURE CREDITS

⎯⎯◇⎯⎯

**Front cover**: Copyright The John Cowan Archive; **Frontispiece**: Stephane Cardinale/Corbis Entertainment/ Getty Images; **Expedition: Fashion from the Extreme** 1: Photograph by Irving Penn, *Yeti (Front View)*, New York, 1990 © The Irving Penn Foundation, image courtesy of Miyake Design Studio; 2: Courtesy ALTUZARRA; 3: Courtesy ALTUZARRA; 4: Library of Congress; 5: Library of Congress; **The Explorers Club: A Brief History** 6–17: The Explorers Club Research Collections; **Dress, Image, and Cultural Encounter in the Heroic Age of Polar Exploration** 18: 3000.32.1801; Gift of Donald and Miriam MacMillan; Courtesy of the Peary-MacMillan Arctic Museum and Arctic Studies Center, Bowdoin College; 19: Photographer unknown; 20: 2006.4.39; Gift of Margaret Tanquary Corwin; Courtesy of the Peary-MacMillan Arctic Museum and Arctic Studies Center, Bowdoin College; 21: 1966.129.1; Gift of Donald and Miriam MacMillan; Courtesy of the Peary-MacMillan Arctic Museum and Arctic Studies Center, Bowdoin College; 22: 2007.8.3; Estate of Raymond F. DeVinney; Courtesy of the Peary-MacMillan Arctic Museum and Arctic Studies Center, Bowdoin College; 23: 1966.129.2; Gift of Donald and Miriam MacMillan; Courtesy of the Peary-MacMillan Arctic Museum and Arctic Studies Center, Bowdoin College; 24: Photograph by Edward Curtis; Library of Congress; 25: Postcard by Kawin & Co.; 2000.1.14; In memory of Dr. H. Franklin Williams; Courtesy of the Peary-MacMillan Arctic Museum and Arctic Studies Center, Bowdoin College; 26: Photographer unknown; Library of Congress; 27: Photographer unknown; Owner: National Library of Norway; 28: Photographer unknown; Owner: National Library of Norway; 29: Photographer unknown; Owner: National Library of Norway; 30: Photographer Anders Beer Wilse; Owner: National Library of Norway; 31: Photograph by Herbert Ponting; Scott Polar Research Institute, University of Cambridge; **Fashion from the Extreme: The Poles, Highest Peaks, and Beyond** 32: Photograph by John Cowan. Copyright The John Cowan Archive; 33: Martin and Osa Johnson Safari Museum; 34: Martin and Osa Johnson Safari Museum; 35: Public domain; 36: Photograph by Franco Rubartelli; 37: Photograph by Frank Conner; Courtesy of Universal Studios Licensing LLC; 38: Public domain; 39: Photographer unknown; Image #2A18808; American Museum of Natural History Library; 40: Photographer unknown; Image #2A18823; American Museum of Natural History Library; 41: *Vogue*, December 1, 1917; 42: Photograph by Julius Kirschner; Image #37869; American Museum of Natural History Library; 43: Photograph by Kay C. Lenskjold; Image #37764; American Museum of Natural History Library; 44: *Vogue* Paris, January 15, 1921; Illustration by Harriet Meserole; 45: Public domain; 46: Photograph by Irving Penn, Peter & Dagmar Freuchen, New York, 1947 © The Irving Penn Foundation; 47: Photograph by Irving Penn. © Condé Nast; 48: Photograph by Irving Penn. © Condé Nast; 49: *Harper's Bazaar*, October 1962; Photograph by Richard Avedon; © The Richard Avedon Foundation; 50: *Vogue*, November 1964;

Photograph by John Cowan; Copyright The John Cowan Archive; 51: Rudolph Martin Anderson, 1916, Canadian Museum of History, 39026; 52: Photo Patrice Stable; 53: Photo Patrice Stable; 54: Rose Hartman/Archive Photos/ Getty Images; 55: Ron Galella/Ron Galella Collection/Getty Images; 56: firstVIEW.com; 57: firstVIEW.com; 58: firstVIEW.com; 59: Photograph by Arthur Elgort; 60: Stephane Cardinale/Corbis Entertainment/Getty Images; 61: Photograph by Hong Jang Hyun; 62: Courtesy of Moncler; 63: Photograph courtesy of the Eddie Bauer Archives; 64: Photograph courtesy of the Eddie Bauer Archives; 65: Photograph courtesy of the Eddie Bauer Archives; 66: Photograph by George Hoyningen-Huene; 67: *The Times, Everest Colour Supplement*, September 22, 1953; 68: Photograph by J. B. Noel, © J. B. Noel / Royal Geographical Society; Royal Geographic Society: Image number: S0020258; 69: Photograph by Hans Feurer; 70: Photo courtesy of the Eddie Bauer Archives; 71: Photograph by Juan Ramos; 72: *Vogue*, September 1976. Photograph by Arthur Elgort; 73: Photograph by Arthur Elgort; 74: Photograph by Arthur Elgort; 75: U.S. Naval Institute; 76: Photograph by Peter Wories; 77: Photographer unknown; 78: Photograph by Andy Hilfiger. Courtesy: H2o Ice Water; 79: Courtesy of Comme des Garçons; 80: Richard Young/ Rex/Shutterstock; 81: Courtesy ALTUZARRA; 82: Photograph by Jackie Nickerson; 83: Photographer unknown; Balenciaga; 84: The Museum at FIT, 2001.100.1; Donated by Fortunée A. Lorant, Paris; 85: Tristram Kenton / Royal Opera House / ArenaPAL; **Fur: The Final Frontier** 86: Imagno/Hulton Archive/Getty Images; 87: *Vogue*, November 1977; Photograph by Eisuke Ishimuro; 88: Royal Collection Trust/© Her Majesty Queen Elizabeth II 2016; 89: Gemäldegalerie Berlin; 90: Courtesy of the David Winton Bell Gallery, Brown University; 91: Courtesy Owenscorp / Valerio Mezzanotti; 92: The Texas Fashion Collection, College of Visual Arts and Design, University of North Texas. Gift of Claudia de Osborne; 93: Philadelphia Museum of Art, 1969-232-55a, Gift of Mme Elsa Schiaparelli, 1969; 94: 2011.5.20; Museum Purchase; Courtesy of the FIDM Museum at the Fashion Institute of Design & Merchandising, Los Angeles, CA; Photograph by Brian Sanderson; 95: ©Victoria and Albert Museum, London; 96: ©Victoria and Albert Museum, London; 97: The Museum at FIT, 2010.21.1, Gift of Ambassador Joseph Verner Reed; 98: John Kobal Foundation/Moviepix/Getty Images; 99: John Rawlings/Condé Nast Collection/Getty Images; **Looking Back at the Future: Space Suits and Space Age Fashion** 100: © The Richard Avedon Foundation;; 101: Photographer unknown; Grumman Aerospace Corporation; Collection of the family of Leonard Matero; 102: From G. Le Faure and H. de Graffigny, *Aventures extraordinaires d'un savant russe*, illustrations by J. Cayron, Henriot, and L. Vallet (1889); 103: *Life*, January 6, 1958; 104: ILC Dover, LP; 105: Photo by Mark Avino, Smithsonian National Air and Space Museum (NASM 2004-55445); 106: Peter Knapp/Elle/Scoop; 107: Photograph

by William Klein; 108: Photograph by William Klein; 109: The Museum at FIT, 78.170.5; Gift of Bernie Zamkoff; 110: The Museum at FIT, 2007.46.75; Donated in memory of Isabel Eberstadt by her family; 111: The Museum at FIT, 77.183.2CD; Gift of Ruth Sublette; 112: The Museum at FIT, 2014.56.2; Gift of Abel Rapp; 113: *Vogue*, November 1, 1969; 114: Pierre Cardin, Cosmocorps collection, 1967, Yoshi Takata / DR; 115: The Museum at FIT, 72.91.30; Gift of Lauren Bacall; 116: The Museum at FIT, 91.128.10; Gift of CITICORP; 117: The Museum at FIT, 70.62.1; Gift of Lauren Bacall; 118: The Museum at FIT, 87.92.4; Gift of Ms. Liz Bader; 119: Photograph by Richard Avedon; © The Richard Avedon Foundation; 120: Photograph by Richard Avedon; © The Richard Avedon Foundation; 121: The Museum at FIT, 81.48.1; Gift of Montgomery Ward; 122: The Museum at FIT, 81.48.2; Gift of Montgomery Ward; 123: Photo by HIRO; 124: *Aeroplane Dress* (film stills), film by Marcus Tomlinson, dress and model styling by Hussein Chalayan; production by Premiere Heure / Marcus Tomlinson; copyright Marcus Tomlinson; **Ocean Exploration: Fashions from the Deep** 125: *Vogue*, July 2010, Photograph by Patrick Demarchelier/*Vogue* © Condé Nast; 126: Photograph by Myrabella; 127: OAR/National Undersea Research Program (NURP), public domain; 128: *Vogue*, July 1951, p. 46, photograph by Irving Penn © Condé Nast; 129: Public domain; 130: Hugh Bradner Papers, Special Collections & Archives, UC San Diego; 131: Image courtesy of O'Neill; 132: *Vogue*, September 15, 1967, photograph by Arnaud de Rosnay, courtesy of Arnaud de Rosnay estate; 133: *Vogue*, May 1, 1971 pp. 136–37, photograph by Irving Penn © Condé Nast; 134: *Vogue*, May 1, 1971 pp. 136–37, photograph by Irving Penn © Condé Nast; 135: *Harper's Bazaar*, May 1963 p. 89, photograph by James Moore; 136: *Vogue*, 1965, p. 220, photograph by Irving Penn © Condé Nast; 137: *Vogue*, April 1, 1970, p. 127, photograph by David Bailey; 138: *Harper's Bazaar*, May 1966, pp. 168–69, photograph by Bob Richardson / Art Partner; 139: Parkway Fabricators 1969 catalogue, public domain; 140: *L'Officiel*, no. 683, 1982, p. 120, Photograph by Claus Wickrath; 141: *L'Officiel*, no. 683, 1982, p. 121, Photograph by Claus Wickrath; 142: Photograph by Clive Arrowsmith. FRPS; 143: *L'Officiel*, no. 643, 1978, p. 154–55, (left) photograph by T.P. Trosset, (right) Michel Picard; 144: *Vogue*, June 1, 2011, p. 140, Raquel Zimmermann/dna model management, © Craig McDean / Art + Commerce; 145: Image courtesy of Christian Francis Roth; 146: *Vogue*, January 1, 1991, photograph by Guy Marineau; 147: The Museum at FIT, 94.126.1. Gift of DKNY; 148: Image courtesy of firstview.com; 149: Image courtesy of Pierre Hardy; 150: Photograph by Richard Pierce; 151: Photograph by Marcio Madeira. Image courtesy of firstview.com; 152: Photograph by Marcio Madeira. Image courtesy of firstview. com; 153: Photograph by Dan and Corina Lecca; 154: Photograph by Dan and Corina Lecca; 155: Image courtesy of firstview.com; **Back cover**: © CHANEL, Photograph by Olivier Saillant